Breeze into
JAPANESE

Breeze into JAPANESE

PRACTICAL LANGUAGE FOR BEGINNERS

KAZUKO IMAEDA

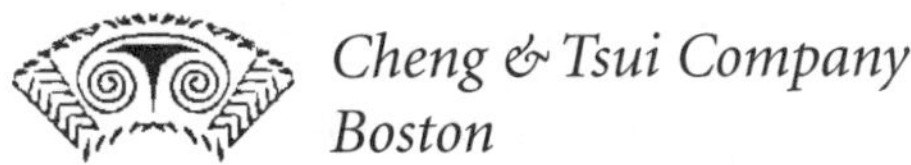

Cheng & Tsui Company
Boston

10 09 08 07 06 05 04   6 5 4 3 2 1

Printed in the U.S.A.

Published by
Cheng & Tsui Company
25 West Street
Boston, MA 02111-1213 USA
Fax (617) 426-3669
www.cheng-tsui.com
"Bringing Asia to the World"™

Library of Congress Cataloging-in-Publication Data

Imaeda, Kazuko.
Breeze into Japanese : practical language for beginners / Kazuko Imaeda.
     p.   cm.
  ISBN 0-88727-422-6 (pbk.)
  1. Japanese language—Conversation and phrase books—English. I. Title.
  PL539.I43 2003
  495.6'3421—dc22

                                    2003023024

Quality Paperback with 2 Audio CDs ISBN 0-88727-422-6

Kintaibashi Bridge, Yamaguchi

# Contents

1. LET'S PRONOUNCE JAPANESE! 1

In this lesson you will learn:

> *Speaking*
> To read and pronounce romanized Japanese characters

> Long Vowels
> Double Consonants

2. LET'S SPEAK JAPANESE! 5

In this lesson you will learn:

> *Speaking*
> To use simple greetings and phrases

3. FOOD, FOOD AND MORE FOOD 9

In this lesson you will learn:

> *Speaking*
> To make simple requests such as asking for food
>
> *Grammar*
> To know the basic differences between English and Japanese grammar
> To understand the role of the particles **wa, ga, o, to** and **ka** in Japanese

> Conversation: May I Have Tempura Please?

7. FOCUS ON ACTION: VERBS   53

In this lesson you will learn:

Speaking
To talk about what people do or don't do
To ask "Would you like to _?"

Grammar
To use **V•masu**-verbs
To use the interrogative pronouns **nan** and **nani**
To understand how to indicate future tense with **V•masu**-verbs

8. THE MIGHTY LITTLE WORDS: JAPANESE PARTICLES   69

In this lesson you will learn:

Speaking
To talk about how and where something is done
To ask how to say something in Japanese/English
To talk about doing things with others
To ask if your listener agrees
To make an exclamation

Grammar
To expand action sentences with the particles **de** and **to**
To use the particle **de** with the verb **desu**
To use the particles **ne** and **yo** at the end of sentences
To understand word order in Japanese sentences

Contents

9. NUMBERS, DATES AND TIMES — 83

In this lesson you will learn:
    Speaking
    To tell someone your telephone number
    To ask how much something is
    To tell and ask the date
    To tell and ask the time
    Grammar
    To understand the suffixes associated with numbers

In this lesson you will learn:

Speaking

To talk about daily routines and habits

To talk about people doing the same things as others

To talk about people doing several things

To express to whom or for whom something is done

To ask somebody to join you in an activity

Grammar

To understand the role of the particles **mo** and **ni**

To use more transitive verbs

To expand basic sentence structure to indicate time of action

To understand the difference between specific time and general time in time expression

In this lesson you will learn:

Speaking

To talk about people going to and coming from places and events

To describe transportations to get to places

To talk on the telephone

Grammar

To use the verbs of motion

To understand the roles of the particles **e, kara, ni** and **made**

Contents

15. YOKO IS MORE BEAUTIFUL THAN I AM. BUT HANAKO IS THE MOST BEAUTIFUL OF ALL.   163

In this lesson you will learn:

    Speaking
    To describe how something is done
    To talk with the words "very" and "not very"
    To make comparisons

    Grammar
    To use adverbs
    To convert the adjectives you've learned into adverbs
    To understand comparisons of adjectives
    To use the comparative degree with the particle **yori**
    To use the superlative degree with the adverbs **ichi-ban** and **mottomo**

16. THAT DARNED CAT IS IN MY GARDEN!   175

In this lesson you will learn:

    Speaking
    To talk about positions or locations of things, people and shops
    To express "to have"

    Grammar
    To use the verbs **arimasu** and **imasu**
    To understand the difference between the particles **ni** and **de**

17. I'M LOST! WHERE IS THE STATION?   187

In this lesson you will learn:

Speaking
To use words such as "on," "beside," "above" and "below" to describe the location of things
To use words such as "before" and "after" to talk about when you do something
To ask for directions, and understand directions that are given to you

Grammar
To use the particle **no** to connect two nouns
To use the particles **mae** and **ato**
To understand the expressions associated with directions

18. IT WILL RAIN TOMORROW!   199

In this lesson you will learn:

Speaking
To talk about things that happen naturally
To talk about people causing things to happen
To talk about things that are being done
To talk about the weather
To talk about what people can do and understand

Grammar
To understand the differences between Japanese and English intransitive verbs
To understand when to use the particles **ga** and **wa** after a subject
To use the verbs **dekimasu** and **wakarimasu**

19. IT ALL HAPPENED YESTERDAY — 211

In this lesson you will learn:

Speaking
To talk about what people did or didn't do in the past
To say when people do or did things

Grammar
To use the past tense
To understand the relative time expressions

20. TOMORROW IS ANOTHER DAY! — 223

In this lesson you will learn:

Speaking
To express your plans and goals for the future
To talk about changes you anticipate in the future

Grammar
To use future tense
To use the verb **narimasu**

21. SHALL I SUGGEST? OR SHALL I DEMAND? — 235

In this lesson you will learn:

Speaking
To suggest that someone do things with you: "Let's ___"
To order someone to do something
To visit a doctor and describe how you feel physically

Grammar
To use **V•mashō** to make a polite request
To use **V•nasai** to make an imperative sentence

22. SOME AND ANY — 247

In this lesson you will learn:

Speaking

To express quantities with the words "some" and "any"

Grammar

To understand the use of **ka, demo** and **mo** after interrogatives

23. DESIRES — 253

In this lesson you will learn:

Speaking

To talk about your desires and wishes in both the present and the past

To use phrases starting with "which," "that," and "where" to describe people, places, and things

Grammar

To use **V•tai** verbs

To expand sentence structure with adjective clauses

In this lesson, you will learn:
To read Japanese characters called hiragana

In this lesson, you will learn:
To read Japanese characters called katakana

In this lesson, you will learn:
Some kanji

Japanese Customs and Culture

Writing Exercises

Acknowledgments

I thank Professor Mitsuru Shimpo, Professor Kuninosuke Imaeda and Dr. Mari Imaeda for carefully proofreading the manuscript.

I thank Mr. Todd Marshall-Taylor and the University of Waterloo for use of the language laboratory, Ms. Meiko Ando for drawing some of the illustrations, and Mr. Masahiko Yokouchi for helping to record the CDs.

Finally, I thank my publisher Ms. Jill Cheng, my directorial editor Ms. Kristen Wanner, my production manager Ms. Sandra Korinchak, and all the people involved in the production of my book at Cheng & Tsui Company. They have always been very helpful and courteous.

 # Introduction

This book will enable you to teach yourself Japanese. The contents have been carefully chosen to provide you with the essential minimum for saying whatever you are likely to want to say. However, this book is more than simply a "conversational survival manual": *Breeze into Japanese* has been designed to teach Japanese step by step as logically as possible, and the teaching approach it uses will give you not just the ability to ask for post card stamps in Tokyo, but also a solid grammatical understanding of the language and a firm foundation for more advanced studies in Japanese.

Breeze into Japanese is designed so that you may focus only on speaking Japanese and understanding spoken Japanese. You may learn to read and write some Japanese as well. It all depends on what you wish! If you are interested in reading and writing Japanese, you'll want to spend time on the writing practice exercises found throughout the book. Typically, five characters are introduced in each exercise and they may be studied whenever you are ready to do so. Lessons 24, 25 and 26 will also be important to you, since they introduce and explain the written language.

How Rōmaji Will Help You Breeze into Japanese

Japanese sentences are written in a combination of characters called kanji, hiragana and katakana. **Kanji** consists of old Chinese characters, derived from ideograms (symbols used to represent ideas) and pictographs (pictures); each kanji has a complete meaning. Hiragana and katakana are more like two sets of "alphabetical fonts" in the English language. They are phonetic syllabic characters: each character represents a sound without any meaning. For every syllabic character in hiragana, there is a corresponding syllabic character in katakana. **Hiragana** is used in writing Japanese when kanji characters are not available or when a writer does not know them. **Katakana** is used for foreign words, other than Chinese, which are now a part of Japanese vocabulary. And a system of romanized spelling, **rōmaji**, is used to express Japanese sounds with the English alphabet.

Throughout lessons 1 to 23 of *Breeze into Japanese*, rōmaji is used to represent Japanese sounds. There are several reasons for this. First, learning Japanese through unfamiliar written symbols delays the process of learning spoken Japanese and causes confusion. Second, the reading of Japanese is a process which requires in-depth study in itself, and unless you have first mastered some spoken Japanese, you are unlikely to make easy headway with the written language.

The transition from rōmaji to hiragana is introduced in lesson 24; katakana and some kanji characters are introduced in lessons 25 and 26.

Symbols to Guide You

Throughout this book, you will see the following symbols:

 This symbol, at the beginning of a lesson, tells you what you will be learning in the lesson.

 This symbol, at the end of a lesson, tells you what you must remember from the lesson to proceed to the next lesson.

 This symbol denotes sections which are on the audio CDs.

 This symbol highlights basic sentence structures, phrases and grammatical rules which are important and which you should memorize.

 This symbol highlights information about Japanese culture, customs and events in history.

A Note about the Conversations

Conversations are included from time to time to reinforce what you have learned so far. In Japanese, the spoken language and the written language can seem to be very different. This is because when Japanese people talk, they omit parts of a sentence that may be understood from the context or situation. For example, if a speaker is talking about himself, it is common for him to omit the subject, "I," from the second sentence onward since it is understood without saying. For the sake of understanding the conversations clearly, throughout the book you'll see that those "omitted" parts are included in lighter print and enclosed in parentheses. When you practice the conversations aloud, you should omit the parts in parentheses—just as a Japanese native speaker would. (By the way, all the sentences in examples are written in full.)

Levels of "Politeness" in Japanese Speech

There are four levels of speech style in Japanese: polite speech, plain speech, honorific speech and rude language. **Polite speech** is used in formal situations, in business, in the classroom, when addressing audiences, when shopping, and when speaking to strangers or superiors. **Plain speech** is used in informal, everyday situations among family, friends, equals or when addressing children. **Honorific speech** is used to show respect to one's superiors, or to customers. **Rude language** is used towards inferiors, or as insults. Throughout this book, I have used the polite form of the Japanese language: it is safer to be polite than plain, and honorific speech is not expected of non-native speakers.

A Note about the Verbs

In English, a verb's tenses, voices, numbers, etc. are expressed by changing the form (*eat, eats, ate, eaten, eating*) and using the auxiliary verbs "to be" (*am* eating, *will* eat, *will be* eating) and "to have" (*have* eaten, *had* eaten). A Japanese verb operates in a similar way. A Japanese verb conjugates (meaning it changes its ending), just as an English verb changes its form, and auxiliaries are attached at the end of a verb, just as auxiliaries are put in front of a verb in English. In Japanese, various verbs, adjectives and particles function as auxiliaries.

There are six forms for a verb and many auxiliaries in Japanese. The verbs I have introduced in this book, namely **V•masu,** are not the basic form; rather, they are one of many variations. In fact, **V•masu** is one of the six verb forms plus the auxiliary verb **masu. Masu** expresses the polite speech style and it is **masu** that conjugates to form various tenses for the polite speech style. Unlike English, which uses the basic verb form (e.g., *eat, sleep, read*) most frequently in everyday life, Japanese uses one of the variations, namely **V•masu,** most commonly, and it is those verbs that you will learn in this book. I shall call them **V•masu**-verbs collectively.

Singular and Plural—One and the Same!

Most Japanese nouns and pronouns remain the same word whether they're in singular or plural form. Hence Japanese nouns and pronouns must be translated according to their context within a sentence. For example, samurai can mean *a warrior* or *warriors*. The English translations for most nouns and pronouns have been put in the singular form in the examples in this book, although they could just as easily have been put in the plural form. (Explanations are given in detail in lesson 3.)

A Few More Notes before You Begin

The prefix **o** enclosed in parentheses—that is, (**o**)—indicates that **o** is a term of politeness rather than a part of the word itself, and it is excluded in the glossary. Hyphens (-) between syllables of words are included in order to clarify and aid the pronunciation, and they are included in the glossary.

Whenever a word is defined as belonging to one part of speech or grammatical group in English and another in Japanese, I have used the definition of English grammar in this book. Any differences in definition are pointed out for you with footnotes. I have followed the latest *Kokugo Jiten,* published by Shōgakkan on 1 January 2002, for the definitions of Japanese grammar.

You may obtain the answers to the exercises by visiting www.cheng-tsui.com, and any comments or questions may be sent to kazukoimaeda@sympatico.ca.

Enjoy your learning.

Let's Pronounce Japanese!

Speaking
To read and pronounce romanized Japanese characters

にほんご	ニホンゴ	日本語
JAPANESE WRITTEN IN HIRAGANA	*JAPANESE* WRITTEN IN KATAKANA	*JAPANESE* WRITTEN IN KANJI

italiano	français
ITALIAN WRITTEN IN ITALIAN	*FRENCH* WRITTEN IN FRENCH

The first thing you must learn when you start learning any foreign language from a book is to read words in that language. Because Japanese characters are so totally different from English characters, learning Japanese is not the same as learning French or Italian. In the examples above, you may be able to read the words in French or Italian, more or less, even if you have never learned the languages before, because they use the same letters as English. But you cannot even remotely guess what the words say in Japanese. So how can you learn Japanese from a book if you can't read it?

To solve this problem, the Japanese words in this book are written in romanized characters, using a system of phonetic transcription called rōmaji in Japanese.

JAPANESE SYLLABLES

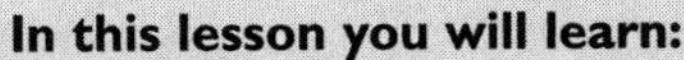 In pronouncing Japanese, each syllable, the fancy word for an individual sound, receives approximately equal stress and time. Study the Japanese syllables below carefully until you are familiar with them.

a	*i*	*u*	*e*	*o*		*ga*	*gi*	*gu*	*ge*	*go*		*kya*	*kyu*	*kyo*
ka	*ki*	*ku*	*ke*	*ko*		*za*	*ji*	*zu*	*ze*	*zo*		*sha*	*shu*	*sho*
sa	*shi*	*su*	*se*	*so*		*da*			*de*	*do*		*cha*	*chu*	*cho*
ta	*chi*	*tsu*	*te*	*to*		*ba*	*bi*	*bu*	*be*	*bo*		*nya*	*nyu*	*nyo*
na	*ni*	*nu*	*ne*	*no*		*pa*	*pi*	*pu*	*pe*	*po*		*hya*	*hyu*	*hyo*
ha	*hi*	*fu*	*he*	*ho*								*mya*	*myu*	*myo*
ma	*mi*	*mu*	*me*	*mo*								*rya*	*ryu*	*ryo*
ya		*yu*		*yo*								*gya*	*gyu*	*gyo*
ra	*ri*	*ru*	*re*	*ro*								*ja*	*ju*	*jo*
wa				*wo*								*bya*	*byu*	*byo*
n												*pya*	*pyu*	*pyo*

Because we shall often be using the term *vowel* in this book, it is important to understand exactly what it means. In English there are six vowels, *a, e, i, o, u* and *y* (every English word must contain at least one vowel). But the Japanese government standardization decrees that there are five vowels, **a, i, u, e** and **o**, in Japanese.

A note of caution is essential with regard to the syllables **ra, ri, ru, re** and **ro**. In fact, Japanese has no sound equivalent to English *r*; the syllables **ra, ri, ru, re** and **ro** are pronounced as **la, li, lu, le** and **lo** in English. However, because the Japanese government standardization of rōmaji calls for writing **ra, ri, ru, re** and **ro,** I have used these syllables also.

HOW TO READ A JAPANESE WORD

The easiest way of pronouncing a Japanese word is to break it up using a slash (/) after every vowel (**a, i, u, e, o**) and reading each syllable separately.

Examples

O/ya/su/mi/na/sa/i/	*Good night*
Ta/da/i/ma/	*I am back (now)*

When the characters between the two slashes start with **n,** you must do a test. If this **n** is not followed by a vowel or a **y,** it is a syllabic **n**—pronounced separately—and you put a slash after the **n.**

Examples

Ko/nba/nwa/	*Good evening*

The **n** is not followed by a vowel or a **y,** and so it is a syllabic **n.** Therefore, you put a slash after the **n. Ko/n/ba/n/wa/**

Similarly, **Go/me/nna/sa/i/** *Sorry* becomes **Go/me/n/na/sa/i/.**

Long Vowels

When a vowel has a bar over it, the effect is to lengthen it to almost double the length of the regular vowel. The difference between a long vowel and a regular vowel is important in Japanese, since the meanings of many words change according to the lengths of the vowels.

Examples

obasan aunt	*obāsan grandmother*
tori bird	*tōri street*
ojisan uncle	*ojīsan grandfather*

I have used the following system to indicate long vowels.

ā is pronounced as **a/a/**	**ē** is pronounced as **e/e/**
ī is pronounced as **i/i/**	**ō** is pronounced as **o/o/**
ū is pronounced as **u/u/**	

          Lesson 1: Let's Pronounce Japanese!

🔘 *Examples*

O/ha/yō/go/za/i/ma/su/	*Good morning*

This is pronounced as **O/ha/yo/o/go/za/i/ma/su/**.

A/ri/ga/tō/	*Thank you*

This is pronounced as **A/ri/ga/to/o/**.

O/bā/sa/n/ is pronounced as **o/ba/a/sa/n/**.

O/jī/sa/n/ is pronounced as **o/ji/i/sa/n/**.

Double Consonants

Double consonants (**kk, pp, tt, ss**) are given twice the length of a single one. The first consonant is a momentary silent pause, equivalent in time of one syllable of Japanese, and the second consonant is pronounced as usual.

🔘 *Examples*

Nippon	*Japan*	is pronounced as *Ni/*(short pause)*/po/n/*
zasshi	*magazine*	is pronounced as *za/*(short pause)*/shi/*
gakkō	*school*	is pronounced as *ga/*(short pause)*/ko/o/*
kippu	*ticket*	is pronounced as *ki/*(short pause)*/pu*

Although you don't need to practice this right away, you should be aware of the following. The vowels **i** and **u** are whispered (almost not pronounced) when they occur between a pair of **f, h, k, p, s, t, ch, sh** and **ts**, or when they occur at the end of a sentence after **f, h, k, p, s, t, ch, sh** and **ts**. The most noticeable whispering sounds are those of **u** for the verbs **V•masu** and **desu** when they occur at the ends of sentences. You will notice this on the CDs: they sound like "**V•mas**" and "**des**" sometimes, and "**V•masu**" and "**desu**" other times.

EXERCISES

1.1. 🔘 *Listen to the sound of each syllable, and write down the rōmaji for that syllable. You may use the syllable table on page 1.*

1. _______	2. _______	3. _______	4. _______	5. _______
6. _______	7. _______	8. _______	9. _______	10. _______
11. _______	12. _______	13. _______	14. _______	15. _______
16. _______	17. _______	18. _______	19. _______	20. _______

1.2. *Listen to the words carefully, and write them down in rōmaji. You may use the syllable table on page 1.*

1.__________   2. ___________   3. __________

1.3.  *Listen to each word, find it in the list below, and mark its letter in the blank.*

1. __*a*__ 2. ______ 3. ______ 4. ______ 5. ______ 6. ______ 7. ______ 8. ______ 9. ______

a. *Nippon* b. *tōri* c. *ojisan* d. *obasan* e. *gakkō* f. *ojīsan* g. *tori* h. *obāsan* i. *zasshi*

1.4. Rewrite the following words adding slashes (/) and "(short pause)s" to indicate their syllables, and then practice their pronunciation.

1. *hajimemashite* ____

2. *okaerinasai* ____

3. *konnichiwa* ____

4. *sumimasen* ____

5. *otōsan* ____

6. *okāsan* ____

7. *koppu* ____

8. *kitte* ____

What you must remember from this lesson to proceed to the next lesson:

Each Japanese syllable receives approximately equal stress and time.

The procedure for reading a Japanese word:

1. Put a slash (/) after every vowel (**a, i, u, e, o**).
2. Check whether any character groups between two slashes start with **n**. If they start with **n** and if the **n** is not followed by a vowel or a **y**, put a slash after the **n**.
3. If a vowel (**a, i, u, e, o**) has a bar over it, replace it with **a/a, i/i, u/u, e/e, o/o**.
4. If there is a double consonant (**kk, pp, tt, ss**), replace it with (silent pause)/**k**, (silent pause)/**p**, (silent pause)/**t**, (silent pause)/**s**.

Lesson 1: Let's Pronounce Japanese!

2 Let's Speak Japanese!

Speaking
To use simple greetings and phrases

In the previous lesson, you learned to read Japanese words. In the English language, a syllable may be pronounced differently depending on what comes before and after it. For example, *"the"* is pronounced differently in *"the"* and *"theater."* In the Japanese language, syllables are always pronounced the same way, no matter where in words they appear, and this makes it much easier to learn the language.

In this lesson, you will be learning simple greetings and phrases such as "Good morning," "Good afternoon," "I am sorry" and "How are you?". You will be surprised by the power of these simple greetings and phrases accompanied by your charming smile: in no time, you will have plenty of Japanese friends. Since these greetings and phrases will be used constantly, they should be memorized.

SIMPLE GREETINGS AND PHRASES

Here is a list, continuing on the next page, of simple greetings and phrases which are fairly straightforward to use. Practice them with the CD:

Ohayōgozaimasu.	*Good morning.*
Konnichiwa.	*Good afternoon, Good day.*
Konbanwa.	*Good evening.*
Oyasuminasai.	*Good night.*
Sayōnara.	*Good-bye.*
Dewa mata.	*See you.*
Hajimemashite.	*How do you do?*
Dōzo yoroshiku	*Pleased to meet you.*
(O)genki desu ka.	*How are you?*
Hai genki desu.	*I am fine.*
Hai okagesamade.	*I am fine, thank you.*

Dōzo.	*Please.*

Gomennasai.	*Sorry.*
Sumimasen.	*Excuse me, Pardon me.*

Arigatō.	*Thank you.*
Dō itashimashite.	*You are welcome.*

Whenever you come home from work, school, shopping, traveling and so on, you say **tadaima,** *I am back (now),* as a greeting. Whoever is there will acknowledge you by saying **okaerinasai,** *welcome back.*

Tadaima.	*I am back (now)*
Okaerinasai.	*Welcome back.*

Whenever you start to eat or drink something, you say **itadakimasu,** implying gratitude to the person who prepared or offered it, good fortune for being able to afford it, etc. When you finish, you say **gochisōsama,** *thank you, it was delicious,* to the person who prepared or offered it. **Itadakimasu** is also used when you take a gift, implying both acceptance and gratitude.

Itadakimasu.	*Thank you for the gift (when receiving it).*
	Thank you for the food (before eating).
Gochisōsama.	*Thank you for the delicious food (after eating).*

Whenever you are introduced, you say **hajimemashite, dōzo yoroshiku.** The phrase **dōzo yoroshiku** used after **hajimemashite,** *how do you do?,* expresses desire for a friendly relationship in the future and may be thought as *please be good to me in the future* or *pleased to meet you.*

After you ask a favor, you say **dōzo yoroshiku** by itself. It means *please take good care of the matter I asked.* It is also used after _ **ni,** *to* _, to express kind regards to a person or persons not present, and it is translated as *please give my regards to _.*

Dōzo yoroshiku.	*Pleased to meet you (in introductions).*
	Please do as I requested (after asking for a favor).
____ ni dōzo yoroshiku.	*Please give my regards to ____.*

JAPANESE CUSTOMS AND CULTURE

Bowing

Japanese people bow to each other on occasions when Westerners shake hands, when greeting someone or saying good-bye, and when expressing gratitude or apology. When you bow, you bend from the waist. Also, you don't change the angle of your head and your eyes should be looking slightly downward. The legs are kept straight and the heels should be together. A man's arms are held close to his sides and a woman's hands are put together in front, lightly touching each other. The lower ranking person (age, social status, business relations, etc., determine the rank) holds the bow lower and longer than does the higher ranking person.

 Lesson 2: Let's Speak Japanese!

Bowing was, and still is, a very important part of everyday life and a way to show your respect for others, especially superiors. During the time when samurai (warriors) ruled Japan—from the end of the twelfth century to the middle of the nineteenth century—a commoner lost his life if he did not bow to a samurai to show his respect. Samurai had a right to slice off the head of a commoner anytime the latter appeared lacking in respect. Even a foreigner did not escape this fate. In 1862, Charles Richardson, an Englishman, was out hunting when he encountered a procession of a daimyō (a local feudal lord). Because he did not dismount from his horse and bow to the daimyō, he was

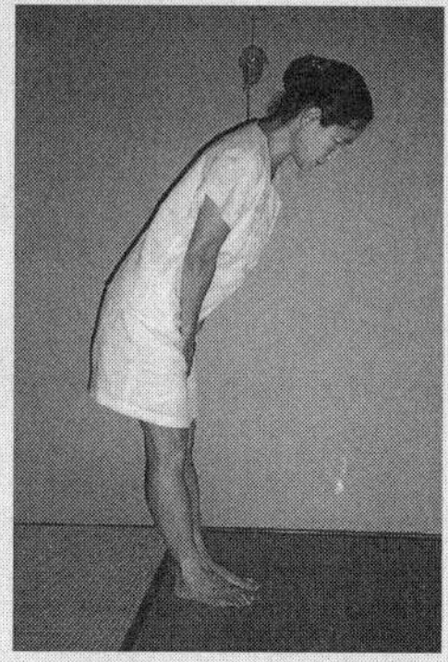
Proper way of bowing.

chased, caught and killed by the daimyō's retinue. (It was customary in those days for commoners to sit on dirt roads with their heads bowed to the ground whenever a daimyō passed with his retinue.) The British government was furious with the event and demanded a large compensation from the Shōgun (absolute military ruler of Japan under whose authority daimyō ruled locally) and the daimyō, as well as punishment of the attackers. The demands were completely ignored by the Shōgun's government and the British government subsequently sent its navy to Japan in retaliation.

Feudal lords built castles for fortification against enemies. Himeji Castle, Himeji.

When Japanese people talk face to face, they do not make eye-to-eye contact. They view it as intimidating, and it is interpreted not as a sign of interest and respect, but as an indication of the speaker's defiance. Sometimes, Japanese people smile not just when they are happy or amused, but also when they are sad or embarrassed, to hide their feeling or embarrassment. Japanese people generally refrain from showing negative emotions in public because they do not want to make other people feel uncomfortable.

Some Characteristics of Japanese Society and People

As soon as a Japanese child starts to go to kindergarten, he is encouraged to work in a group, and this trend continues throughout his life. He gains a strong sense of belonging to a group whose interests may sometimes override his own: there is a tendency to conform to the character of his group rather than develop his own individual personality. A Japanese person may belong to many groups, and everyone is conscious of his rank in the group. Any individual who stands out in a group might be treated with suspicion or even be isolated. Japanese hate to be laughed at or singled out in any way, tending to be bold in groups but very timid alone. The Japanese language has different forms of addressing and talking to people according to their positions on the social scale. Guns are illegal in Japan and even the police do not carry them. The crime rate is very low and, for example, lost wallets are usually turned in to police stations. Japanese society is that of "men first" and not "ladies first": men do not open the doors for women. Although it may be common in Western cultures to do so, Japanese hardly show any affection, feelings or anger in public: they never embrace, cry, kiss and so on in public places. For the Japanese, calmness and harmony are high ideals. While kissing or hugging in public is treated as improper, it is becoming more and more prevalent among young people in their teens and twenties due to the influence of the West. Almost every Japanese person has brown eyes and black hair because there were no interracial marriages until fairly recently. However, many young Japanese men and women dye their hair to be fashionable.

EXERCISES

2.1. In this exercise, you are going to speak Japanese with me. I shall speak to you first, and I want you to reply to me. You may check your replies against the correct answers recorded at the end of this exercise.

2.2. Listen to the track for Exercise 2.1 again, and choose from below the context in which each greeting you hear should be used.

1. ___d___ 2. ______ 3. ______ 4. ______ 5. ______ 6. ______ 7. ______ 8. ______

a. greeting in the morning

b. when you are introduced to a stranger

c. greeting in the afternoon

d. when you come home from school

e. greeting in the evening

f. when you go to bed

g. after eating

h. when you part from a friend

What you must remember from this lesson to proceed to the next lesson:
All the simple greetings and phrases.

     Lesson 2: Let's Speak Japanese!

3   Food, Food and More Food

You are now able to greet people you see, and I hope that you have broken the ice with your charming smile. The next step is to go out into town for shopping and dining.

In this lesson, you will learn to ask for things such as an apple or a steak: you will learn to say sentences such as "May I have a steak please?," "May I have a coffee please?," and so on. Also, you are going to venture out to restaurants.

BASIC DIFFERENCES BETWEEN ENGLISH AND JAPANESE

There are several basic differences between English and Japanese, and I shall mention them briefly. (If you have forgotten English grammar, or are interested in more detail, take a look at the Appendix.)

Japanese nouns have no special forms to show whether they are singular or plural (both *an apple* and *apples* have the same form in Japanese). There are no articles (*the, a, an*) in Japanese. Hence **ringo** means *an apple, apples, some apples, the apple,* or *the apples*. Which translation to choose may usually be decided from the context without ambiguity. Similarly, most Japanese pronouns have no special forms to show whether they are singular or plural. Hence *this* and *these* have the same word, **kore,** in Japanese.

Japanese verbs do not have different forms to indicate whether their subjects are singular or plural or whether they are first person, second person or third person. Hence the verbs *am, is* and *are* all have the same verb, **desu,** in Japanese. Japanese verbs are placed at the ends of sentences or just before them if **ka/ne/yo** is placed at the ends. Japanese verbs conjugate (meaning they change their endings). Similarly, Japanese adjectives also conjugate.

PARTICLES

Let us consider the sentence *The cat chases the mouse.* The easiest way to analyze a sentence is to look first for the verb of the sentence. The action word in the sentence is *chases,* and hence *chas-*

es is the verb of the sentence. The subject is the person/thing which chases, and it is *the cat* which chases. What *the cat chases* is the direct object, and it is *the mouse* which is chased. The meaning of the sentence is very different if *the cat* and *the mouse* are interchanged, that is: *the mouse chases the cat*. In an English statement with an active verb, a subject must come before the verb and a direct object must come after the verb.

In Japanese, words are combined together quite differently from English to form sentences. Japanese has little words called particles, and they are usually made out of one or two syllables (such as **wa, ga** and **o**).

Particles are placed after words to indicate their purposes in sentences. For example, **o** is placed after direct objects and **wa/ga** is placed after subjects in statements.

Hence, wherever a subject or a direct object is placed in a sentence, there is no confusion as to which word is the subject and which word is the direct object. Only verbs have fixed locations in sentences: verbs in Japanese come at the ends of sentences or just before them if **ka/ne/yo** is placed at the ends. Japanese prepositions and conjunctions are members of the particle category.

MAY I HAVE AN APPLE PLEASE?

The simplest way to ask for something is to use the sentence structure

object **o kudasai.**

Kudasai, the last word in the sentence, is the verb meaning *May I have ___ please?*

O is the particle which indicates that the preceeding word is the direct object of the verb **kudasai.**

Examples

Ringo o kudasai.	*May I have an apple please?*
Orenji o kudasai.	*May I have an orange please?*

 Here are some fruits and vegetables that we'll use in this lesson.

Nouns

kudamono fruits

banana banana	*orenji* orange	
budō grape	*painappuru* pineapple	
ichigo strawberry	*ringo* apple	
mikan tangerine	*sakuranbo* cherry	
momo peach	*suika* watermelon	
nashi pear	*tomato* tomato	

yasai vegetables

daikon large white radish
hakusai Chinese cabbage
jagaimo potato
kyūri cucumber
ninjin carrot
tamanegi round onion

You know by now that **banana** may be translated as *a banana, bananas, some bananas, the banana* or *the bananas*, depending on the context of a sentence.

            Lesson 3: Food, Food and More Food

That was easy, wasn't it? But now, you are more ambitious: you don't want just apples. You want apples and tangerines.

 The particle **to,** when used between nouns, is translated as *and* or *both __ and __.*

Examples

ringo to mikan	*an apple and a tangerine*
banana to mikan	*a banana and a tangerine*
Ringo to mikan o kudasai.	*May I have both an apple and a tangerine please?*

 The particle **ka,** when used between nouns, acts like the English *or* or *either __ or __.*

Examples

ringo ka orenji	*an apple or an orange*
yasai ka kudamono	*vegetables or fruits*
Ringo ka orenji o kudasai.	*May I have either an apple or an orange please?*

LET'S GO TO A RESTAURANT

One of the alluring features of walking Japanese streets is the mouth-watering displays of food in the show windows of restaurants. In front of most restaurants in Japan, you will usually find a window display of models of various Japanese dishes. Although made of colorful plastics, they look very appetizing and you can't avoid looking at them. They are everywhere! The names for the dishes and their prices are displayed beside them. You can choose the dish you want to order before you enter the restaurant and be sure of what you will get.

Let us now investigate these attractive dishes since it is important to know what they actually are—looks are sometimes misleading. The names of the dishes and their translations (or description of the contents in case there is no exact translation) are as follows:

Some Typical Japanese Dishes

donburi	*bowl of cooked rice with toppings of meat, fish, eggs and vegetables*
hanbāgā	*hamburger*
jūsu	*juice*
karēraisu	*Indian curry*
kōhī	*coffee*
okonomiyaki	*meat and vegetable pancake*
pan	*bread*
rāmen	*ramen (noodles in a hot soup with some garnishing)*
sandoicchi	*sandwich*
sarada	*salad*

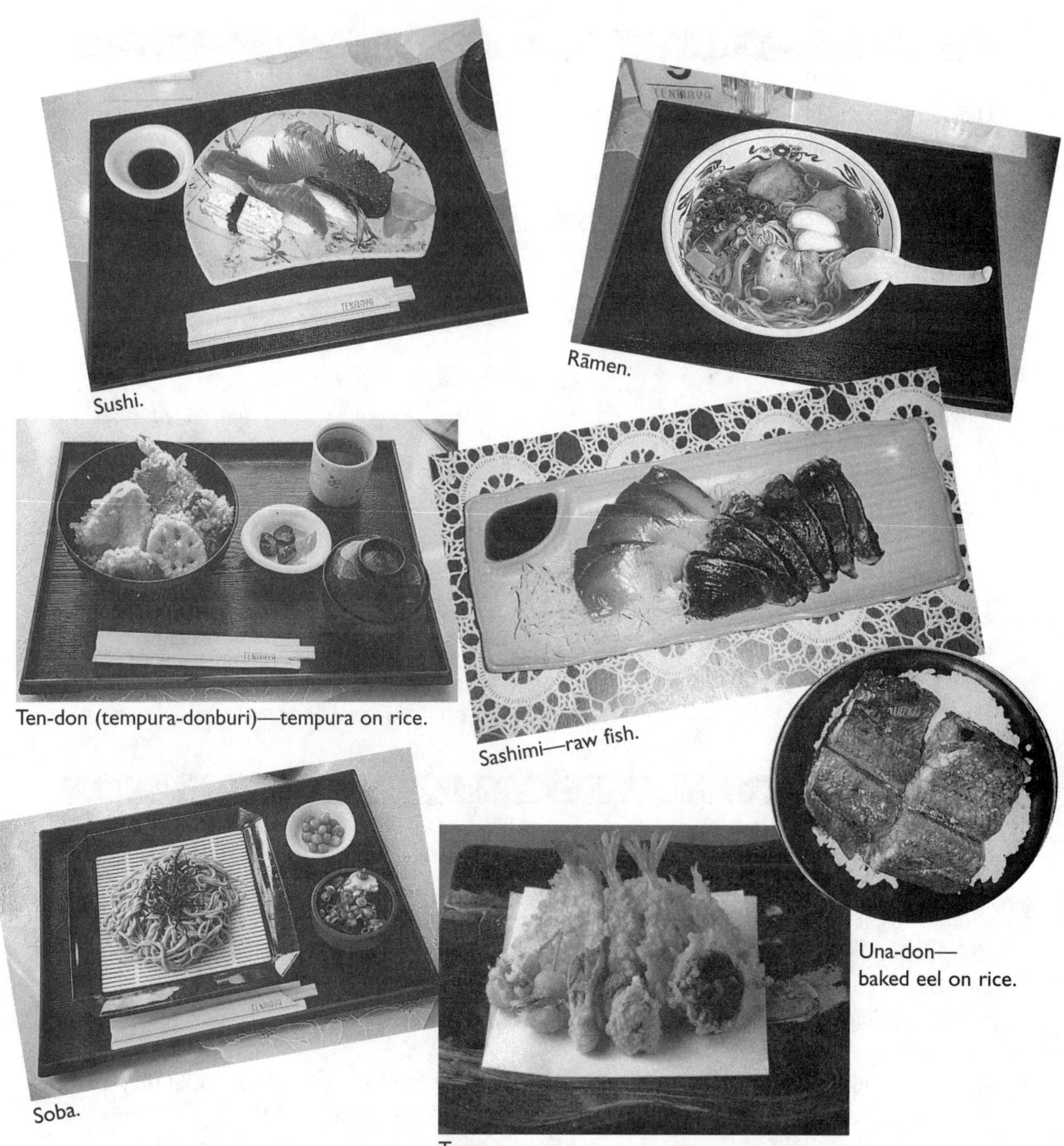

Sushi.

Rāmen.

Ten-don (tempura-donburi)—tempura on rice.

Sashimi—raw fish.

Una-don—
baked eel on rice.

Soba.

Tempura.

soba	buckwheat noodles eaten either with a cold dipping sauce or in a hot broth
sukiyaki	meat and vegetables cooked in sweetened soy sauce
sushi	raw fish placed on top of vinegared rice balls; fish, vegetables and cooked eggs mixed in, or rolled with, vinegared rice
sutēki	steak
tenpura	tempura (pieces of food coated with thin batter and then deep fried)
tonkatsu	pork cutlet
udon	thick noodles in hot soup, garnished with meat and vegetables
yakisoba	fried noodles with meat and vegetables (Chinese chow mein)
yakitori	small chicken pieces skewered and barbequed with sauce

     Lesson 3: Food, Food and More Food

Now, you are ready to go into a restaurant; you know what you want to order and how to order it. As soon as you step one foot into a restaurant, you will hear **irasshaimase** from waiters. Sometimes **irasshaimase** is said gently with a deep bow by the waiter in charge; more often, however, it is said loudly by many of them, one after another, from all quarters.

Irasshaimase is a greeting to a customer when he or she comes into a restaurant or a shop. It is translated as *Hello and welcome!* or *Come in!*

You usually don't reply to these greetings unless you are friendly with the waiters or the shop clerks. From a waiter's or a clerk's point of view, you, a customer, must be cherished, and your entrance stirs up so many welcoming greetings to make you feel good. You may also be greeted with **irasshaimase** when you visit someone's home.

 Conversation: May I Have Tempura Please?

Tom, an American, has just moved to Japan with his family. This is his first visit to a Japanese restaurant.

Waitress:	*Irasshaimase.*	*Hello and welcome!*
Tom:	*Konnichiwa.*	*Good afternoon.*
	Tenpura o kudasai.	*May I have tempura please?*
Waitress:	*Hai.*	*Certainly (Yes).*

The waitress comes back with a dish of tempura.

| Waitress: | *Dōzo.* | *Please.* |
| Tom: | *Arigatō.* | *Thank you (for bringing the food).* |

EXERCISES

3.1. *Listen and choose from below which food item I have requested. In questions 1 through 3, I am asking for these items in a restaurant; in questions 4 through 8, I am asking my sister to get them for me.*

1. __*d*__ 2. _______ 3. _______ 4. _______ 5. _______ 6. _______ 7. _______ 8. _______

a. sandwich   b. watermelon   c. apple   d. coffee   e. bread   f. tangerine   g. potato   h. steak

3.2. Translate into English:

1. *Banana o kudasai.* ____

2. *Sushi o kudasai.* ____

3. *Sutēki to pan* ____

4. *Sutēki to pan o kudasai.* ____

5. *Kōhī ka jūsū* ____

6. *Kōhī ka jūsū o kudasai.* ____

7. **Ringo to mikan to banana o kudasai.** ____

Translate into rōmaji:

8. May I have apples please? ____

9. May I have Indian curry please? ____

10. A banana or an orange ____

11. May I have a banana or an orange please? ____

12. Tempura and soba ____

13. May I have tempura and soba please? ____

14. May I have coffee, bread and a pork cutlet please? ____

____

3.3.  *You are in a restaurant. Ask a waiter for the following familiar dishes, using the sentence structure _ o kudasai. Say each sentence aloud. You may check what you have said against the correct answers recorded on the track for Exercise 3.3.*

1. hamburger   2. juice   3. salad   4. steak   5. coffee and sandwich

You are in a hospital with a broken leg. Ask your friend to pass the following fruit.

6. banana   7. orange or apple   8. strawberry and pear

What you must remember from this lesson to proceed to the next lesson:

Particles are put after words to indicate their purposes in a sentence.

The particle **o** is placed after a direct object (except for direct replies).

The particle **wa/ga** is placed after a subject (except for direct replies).

Verbs are placed at the ends of sentences or just before them if **ka/ne/yo** is placed at the ends.

_ o kudasai implies *May I have _ please?*

     Lesson 3: Food, Food and More Food

4 Introduce Yourself!

In this lesson you will learn:

Speaking
To introduce yourself and others
To describe what people, places, and things are

Grammar
To use the link-verb **desu** to form simple sentences
To use suffixes to address other people
To use the pronouns **kore, sore,** and **are**

Sentences are made from subjects and predicates, and intransitive verbs of being (those that have basically the same meaning as the verb *to be*), known also as link-verbs, require complements to complete the sentence. The function of verbs of being (link-verbs) is to link subjects with complements. In other words, *is* in the sentence "A is B" is a link-verb. Here are some sentences using verbs of being (link-verbs).

I *am* Tom.

This *is* a dog.

The various parts of the sentences may be classified as follows.

SUBJECT	PREDICATE	
	Verb of Being	*Complement*
I	am	Tom
This	is	a dog

In this lesson, you will learn to introduce yourself and others using verbs of being (link-verbs): you will learn to say sentences such as "I am Tom," "I am a Canadian," "This is (my) father," "This is (my) dog," "That is the station," "That is a school," and so on.

LINK-VERBS: IS, AM, ARE

To link subjects with complements, you use the intransitive verb **desu*** in Japanese.

subject **wa** complement **desu**

This sentence structure is used to identify some thing/one/place with some other thing/one/place. The particle **wa** follows a subject, and the complement is placed before the intransitive verb **desu,** which is placed at the end of the sentence.

*Although **desu** is defined as an auxiliary verb in Japanese grammar, I shall define it as a link-verb since its main function is to equate one thing with another, which is one of the functions of the English link-verb *to be*.

Because Japanese verbs have no special forms to show whether their subjects are singular or plural, or whether they are of the first ("I/we"), second ("you") or third ("he/she/it/they") person, **desu** is translated as *is, am* or *are*.

I Am Tom, I Am an American, I Am a Student

Let us now learn important personal pronouns.

🔘 *Personal Pronouns*

boku I, me (for boys)	*watashi* I, me (except boys)
anata you	

You may notice that boys use **boku** while everybody else uses **watashi** for *I* or *me*.

It is now a matter of putting **watashi** (or **boku**) for the subject and your name for the complement in the sentence structure _ **wa** _ **desu** to introduce yourself. I shall write the English names with English spelling, and not with Japanese (e.g., Tom and not **Tomu**).

🔘 *Examples*

Watashi wa Tom desu.	*I am Tom.*
Boku wa Tom desu.	*I am Tom.*

Let us now look at the following vocabulary of nationalities, occupations and so on. By putting these nouns in the place for the complement, you may talk a lot more about yourself.

🔘 *Nouns*

Amerika-jin American person	*gakusei* student (of a school)
Doitsu-jin German person	*ha-isha* dentist
Furansu-jin French person	*isha* physician, medical doctor
Igirisu-jin British person	*kaishain* white-collar worker
Kanada-jin Canadian person	*kangofu* nurse
Nihon-jin Japanese person	*seito* student (in general)
gaijin foreigner	*sensei* teacher
	uētā waiter
akachan baby	*uētoresu* waitress
kodomo child	
otona adult	
tomodachi friend	

🔘 *Examples*

Watashi wa Amerika-jin desu.	*I am an American.*
Watashi wa gakusei desu.	*I am a student.*

You may have noticed from the vocabulary above that words describing people of different nationalities always have **jin** at their ends (e.g., **Amerika-jin**). **Jin** is a suffix added to the name of a country to stand for its person/people. Although Japanese nouns have the same form for singular and plural (both *an apple* and *apples* are **ringo** in Japanese), an exception applies to people.

Lesson 4: Introduce Yourself!

For people, we put **tachi** after the nouns and personal pronouns to make them into the plural form. Hence **watashi-tachi** means *we* and **Amerika-jin-tachi** means *American people.*

Suffixes

-jin is added to the name of a country to stand for its person/people.
-tachi is added to make a person into a plural form; e.g., *watashi-tachi, we.*

A Japanese person has two names, a family name and a given name, and uses them in that order (for example, Hepburn Audrey). You may address or speak of a person by her family name or by a given name, according to your degree of acquaintance with her, just as in English, but the following suffix must be added to either of them.

Suffixes

-chan is added after the names of small children and especially after the names of girls; e.g., *Amy-chan, Amy.*
-kun is added after the names of boys; e.g., *Bob-kun, Bob.*
-san is added after names; it is comparable to Mr., Mrs., Miss or Ms.; e.g., *Kelly-san, Mr./Mrs./Miss/Ms. Kelly; Betty-san, Betty.*
-sensei is added after the names of teachers (of any kind) and medical doctors; e.g., *Kelly-sensei, Mr./Mrs./Miss/Ms./Dr. Kelly.*

Suffixes should never be used when you are speaking about yourself. When you address or speak of a teacher (of any kind) or a medical doctor, **sensei** must be added to the name. Teachers and medical doctors have a high social status in Japan, and, in the culture where showing respect for one another is important, it would be rude not to add **sensei** after their names.

 ## Examples

Anata wa Kelly Tom-san desu.	*You are Mr. Tom Kelly.*
Anata wa Makoto-kun desu.	*You are Makoto.*
Hanako-chan wa akachan desu.	*Hanako is a baby.*

THIS, THAT AND THAT (OVER THERE): *KORE, SORE* AND *ARE*

You now know how to address other people. The next step is to introduce and talk about other people. To do that, you need to learn pronouns such as *this* and *that* so that you are able to say sentences like "This is Tom" and "That is Helen."

While the English language has only "this" and "that," the Japanese language has **kore, sore** and **are** to indicate "this" and "that" for a thing or person.

Pronouns

kore *this;* indicates a thing/person "near the speaker."
sore *that;* indicates a thing/person "near the listener."
are *that;* indicates a thing/person "away from the speaker and the listener."

Now you are able to introduce your friends to your family.

 **Examples**

Kore wa Smith-san desu.	*This is Mr. Smith.*
Kore wa Hanako-san desu.	*This is Hanako.*

When you are introducing or referring to other people to whom you have to show your respect, such as teachers, medical doctors, your friend's father, etc., you use **kochira, sochira** and **achira.**

 **Pronouns**

kochira *this;* indicates a person "near the speaker."

sochira *that;* indicates a person "near the listener."

achira *that;* indicates a person "away from the speaker and the listener."

This Is (My) Family

You have introduced your friends to your family, and now you need to introduce your family to your friends, using the following vocabulary. They usually mean "*my* family," "*my* grandfather," "*my* father," etc., unless specified otherwise.

          Lesson 4: Introduce Yourself!

Nouns

kazoku family

ojīsan grandfather	*obāsan grandmother*
otōsan father	*okāsan mother*
onīsan older (elder) brother	*onēsan older (elder) sister*
otōto younger brother	*imōto younger sister*
ojisan uncle	*obasan aunt*

Examples

Kore wa otōsan desu.	*This is (my) father.*
Otōsan wa sensei desu.	*(My) father is a teacher.*
Kore wa otōto desu.	*This is (my) younger brother.*
Otōto wa gakusei desu.	*(My) younger brother is a student.*

It is interesting to note that there are two distinct words for *brother* (as well as *sister*) in Japanese, meaning "older brother" and "younger brother" (as well as "older sister" and "younger sister"). In the Japanese culture, it is important to distinguish whether a brother/sister is older or younger than yourself since anyone older than you has more "clout" than you have. Older people are/were respected automatically. That is why **san** is a part of words for **ojīsan, otōsan, onīsan, ojisan, obāsan, okāsan, onēsan** and **obasan** while **boku, watashi, otōto** and **imōto** do not have **san** in them.

When a Japanese person talks to or refers to an older person in the family, that older person is called or referred to as **ojīsan, otōsan, onīsan,** and so on, but the younger family member is referred to or called by their name without **san** after it.

Japanese have different words for *wife* and *husband,* depending on whose husband and whose wife, as may be seen below.

Nouns

kanai my wife	*okusan somebody else's wife*
shujin my husband	*goshujin somebody else's husband*

It is interesting that **shujin** means *master* as well as *my husband* and **goshujin** means *master* (used with respect) as well as *somebody else's husband.* Well, you may draw whatever conclusion you like from that!

This Is (My) Cat

Here are the names of some common animals.

Nouns

dōbutsu animals

ahiru duck	*neko cat*	*tora tiger*
buta pig	*nezumi mouse, rat*	*tori bird*
hebi snake	*raion lion*	*uma horse*

inu *dog*	risu *squirrel*	usagi *rabbit*
kirin *giraffe*	saru *monkey*	ushi *cow*
kuma *bear*	tanuki *badger*	zō *elephant*

Examples

Kore wa ushi desu.	This is a cow.
Sore wa inu desu.	That is a dog.
Are wa neko desu.	That (over there) is a cat.
Kore wa inu to neko desu.	These are a dog and a cat.

A FEW WORDS ABOUT BASIC CONVERSATIONS

When you begin to speak a foreign language, you should always remember to say what you want to say in simple sentences. Any complicated sentence you may want to say should be changed into simple sentences to avoid any mistakes you might otherwise make. For example, instead of saying "I am going to town to buy books," you could say "I am going to town; I am going to buy books there." In this way, you will avoid mistakes; at the same time, you may be able to come up with the sentences much faster than you could construct a more complicated sentence. For the person listening to you, it is easier to understand simple sentences than more complicated ones, with or without mistakes.

When Japanese people speak, they omit parts of sentences that may be understood from the context or situation. To help you understand the conversations clearly in this book, such parts are included and enclosed in parentheses. While practicing the conversation pieces, omit the parts in parentheses. It should be noted that, when a word is omitted from a conversation, the particle which defines the purpose of the word in the sentence is omitted with it. For example, if a subject is omitted from a sentence, the particle **wa** which defines the preceding word to be the subject in the sentence is omitted also, as shown in the following conversation.

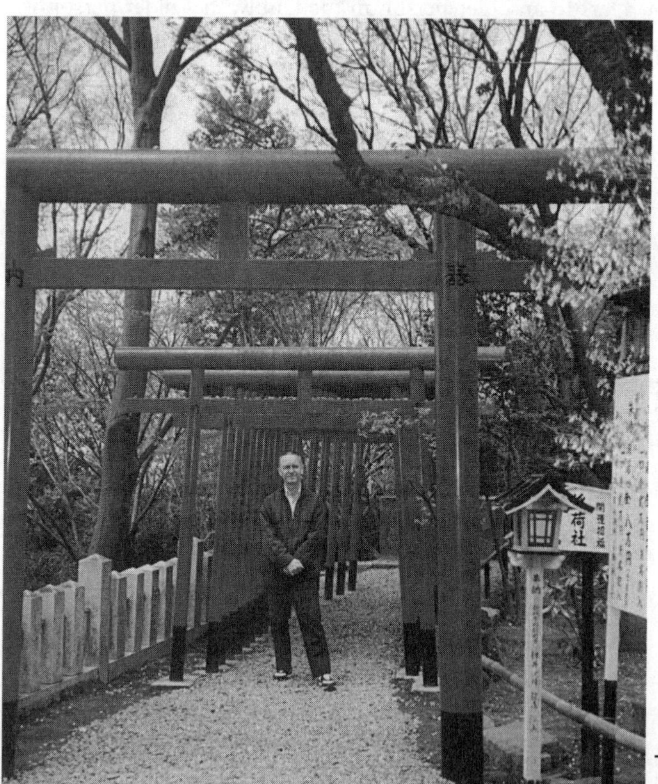

Torii, the gateways
to a shrine.

   Lesson 4: Introduce Yourself!

Conversation: How Do You Do?

Tom meets Makoto who is walking with his sister Sachiko. Take care to see which parts of the sentences are omitted.

Tom:	*Konnichiwa (Makoto-kun).*	*Good afternoon, Makoto.*
Makoto:	*Konnichiwa (Tom-kun).*	*Good afternoon, Tom.*
	Kore wa Sachiko desu.	*This is Sachiko.*
	(Kore wa) imōto desu.	*This is (my) younger sister.*
Sachiko:	*Hajimemashite.*	*How do you do?*
	Dōzo yoroshiku.	*Pleased to meet you.*
Tom:	*Hajimemashite.*	*How do you do?*
	(Boku wa) Tom desu.	*I am Tom.*
	Dōzo yoroshiku.	*Pleased to meet you.*

JAPANESE CUSTOMS AND CULTURE

Japanese Families and Their Lives

Until about 1970, it was not unusual to see three generations living together in the same house in Japan. In fact, traditionally, an eldest son is expected to live with his parents after he gets married, and his wife is expected to look after her parents-in-law in their old age. In return, he inherits his parents' fortune. A Japanese man spends much of his time with his work; he rarely spends time with his family and is often unaware of what is going on at home. He usually gets up early to take a long commute to work and comes home after his children have gone to bed. On the other hand, his wife's work revolves around her family. A woman usually quits her job when she gets married and, unless there is a financial need, she stays at home. The wife looks after the family finances and the husband gets his allowance from his wife. A husband and a wife have separate social lives except for a few social gatherings, such as weddings and funerals. A Japanese child spends his time between school and homework. He rarely has any time for anything else for the following reason. In Japan, great importance is placed on one's university degree once one gets out into the world. A person's career advancement and capabilities in the society are more or less decided and/or restricted by the degree he or she has obtained. This in turn makes parents push their children to aim for good universities, and in preparation for that, good high schools, good secondary schools and even good primary schools.

THIS, THAT AND THAT (OVER THERE) FOR PLACES

Unlike the English language, Japanese has many different words for *this* and *that*. When you talk of a "thing/person," you use **kore, sore** and **are** (**kochira, sochira** and **achira** are used to refer to your superiors). When you talk about *this* and *that* related to a "place," you must use **koko, soko** and **asoko.**

🔊 *Pronouns*

koko *this (place);* used to indicate "the place near the speaker."

soko *that (place);* used to indicate "the place near the listener."

asoko *that (place over there);* used to indicate "the place away from both the speaker and the listener."

The following is a vocabulary of places to increase your speaking power with the sentence structure **_ wa _ desu.**

 **Nouns**

basu-sutoppu bus stop	*daidokoro* kitchen
byōin hospital	*furoba* bathroom
depāto department store	*heya* room
dōbutsuen zoo	*ima* family room
eki (railway) station	*niwa* garden
gakkō school	
ginkō bank	
hikōjō airport	*otearai* washroom (polite)
hoteru hotel	*toire* washroom
hon-ya bookstore	*apāto* apartment
jinja shrine	*ie* house, home
kōen park	*manshon* high-class apartment
omocha-ya toy shop	*uchi* house, home
resutoran restaurant	
ryokan Japanese inn	*kawa* river
(o)tera temple	*mizūmi* lake
yōchien kindergarten	*umi* sea
yūbinkyoku post office	*yama* mountain

Examples

Koko wa depāto desu.	*This (place) is a department store.*
Soko wa dōbutsuen desu.	*That (place) is a zoo.*
Asoko wa eki desu.	*That (place over there) is a (railway) station.*

 If you want to experience the yesteryear of Japan, you should stay in a **ryokan,** a Japanese inn. You will get personal attention from a maid who will serve you meals in your room, lay a futon on tatami for your sleeping, as well as give any other personal attention that is required. A ryokan is often located near hot springs. Dinners and breakfasts are included in the cost.

 **Jinja,** a Shinto shrine, is not simply a burial ground, nor simply a place of worship. It is also a gathering place for the spirits who live on after the death of their bodies (see page 230 for more detail).

 **Manshon,** originating from the English word *mansion,* is pronounced almost as *mansion* in English. However, it is far from being a great big house as you would think: it is merely a modest-sized apartment in Japan.

    Lesson 4: Introduce Yourself!

4.1. 🔘 *Someone is introducing herself/himself to you. Listen carefully and answer the following questions in rōmaji by filling in the blanks.*

1. Who am I? *Anata wa* <u>*Hanoko*</u> *-san desu.*

   Am I Japanese, American or Canadian? *Anata wa* ___________ *-jin desu.*

   Am I a teacher? A student? *Anata wa* ___________ *desu.*

2. Who am I? *Anata wa* ___________ *-kun desu.*

   Am I Japanese, American or Canadian? *Anata wa* ___________ *-jin desu.*

   Am I a teacher? A student? *Anata wa* ___________ *desu.*

4.2. When addressing the people below, what do you put after each of their names? Write **chan, san, kun,** *or* **sensei** *in the blanks.*

1. Mr. Kelly, your school teacher. *Kelly-* ___________

2. Hiroshi, a boy about 12 years old. *Hiroshi-* ___________

3. Noriko, a girl about 5 years old. *Noriko-* ___________

4. Dr. Nakamura, your physician. *Nakamura-* ___________

4.3. 🔘 *Listen to Tom as he introduces a member of his family. Answer the questions in English.*

1. Whom did Tom introduce? ____

2. Whom did Tom introduce? ____

3. Whom did Tom introduce? ____

4. Whom did Tom introduce? ____

4.4. 🔘 *Listen to the track for Exercise 4.3 again, and fill in the blanks with the correct words in rōmaji.*

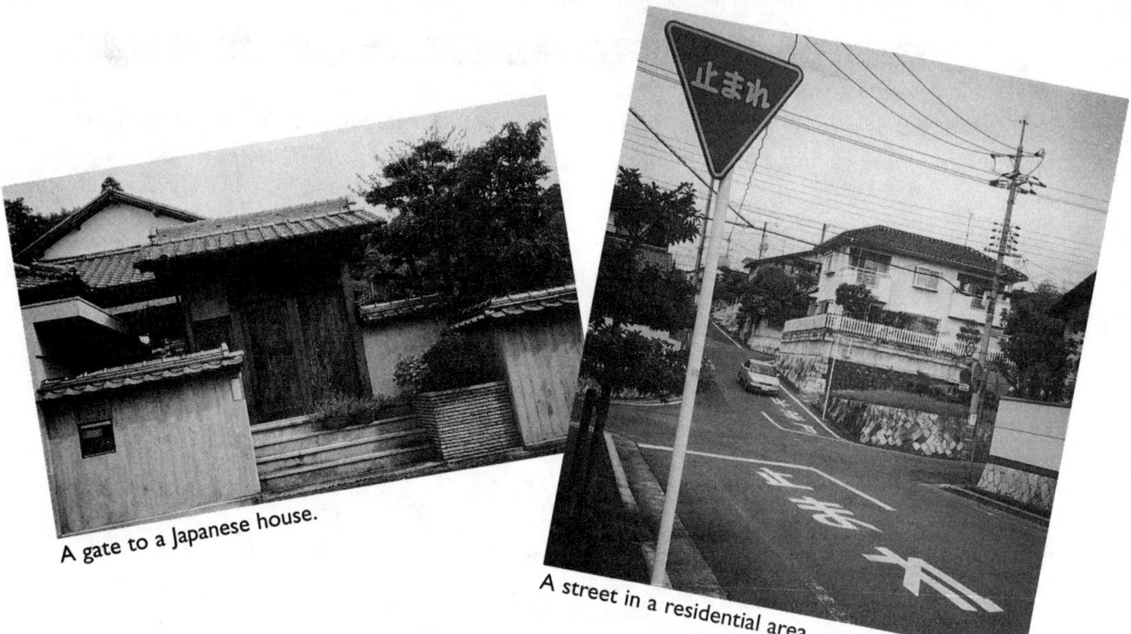

A gate to a Japanese house.

A street in a residential area.

1. What does Tom's father do? *Otōsan wa* ______________ *desu.*

2. What does Tom's mother do? ______________ *wa* ______________ *desu.*

3. What nationality is Tom's mother? ______________ *wa* ______________ *desu.*

4. Are Tom and his brother Ken both students? Yes, __________ *to* ___________ *wa gakusei desu.*

5. How do you know that Ken is older than Tom? *Ken wa* ______________ *desu.*

6. What is Cute? *Cute wa* ______________ *desu.*

4.5. *Imagine yourself visiting a zoo with me. I shall describe what I see. Listen and answer the following in English.*

1. What do I see near me? ____

2. What do I see away from me? ____

3. What do I see very far away from me? ____

4.6. *Write the correct rōmaji pronoun in the blanks:* **kore, sore, are, koko, soko,** *or* **asoko.**

1. To describe the cat you are holding: ______________ *wa neko desu.*

     Lesson 4: Introduce Yourself!

2. To describe the station you are in: _____________ *wa eki desu.*

3. To describe the dog near you, but not too close: _____________ *wa inu desu.*

4. To describe the toilet near you, but not too close: _____________ *wa toire desu.*

5. To describe the horse far away from you: _____________ *wa uma desu.*

6. To describe the airport far away from you: _____________ *wa hikōjō desu.*

4.7.
1. Circle the words that make sense in the blank for the sentence Koko wa _________ desu.
ahiru   eki   hoteru   inu   saru   hon-ya   hikōjō   byōin   otearai

2. Circle the words that make sense in the blank for the sentence Soko wa _________ desu.
daidokoro   niwa   risu   resutoran   (o)tera

3. Circle the words that make sense in the blank for the sentence Asoko wa _________ desu.
ie   ginkō   nezumi   ringo   banana   kōen

4.8. Translate into English:

1. Watashi wa Hanako desu. ____

2. Kore wa Amy-san desu. ____

3. Kore wa neko desu. ____

4. Are wa imōto to otōto desu. ____

5. Are wa sensei desu. ____

6. Otōsan wa Amerika-jin desu. ____

7. Koko wa basu-sutoppu desu. ____

8. Asoko wa dōbutsuen desu. ____

Translate into rōmaji:

9. I am Betty. ____

10. We are students. ____

11. This is (my) mother. _______________________________

12. These are pigs and cows. _______________________________

13. Betty is (my) younger sister. _______________________________

14. Robert is a foreigner. _______________________________

15. That (place) is a park. _______________________________

16. This (place) is a hospital. _______________________________

4.9. 🔘 *I want you to introduce me to the following people/buildings/animals, using the sentence structure _ **wa** _ **desu.** Say each sentence aloud. You may check your introduction against the correct answers recorded on the track.*

1. Your younger sister who is beside you _______________________________

2. Your elder sister who is near you _______________________________

3. Your father who is far away _______________________________

4. The cat you are holding _______________________________

5. The bird in the sky _______________________________

6. The bank we are in _______________________________

7. The mountain far away _______________________________

Genkan, a small vestibule where you must take your shoes off before entering any further.

In an outdoor onsen (public bath).

     Lesson 4: Introduce Yourself!

The Japanese Home, Bath and Toilet

Japanese houses and apartments are fairly small compared with Western homes, due to the limited amount of land available for the large population. A Japanese-style room, with the floor made of *tatami* (a thick mat woven from dried stem of *igusa*, or rush grass), may be used as a dining/living room during the day and as a bedroom at night. A futon, an easily foldable and movable light fluffy mattress, is laid on the floor for sleeping. Because people sit and lie down on the floor, people must take their shoes off at *genkan*, a small vestibule near the entrance, before proceeding any further. Slippers may be worn only in rooms without tatami floors (e.g., wooden floors, linoleum floors and carpet floors covering Western-style rooms, kitchens, toilets and corridors). When you are in a toilet, you must use the slippers in the toilet. Toilets and baths are usually separate closet-sized rooms.

Tatami room used as a bedroom at night.

Tatami room used as a living/dining room during the daytime.

When you go into a tatami room, there are certain sitting positions that are proper to use, for formal and more informal situations (see the photos). If a woman sits in any other style than these, for example if she crosses her legs or stretches her legs out, Japanese people will think that she is rude. On the other hand, the informal sitting style for men does involve crossed legs.

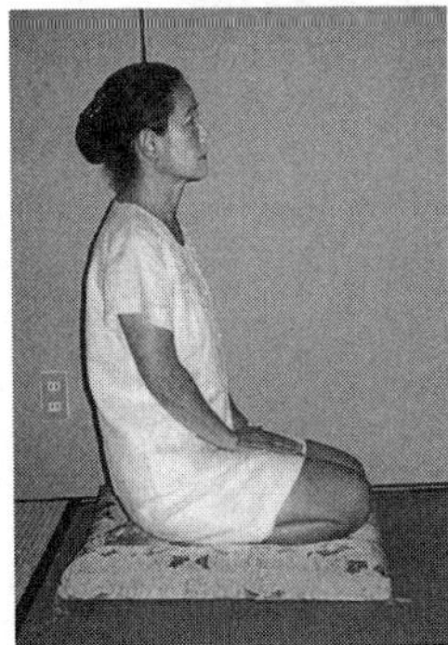

Women's formal sitting pose.

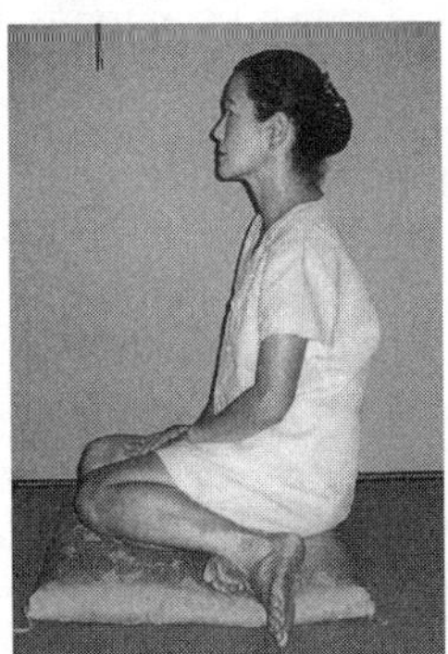

Women's informal sitting pose.

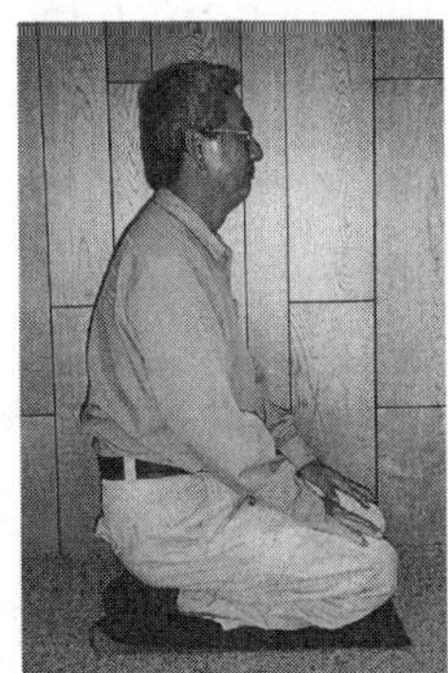

Men's formal sitting pose.

Men's informal sitting pose.

Japanese take baths to relax as well as to cleanse. A Japanese bathtub is kept full of clean hot water which may be used several times by several people before being changed. So you must clean your body entirely outside the tub. The bathing procedure is as follows. You first rinse your body with some tub water before you climb into the tub. After you have warmed up, you climb out of the tub and clean your body with soap. After rinsing yourself thoroughly, you go back into the hot tub again and soak until your heart is content. It is common to share the tub with other people at the same time. For instance, at home a parent shares a bath with a child, a brother shares a bath with another brother, and a sister shares a bath with another sister from time to time. One of the most popular relaxations for Japanese people is going to hot springs where women share public baths with other women and men share public baths with other men.

Although Western-style washroom facilities are becoming more common than traditional ones, and younger people prefer Western-style (because it takes more skill and muscles to use traditional ones!), you may need to use a Japanese toilet. It is usual to squat over it, and never to sit on it. Since no part of the body comes in contact with the toilet, many Japanese people consider it more sanitary than a Western-style toilet. It may be necessary to provide your own tissue paper and handkerchief. Many small restaurants and other establish-

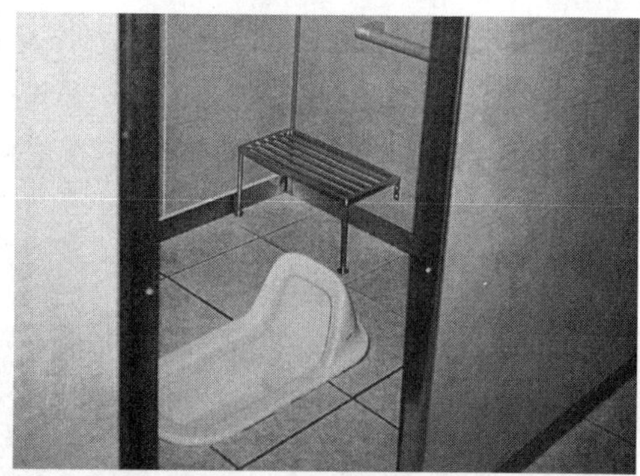
Public Japanese-style toilet.

ments have only one small toilet for both men and women. Knock on the door before entering. If someone is inside, that person will reply. In some places, there are urinals as well as toilet compartments in one big room for both men and women, and a woman may have to walk past a man at the urinal in order to reach a toilet compartment.

WRITING EXERCISE: HIRAGANA FOR *A, I, U, E* AND *O*

For each Japanese character, there is a standard order in which the different parts of the character should be drawn, as well as a standard way of drawing each part. When you write a character for a writing exercise in this book, follow the boxes from left to right for the order of the strokes. There are basically three possibilities for each part of a character, and how it should be drawn, as follows.

1. If the part is vertical or nearly vertical, it is drawn from top to bottom.

2. If the part is horizontal or nearly horizontal, it is drawn from left to right.

3. Otherwise, the part is usually strongly curved, and it is usually drawn from the higher end to the lower end.

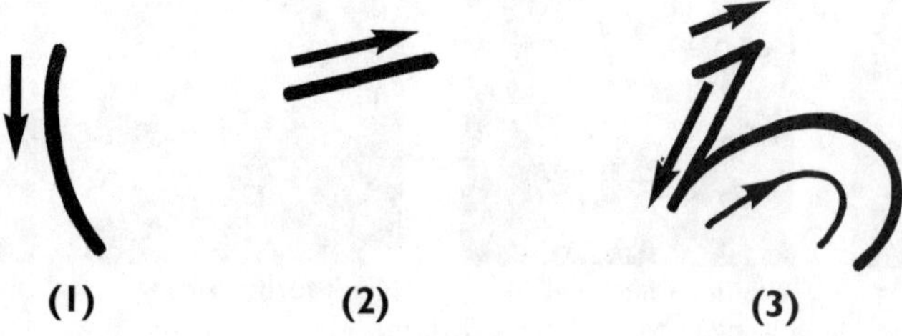

(1)   (2)   (3)

    Lesson 4: Introduce Yourself!

It should be remembered that, once you start to draw a part of a character, you continue it until the end of that part.

Practice the five hiragana characters あ， い， う， え and お.

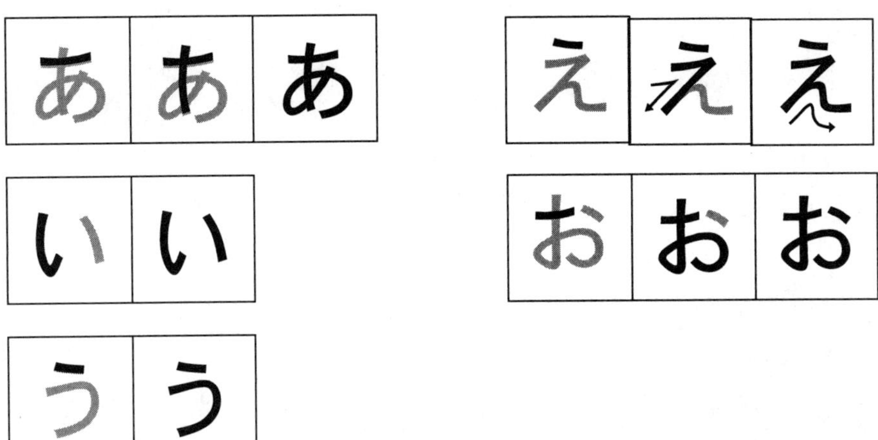

What you must remember from this lesson to proceed to the next lesson:

To identify a subject with a complement, you use the sentence structure

subject wa **complement** desu.

The particle **wa** follows a subject,
a complement is placed before the verb **desu** and
the verb **desu** is translated as *am/is/are.*
Kore/sore/are are used for *this/that/that (over there)* for "person/thing."
Koko/soko/asoko are used for *this/that/that (over there)* for "place."

5 Asking and Answering Questions

In this lesson you will learn:

Speaking
To ask and answer yes and no questions
To talk about family members

Grammar
To make negative statements and questions out of affirmative statements
To use the question particle **ka**

So far, you have learned the sentence structure _ **wa** _ **desu** for statements such as "I am Tom," "This is a cat," and "That is a hospital."

In this lesson, we shall extend the sentence structure _ **wa** _ **desu**. You will learn how to ask questions such as "Are you Tom?," "Is this a cat?," "Is that the hospital?," and so on. After that, you will learn to make negative statements such as "I am not Tom," "This is not a cat," "This is not a hospital." You will also learn to use interrogative (question) pronouns like "who," "what," "where" and "which one" so that you may ask questions such as "Who are you?," "What is this?," "Where is the hospital?," "Who is Tom?," to complete your learning of the sentence structures based on _ **wa** _ **desu**.

QUESTIONS AND ANSWERS

Are You Makoto? Is This an Apple?

In English, you make a question from a statement by placing the verb before the subject and putting a question mark at the end. For example, the statement "This is a cat" is made into a question by placing the verb *is* before the subject *this* and putting "?" at the end: "Is this a cat?"

Japanese simply puts the particle **ka** at the end of a statement to convert it into a question. Because **ka** at the end of a sentence implies that it is a question, no question mark is used in Japanese. Although there is no accent in Japanese, the particle **ka** for a question is pronounced with slightly higher pitch.

Examples

Kore wa tenpura desu.	*This is tempura.*
Kore wa tenpura desu ka.	*Is this tempura?*
Anata wa Makoto-kun desu.	*You are Makoto.*
Anata wa Makoto-kun desu ka.	*Are you Makoto?*
Koko wa eki desu.	*This (place) is a (railway) station.*
Koko wa eki desu ka.	*Is this (place) a (railway) station?*

Yes or No?

That was very easy, wasn't it? To answer questions, you must use "yes" or "no."

Replies

hai yes	*iie* no

Now, you may answer questions as follows.

Hai kore wa tenpura desu.	*Yes, this is tempura.*
Iie kore wa yakitori desu.	*No, this is yakitori.*

Quite often, people abbreviate replies by saying just **hai** or **iie,** just as they say "yes" or "no" in English.

One of the most common abbreviated replies is **hai sō desu** which implies that you agree with what the speaker is saying. Translated according to context, it can mean *yes, it is; yes, I am; yes, that is;* and so on.

Examples

Anata wa Tom-kun desu ka.	*Are you Tom?*
Hai sō desu.	*Yes, I am.*
Asoko wa eki desu ka.	*Is that the station?*
Hai sō desu.	*Yes, it is.*
Are wa Hanako-san desu ka.	*Is that Hanako?*
Hai sō desu.	*Yes, that is.*

When you are talking to a Japanese person, you get an impression that he/she agrees with you always: you hear him/her say **hai** after almost every sentence you utter. If you think that he/she is agreeing with you about everything, you are probably mistaken. A Japanese person acknowledges whatever you are saying with **hai. Hai** merely means that he/she is listening to what you are saying; it should be interpreted as *I am hearing you.* Some people may nod or utter approving sounds instead of saying **hai.**

Well, it is easy to say **hai** to everything the other person is saying. But you cannot go through life agreeing with everything the other person is saying. Sooner or later, you need to disagree and stress the disagreement. For that purpose, you are going to learn negative statements such as "This is *not* a book," "I am *not* Betty," and "This is *not* a toilet."

I Am Not Makoto, This Is Not an Apple

A negative statement for subject **wa** complement **desu** is

subject **wa** complement **de wa arimasen.**

Examples

Kore wa enpitsu desu.	*This is a pencil.*
Kore wa enpitsu de wa arimasen.	*This is not a pencil.*
Anata wa Makoto-kun desu ka.	*Are you Makoto?*
Iie boku wa Makoto-kun de wa arimasen.	*No, I am not Makoto.*
Boku wa Hiroshi desu.	*I am Hiroshi.*
Koko wa Tōkyō desu ka.	*Is this (place) Tokyo?*
Iie koko wa Tōkyō de wa arimasen.	*No, this (place) is not Tokyo.*
Koko wa Nagoya desu.	*This (place) is Nagoya.*

EXERCISES

5.1. *I shall say a statement in Japanese. I want you to convert it into a question and say it back. You may check your replies against the correct answers recorded at the end of this exercise. Then translate the correct answers into English and write them down below.*

1. ____

2. ____

3. ____

4. ____

5. ____

5.2. *Listen to the track for Exercise 5.1 again. This time convert what you hear into negative statements. You may check your replies against the correct answers recorded on the track for Exercise 5.2.*

1. ____

2. ____

3. ____

4. ____

5. ____

5.3. Translate into English:

1. *Sumimasen. Koko wa yūbinkyoku desu ka.*_______________________

   Iie koko wa yūbinkyoku de wa arimasen. _______________________

   Koko wa ginkō desu. _______________________

2. *Tom-kun wa Furansu-jin desu ka.* _______________________

   Iie Tom-kun wa Furansu-jin de wa arimasen. _______________________

   Tom-kun wa Amerika-jin desu. _______________________

3. *Are wa gaijin desu ka.* _______________________

   Iie are wa gaijin de wa arimasen. _______________________

   Are wa Nihon-jin desu. _______________________

4. *Koko wa gakkō desu ka.*_______________________

   *Iie koko wa gakkō de wa arimasen.*_______________________

   *Koko wa yōchien desu.*_______________________

5. *Anata wa Hanako-san desu ka.*_______________________

   Hai sō desu. _______________________

6. Are you Amy? ____

   No, I am not Amy. ____

   I am Betty. ____

7. Is this (place) a toilet? ____

   No, this is not a toilet. ____

   This is a bathroom. ____

8. Are you an American? ____

   No, I am not an American. ____

   I am a German. ____

9. Is this a cat? ____

   No, this is not a cat. ____

   This is a dog. ____

10. Is this (place) a bank? ____

    Yes, it is. ____

INTERROGATIVE PRONOUNS

Who? Where? Which? What?

You may ask more questions such as "Who are you?," "What is this?," "Where are we?," etc., using the following interrogative (question) pronouns.

Interrogative Pronouns*

dare *who*   **doko** *where, which place*   **dore** *which one*   **nan** *what*

*Japanese grammar classifies **dare** as a pronoun, **nan** as a demonstrative pronoun, etc. I have followed the classification of English grammar.

By replacing nouns with interrogative pronouns for simple statements, you may convert them into questions. Let's suppose that you want to make the sentence *What is this?* It is easier to make an interrogative sentence by starting with a simple statement and changing it into a question. To do this, consider a simple statement that could be an answer to the question "What is this?:" for example, **kore wa hon desu,** *this is a book.*

1. You start with the statement **Kore wa hon desu,** *This is a book.*

2. Since *What is this?* is a question, you put **ka** at the end of the statement.

3. Since **hon** is what you don't know and it is a "thing," you replace **hon** with **nan,** *what,* to obtain **Kore wa nan desu ka,** *What is this?*

The systematic chart is as follows.

1. Kore wa hon desu.	*This is a book.*
2. Kore wa hon desu ka.	*Is this a book?*

Replace **hon** with **nan** to get:

3. Kore wa nan desu ka.	*What is this?*

Now you can go one step further. By replacing **kore** with **tenpura** in the above sentence, you get the following sentence:

Kore wa nan desu ka.	*What is this?*

Replace **kore** with **tenpura** to get:

Tenpura *wa nan desu ka.*	*What is tempura?*

Isn't it exciting that you can make a totally different sentence by changing just one word? Well, you are not finished yet: you can go even further. By changing **nan,** *what,* to **dore,** *which one,* in the above sentence, you get the following sentence:

Tenpura wa nan desu ka.	*What is tempura?*

Replace **nan** with **dore** to get:

Tenpura wa **dore** *desu ka.*	*Which one is tempura?*

Let's do the same thing with another sentence, using the question word **dare,** *who.* **Dare** replaces a "person" as follows:

Anata wa Makoto-kun desu.	*You are Makoto.*
Anata wa Makoto-kun desu ka.	*Are you Makoto?*
↓	
Anata wa **dare** *desu ka.*	*Who are you?*
↓	
Sensei *wa* **dare** *desu ka.*	*Who is the teacher?*

Let's try one more example using the question word **doko,** *where.* **Doko** replaces a "place" as follows:

Koko wa yūbinkyoku desu.   This (place) is a post office.
Koko wa yūbinkyoku desu ka.   Is this (place) a post office?

↓

Koko wa **doko** *desu ka.*   Where is this (place)?

↓

Toire *wa doko desu ka.*   Where is the toilet?

 Conversation 1: Are You a Canadian?

This is Tom's first day at his new college. He meets Hanako, who is very eager to make conversation!

Nouns

chizu map	**Amerika** America

Hanako:	*(Anata wa)* **Tom-kun desu ka.**	*Are you Tom?*
Tom:	**Hai sō desu. Anata wa** *(dare desu ka).*	*Yes, I am. And you are?*
Hanako:	*(Watashi wa)* **Hanako desu.**	*I'm Hanako.*
	Dōzo yoroshiku.	*Pleased to meet you.*
Tom:	**Dōzo yoroshiku.**	*Pleased to meet you too.*
Hanako:	*(Anata wa)* **Kanada-jin desu ka.**	*Are you a Canadian?*
Tom:	*Iie (boku wa)* **Kanada-jin de wa arimasen.**	*No, I am not a Canadian.*
	(Boku wa) **Amerika-jin desu.**	*I'm an American.*
Hanako:	*(Kore wa)* **chizu desu.**	*This is a map.*
	Amerika wa doko desu ka.	*Where is America?*
Tom:	*(Amerika wa)* **koko desu*.**	*America is here (this place).*

 Conversation 2: This Is (My) Family

You have learned to pronounce **ka** at the end of an interrogative (question) sentence with slightly higher pitch. When an interrogative sentence is abbreviated and **ka** is omitted from the sentence, as for example at the point marked "**" in the following conversation, the last particle or the last syllable of the last word is pronounced with slightly higher pitch to denote that it is a question.

Tom visits Hanako with a present.

Nouns

namae name	*purezento* present

Tom:	*Konnichiwa.*	*Good afternoon.*
Hanako:	*Konnichiwa. Dōzo.*	*Good afternoon. Please (come in).*
	Tom takes his shoes off and enters the family room.	
Tom:	*(Kore wa)* **purezento desu.**	*This is a present (for you).*
Hanako:	*Arigatō. (Kore wa)* **nan desu ka.**	*Thank you. What is it?*
Tom:	*(Kore wa)* **sakuranbo desu.**	*These are cherries.*

***Koko wa Amerika desu** implies *this is America* while **Amerika wa koko desu** implies *America is here (this place)*, emphasizing *America* by making it the subject of the sentence.

Hanako:	*Kore wa kazoku desu.*	*This is (my) family.*
Tom:	*(Kore wa) okāsan desu ka.*	*Is this (your) mother?*
Hanako:	*Iie (sore wa) okāsan de wa arimasen.*	*No, that's not (my) mother.*
	(Sore wa) onēsan desu.	*That's (my) older sister.*
	Onēsan wa gakusei desu.	*(My) older sister is a student.*
Tom:	*(Kore wa) imōto-san* desu ka.*	*Is this (your) younger sister?*
Hanako:	*Hai (sore wa) imōto desu.*	*Yes, it is.*
Tom:	*Namae wa** (nan desu ka).*	*What's (her) name?*
Hanako:	*(Namae wa) Mari desu.*	*(Her) name is Mari.*
Tom:	*Koko wa doko desu ka.*	*Where is this (place)?*
Hanako:	*(Soko wa) kōen desu.*	*That (place) is a park.*

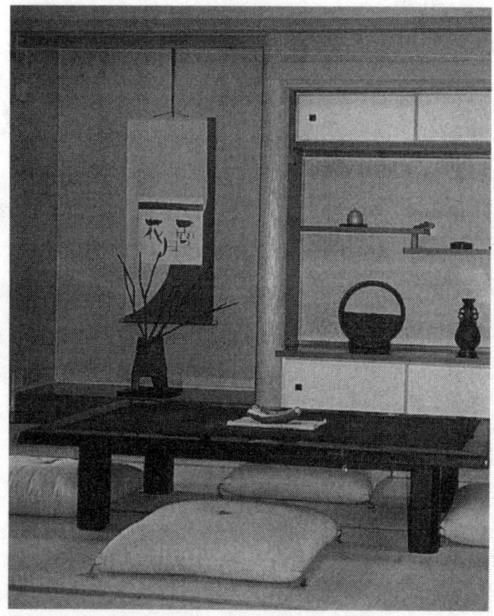

Tatami room used as a sitting room.

EXERCISES

5.4. Look at the pictures on the next page. I shall ask you questions. Reply to each question aloud in a full sentence, as in Exercise 5.3. Correct answers are recorded at the end of this exercise.

1. ____

2. ____

3. ____

*Tom refers to Hanako's younger sister as **imōto-san** while Hanako refers to her as **imōto**.

   Lesson 5: Asking and Answering Questions

(1)   **(2)**   **(3)**

5.5. *Look at the pictures above and do the following three steps for each.*
a. Make a statement by writing rōmaji in the blank.
b. Make the statement (a) into a question.
*c. Write **nan/dare/doko** in the blank to ask what/whom you see.*

1. a. *Kore wa* _______________ *desu. This is (my) grandmother.*

 b. *Kore wa* _______________ *desu ka. Is this (my) grandmother?*

 c. *Kore wa* _______________ *desu ka. Who is this?*

2. a. *Kore wa* _______________ *desu. This is a carrot.*

 b. *Kore wa* _______________ *desu ka. Is this a carrot?*

 c. *Kore wa* _______________ *desu ka. What is this?*

3. a. *Koko wa* _______________ *desu. This is a park.*

 b. *Koko wa* _______________ *desu ka. Is this a park?*

 c. *Koko wa* _______________ *desu ka. Where is this?*

5.6. *Listen to the track for Exercise 5.6. Answer the questions in rōmaji.*

1. ____

2. ____

3. ____

4. ____

5.7. 🔘 *Say the following sentences aloud in Japanese. Correct answers are recorded on the track for Exercise 5.7.*

1. What is this (beside me)?

2. What is that (near you)?

3. What is that (far away)?

4. Who is this (beside me)?

5. Who is that (near you)?

6. Who is that (far away)?

7. Where is this place (we are in)?

8. Where is that place?

9. Where is that place (far away)?

5.8. Translate into English:

1. *Are wa nan desu ka.* ____

   Are wa hon desu. ____

2. *Are wa dare desu ka.* ____

   Are wa Kazuko-san desu. ____

3. *Koko wa doko desu ka.* ____

   Koko wa kōen desu. ____

4. *Sore wa nan desu ka.* ____

   Kore wa sushi desu. ____

5. *Ie wa doko desu ka.* ____

Translate into rōmaji:

6. Who is that (over there)?____

   That (over there) is a teacher. ______________________________________

7. What is this? ____

   That is a Chinese cabbage.____

8. Where is this (place)? ____

This is a department store. ____

9. Who are you? ____

I am Peter. ____

10. Where is the station? ____

5.9. 💿 *I shall ask some questions about Conversation 2. When you hear a question, reply to it aloud in Japanese in a full sentence. Correct answers are recorded at the end of this exercise.*

1. ____

2. ____

3. ____

4. ____

JAPANESE CUSTOMS AND CULTURE

Gift Giving

Japanese people give gifts to express their appreciation for others. They give **ochūgen** (mid-year gifts) to their superiors from early June to mid-July and **oseibo** (year-end gifts) to those to whom they owe favors. Unfortunately, this custom has become very commercialized: department stores have special corners in which to choose ochūgen and oseibo, and they are usually delivered from department stores. Whenever Japanese people travel, it is expected of them to bring back souvenirs for friends, colleagues and all their close acquaintances. When they move into new homes, they give gifts to their new neighbors. Japanese people usually do not open gifts in front of a giver as it is regarded as bad manners. When you visit someone who is ill, do not take a potted plant: "taking root" implies that the illness will take root and will thus be prolonged.

Ochūgen corner of a department store.

Banks and Signatures

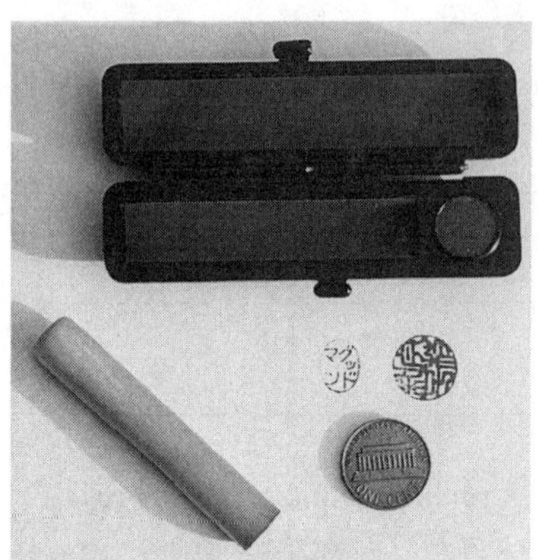

Hanko, hanko case and seals—with a penny to indicate their size. A hanko is used to sign for deliveries, etc., and may be purchased from shelves at hanko-shops. The large seal is from a hanko specially made for important transactions, such as buying/selling houses; it must be registered at the city hall.

All banks, post offices, department stores, and so on, have automated teller machines (ATMs). Once you have opened an account and obtained your access card with PIN (personal identification number used as your electronic signature), you can withdraw/deposit money at any branch. It is much more convenient to use automated teller machines than to use a bank for the following reasons. In Japan, people do not sign their names as in the West. Instead, they use personal seals to sign their names. (Your personal seal has exactly the same significance as your signature would have in the Western world, and so your seal must be kept in a safe place at all times.) Every time you want to withdraw or deposit money at a bank, you must have your personal seal with you. Also, after you have given a withdrawal slip to a teller, you will be given a slip with a number, which designates your place in line, to be called later to receive the money. In other words, you must wait awhile to turn in a withdrawal slip, and again to receive your money. Although each waiting period is only a few minutes, it is fairly inconvenient if you want to make deposits or withdrawals frequently.

Practice the five hiragana characters か， き， く， け *and* こ.

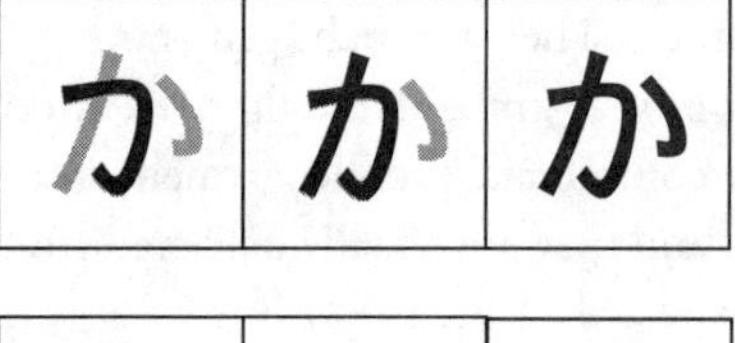

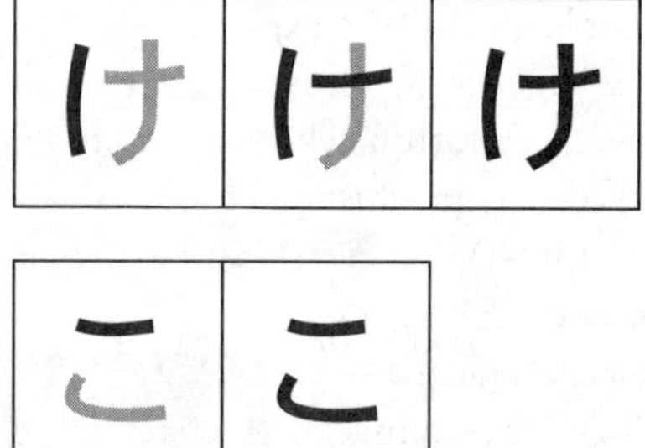

What you must remember from this lesson to proceed to the next lesson:

The particle **ka** is put at the end of a statement to convert it into a question.

The negative sentence for __ **wa** __ **desu** is __ **wa** __ **de wa arimasen.**

6

Is It Yours or Mine?

In the previous lessons, you've learned to introduce yourself, your family, your friends, and so on, by saying "I am Tom," "This is (my) father," etc.

In this lesson, you will learn to say phrases like "*Tom's* book," "*my* book," and "*your* book." The words such as *Tom's*, *my* and *your* are called possessive adjectives because they are adjectives describing *book* and they refer to the possessors of the book. For instance, *Tom* possesses *the book* in the phrase "Tom's book," *I* possess *the book* in the phrase "my book," and *you* possess *the book* in the phrase "your book." The idea of possession is expressed by using the particle **no** in Japanese.

THE PARTICLE *NO*

It's Mine and Not Yours!

 Here is some new vocabulary that will be used in this lesson.

Nouns

enpitsu pencil	*handobaggu* handbag	*isu* chair
hon book	*kaban* briefcase	*tēburu* table
nōto notebook	*kasa* umbrella	*tsukue* desk
pen pen	*megane* eyeglasses	
	saifu wallet, purse	

possessor **No** item/person possessed

The idea of possessive adjective (*my* of "*my* book," *your* of "*your* pencil," *Tom's* of "*Tom's* book," etc.) is expressed by using the personal pronoun (**watashi, anata, Tom**) followed by **no**, followed by the item/person possessed.

Thus **Hanako-san no hon** is equivalent to "Hanako's book." It may be easier to think that **no** has the same function as *'s* in English.

Tom no hon	*Tom's book*
watashi no hon	*my book*
anata no hon	*your book*
watashi no otōsan	*my father*
anata no otōsan	*your father*

The possessors may be not only personal pronouns; they may be nouns, such as a father, a mother, a dog, etc.

Examples

otōsan no isu	*father's chair*
okāsan no isu	*mother's chair*
inu no isu	*dog's chair*

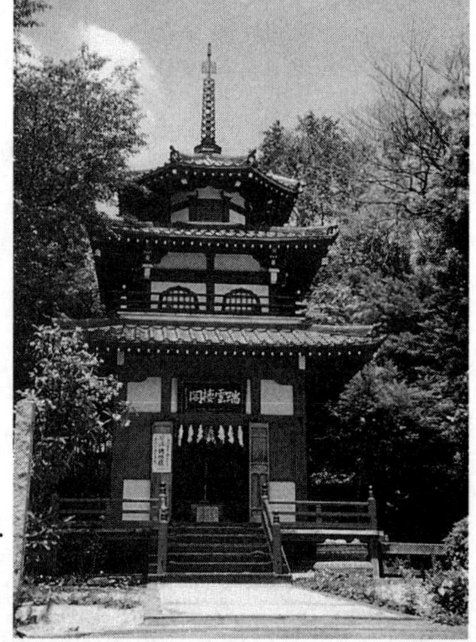

Pagoda.

Conversation 1: What's Your Hobby?

Now, you can be nosey about other people by using the following vocabulary, just as Taro does in the conversation below.

Nouns

kuni *country*	**shumi** *hobby*	**supōtsu** *sports*

Taro:	**Anata no namae wa nan desu ka.**	*What is your name?*
Tom:	(*Boku no namae wa*) **Tom desu.**	*My name is Tom.*
Taro:	(*Anata no*) **shumi wa nan desu ka.**	*What is your hobby?*
Tom:	(*Boku no shumi wa*) **supōtsu desu.**	*It's sports.*
Taro:	**Anata no kuni wa doko desu ka.**	*Where is your country?*
Tom:	(*Boku no kuni wa*) **Amerika desu.**	*My country is America.*

 ## Conversation 2: Is This Yours?

Tom and Hanako sort through a pile of notebooks to find theirs. Notice that **kore wa boku no nōto desu,** *this is my notebook,* may be abbreviated as **boku no desu,** *it's mine.*

Hanako:	(*Kore wa*) **watashi no** (*nōto*) **desu.**	*It's mine.*
	(*Kore wa*) **anata no** (*nōto*) **desu ka.**	*Is this yours?*
Tom:	**Iie** (*sore wa*) **boku no** (*nōto*) **de wa arimasen.**	*No, it's not mine.*
	(*Sore wa*) **Makoto-kun no** (*nōto*) **desu.**	*It's Makoto's.*

My Handbag Was Made in Italy

No between two nouns can also express something other than the possessive adjective idea. If the first noun is a "name of a place," it is the place of origin of the second noun or it describes the location of the second noun.

In other words, **no** makes the "place," which is a noun, into an adjective, so to speak. The following vocabulary lists names of countries and cities around the world which you may designate as the origin of things or location of places.

Nouns

kuni countries		shuto capitals
Chūgoku China	*Kanada Canada*	*Washinton Washington*
Doitsu Germany	*Nihon Japan*	*Pari Paris*
Furansu France	*Nippon Japan*	*Rondon London*
Igirisu Britain		*Tōkyō Tokyo*
Itaria Italy	*gaikoku abroad*	

Examples

Itaria no handobaggu	*Italian handbag*
Nihon no ringo	*Japanese apple*
Tōkyō no eki	*Tokyo station*
Rondon no hikōjō	*London airport*

 Conversation 3: Where Is This?

Hanako points to a location on a map and tests Tom's knowledge of cities in the world.

Hanako:	*Koko wa doko desu ka.*	*Where is this?*
Tom:	*(Koko wa)* **Furansu desu.**	*It's France.*
Hanako:	**Furansu no shuto wa doko desu ka.**	*Where is the French capital?*
Tom:	*(Furansu no shuto wa)* **Pari desu.**	*It's Paris.*
Hanako:	**Igirisu no shuto wa** *(doko desu ka)*	*How about the British capital?*
Tom:	*(Igirisu no shuto wa)* **Rondon desu.**	*It's London.*

School Teacher

No is also used between two nouns where the first noun describes the second noun. In this case, the first noun is neither a "person" nor a "name of a place," and **A no B** is translated as *B of/for/in/on A*.

We can use the following list of languages to practice this use of **no**.

Nouns

Doitsu-go German language	*Itaria-go* Italian language
Eigo English language	*Nihon-go* Japanese language
Furansu-go French language	

The suffix **-go** is added to the name of a country for its language (just as **-jin** is used for its people), e.g., **Furansu-go**, *French language*. There are exceptions to the rule such as **Eigo**, *English*.

Examples

Nihon-go no gakusei	*Japanese language student (student of the Japanese language)*
gakkō no sensei	*school teacher (teacher of a school)*
Eigo no gakkō	*English language school (school for the English language)*
Eigo no hon	*English book (book in the English language)*
supōtsu no hon	*book on sports*

Here are some examples with more than one **no**.

Examples

watashi no Eigo no hon, my English book

> Consider "**eigo no hon**" first. It is translated as *an English book*.
> Then consider "**watashi no** *English book*," and obtain *my English book*.

watashi no gakkō no sensei, teacher of my school

> Consider "**watashi no gakkō**" first. It is translated as *my school*.
> Then consider "*my school* **no sensei**," and obtain *teacher of my school*.

watashi no otōsan no hon, my father's book

> Consider "**watashi no otōsan**" first. It is translated as *my father*.
> Then consider "*my father* **no hon**," and obtain *my father's book*.

Koko wa watashi no sensei no ie desu.	*This (place) is my teacher's house.*

 Conversation 4: Is It a Book in English?

Tom and Hanako are going through a pile of books to find Tom's book.

Hanako:	*(Kore wa)* **anata no** *(hon)* **desu ka.**	*Is this yours?*
Tom:	**Hai** *(sore wa)* **boku no** *(hon)* **desu.**	*Yes, it's mine.*
Hanako:	*(Kore wa)* **Eigo no hon desu ka.**	*Is it a book in English?*
Tom:	**Iie** *(sore wa)* **Eigo no hon de wa arimasen.**	*No, it's not a book in English.*
	(Sore wa) **Furansu-go no hon desu.**	*It's a book in French.*

          Lesson 6: Is It Yours or Mine?

Whose Book? Which Station?: Interrogatives + No

You may ask questions such as "Whose book is this?," "What kind of book is this?," "Which station is this?," etc. using the interrogative (question) pronouns **dare**, *who*, **nan**, *what* and **doko**, *where*. Let's suppose that you want to make the sentence *Whose book is this?* It is easier to make an interrogative sentence (or any other difficult sentence) by starting with a simple statement and changing it into a question. To do this, consider a simple statement that could be an answer to the question "Whose book is this?:" for example, **kore wa watashi no hon desu,** *this is my book.*

1. You start with the statement **Kore wa watashi no hon desu,** *This is my book.*

2. Since *Whose book is this?* is a question, you put **ka** at the end of the statement.

3. Since **watashi** is what you don't know and it is a "person", you replace **watashi** with **dare**, *who,* to obtain **Kore wa dare no hon desu ka,** *Whose book is this?*

The systematic chart is as follows:

1. *Kore wa watashi no hon desu.*	*This is my book.*
2. *Kore wa* watashi *no hon desu ka.*	*Is this my book?*

> *Replace **watashi** with **dare** to get:*

3. *Kore wa* dare *no hon desu ka.*	*Whose book is this?*

Let's do the same thing with another sentence, using the question word **nan,** *what (kind of).* **Nan** replaces a "thing" as follows:

Kore wa Eigo no hon desu.	*This is an English book.*
Kore wa Eigo *no hon desu ka.*	*Is this an English book?*
↓	
Kore wa nan *no hon desu ka.*	*What (kind of) book is this?*

Let's try one more example using the question word **doko,** *where.* **Doko** replaces a "place" as follows:

Koko wa Tōkyō no eki desu.	*This is Tokyo station.*
Koko wa Tōkyō *no eki desu ka.*	*Is this Tokyo station?*
↓	
Koko wa doko *no eki desu ka.*	*Which station is this ?*

 Conversation 5: Whose Eyeglasses Are These?

Hanako visits Tom's house and sees many things which interest her on a table.

Hanako:	*(Kore wa)* **dare no megane desu ka.**	*Whose eyeglasses are these?*
Tom:	*(Kore wa boku no)* **okāsan no** *(megane)* **desu.**	*They're my mother's.*
	(Kore wa) **Itaria no** *(megane)* **desu.**	*They're Italian.*
Hanako:	**Kore wa nan no hon desu ka.**	*What kind of book is this?*
Tom:	*(Kore wa)* **kudamono no hon desu.**	*It's a book on fruit.*
	(Kore wa) **okāsan no** *(hon)* **desu.**	*It's my mother's.*

6.1. 💿 *Say the following phrases aloud in Japanese. Check your answers with the correct answers recorded on the track for Exercise 6.1.*

1. my book

2. your book

3. (my) younger brother's book

4. my father

5. your father

6. Tom's father

6.2. 💿 *Listen to the track for Exercise 6.2. Repeat Japanese after me. Then write who owns what in English.*

1. _teacher's pen_ _______________   2. _______________________

3. _______________________   4. _______________________

5. _______________________   6. _______________________

6.3. Write rōmaji in the blanks to give the following meanings.

1. Hanako's sister: _**Hanako-san**_ *no* _**imōto**_

2. our table: _______________ *no* _______________

3. Tom's country: _______________ *no* _______________

4. British capital: _______________ *no* _______________

5. magazine in the English language: _______________ *no* _______________

6. books on food: _______________ *no* _______________

6.4. 💿 *I shall ask some questions about Conversation 1. Listen to the questions. When you hear a question, reply to it aloud in a full sentence in Japanese. Correct answers are recorded at the end of this exercise.*

1. _______________________________________

2. _______________________________________

6.5. *Listen to the abbreviated replies for the question **kore wa dare no hon desu ka.** Write down whose book it is in English.*

1. *father's* _______________________________

2. _______________________________

3. _______________________________

4. _______________________________

5. _______________________________

6.6. *Write **wa, o, ka, to** or **ni** in the blanks, and translate the sentences into English.*

1. *Koko _________ gakkō desu.* _This is a school._ _______________________

2. *Koko _________ gakkō desu ka.* _______________________________

3. *Koko _________ anata _________ gakkō desu ka.* _______________________

4. *Koko _________ anata _________ onēsan _________ gakkō desu ka.*

____

5. *Pen _________ kudasai.* _______________________________

6. *Pen _________ enpitsu _________ kudasai.* _May I have a pen and a pencil please?_

7. *Pen _________ enpitsu _________ kudasai.* _May I have a pen or a pencil please?_

6.7. *Write **nan, doko** or **dare** in the blanks so that the replies are appropriate.*

1. Question: *Koko wa _________________ no shuto desu ka.*
   Reply: *Koko wa Chūgoku no shuto desu.*

2. Question: *Kore wa _________________ no handobaggu desu ka.*
   Reply: *Kore wa onēsan no handobaggu desu.*

3. Question: *Kore wa _________________ no shashin desu ka.*
   Reply: *Kore wa Itaria no isu no shashin desu.*

6.8. Translate into English:

1. *Sensei no isu* ____

2. *Okāsan no saifu* ____

3. *Hanako-san no otōsan* ____

4. *Kore wa watashi no okāsan desu.* ____

5. *Sore wa watashi-tachi no inu desu.* ____

6. *Are wa gakkō no sensei desu.* ____

7. *Koko wa doko no kuni desu ka.* ____

   Koko wa Itaria desu. ____

8. *Koko wa dare no ie desu ka.* ____

   Koko was Kanada-jin no ie desu. ____

Translate into rōmaji:

9. My friend ________________________________

10. Your family ________________________________

11. This is (my) mother's umbrella. ____

12. May I have my notebook please? ____

13. I am a student of the English language. ____

14. The younger brother's dog's name is Chibi. ____

____

15. What kind of fruit is this? ____

   This is a watermelon. ____

   Lesson 6: Is It Yours or Mine?

Kōrakuen Garden, Okayama.

16. Which station is this? ___________________________________

This is Tokyo station. ___________________________________

Practice the five hiragana characters さ， し， す， せ and そ.

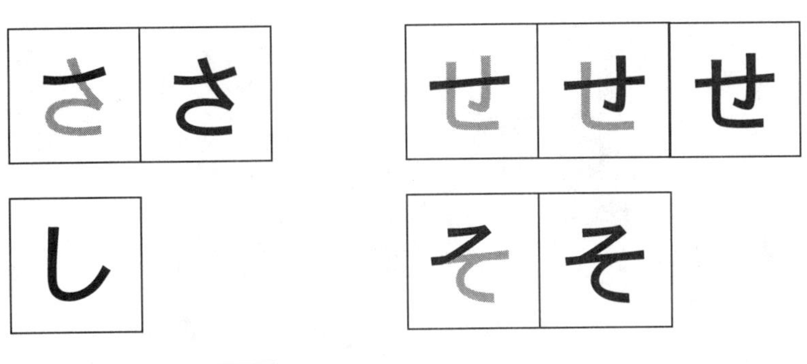

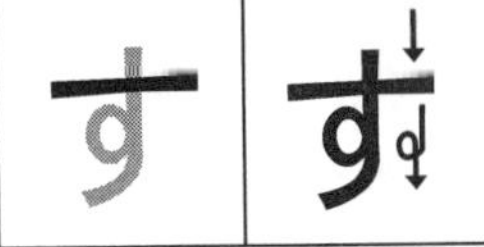

What you must remember from this lesson to proceed to the next lesson:

A (personal-pronoun/noun) No B (noun)

The particle **no** joins two nouns, or a personal pronoun and a noun, related to each other in the form **A no B. A no** is a possessor of **B** (translated as *A's B*), origin of **B,** or describes **B** (translated as *B of/for/in/on A*).

7 Focus on Action: Verbs

In the previous lessons, you learned to use the verb **desu** to equate one thing with another such as "this" with "a dog" with the sentence "This is a dog," "I" with "Betty" with the sentence "I am Betty," etc.

Japanese verbs, which we shall study in this book, may be divided into two groups: **desu** and **V•masu**-verbs.* In this lesson, you will learn to make statements, questions and answers, and negative statements using **V•masu**-verbs.

I EAT STEAK, I DRINK WATER, I LEARN JAPANESE: *V•MASU*-VERBS

Let us look at the list of **V•masu**-verbs. You may realize why I call them **V•masu**-verbs: every verb ends with **masu**. The verbs listed below are transitive verbs (verbs which may have direct objects).

Verbs (Transitive)

araimasu wash	*nomimasu drink*
hanashimasu speak	*okurimasu send*
kaimasu buy	*tabemasu eat*
kakimasu write, draw	*torimasu take*
kikimasu listen to, hear, ask for	*tsukurimasu make*
mimasu see, watch	*urimasu sell*
naraimasu learn	*yomimasu read*

Since you are going to study transitive verbs, you need to learn nouns that may become direct objects for those verbs above, and some are listed below.

*V•masu**-verbs are, in fact, one of the verb forms + an auxiliary verb **masu**. They are used for the polite style of speech, which is the most commonly used speech style, and the one you should use.

 *Nouns*

nomimono drinks	**niku** meat	
(o)cha Japanese green tea	*buta-niku* pork	*shinbun* newspaper
kōcha Indian tea	*gyū-niku* beef	*tegami* letter
miruku milk	*tori-niku* chicken meat	*zasshi* magazine
mizu water		*e* picture, painting
sake Japanese rice wine	*sakana* fish	
wain wine		*eiga* movie
	koe voice, cry	*terebi* television
ame candy	*ongaku* music	
okashi confectionery, sweet, candy	*rajio* radio	*hōkō* direction
	uta song	*kitte* stamp

A transitive **V•masu**-verb has the sentence structure

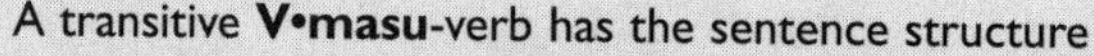

subject **wa** **object** **o** **V•masu.**

The particle **wa** follows the subject, the particle **o** follows the direct object, and the verb **V•masu** is placed at the end.

Examples

Watashi wa inu o araimasu.	*I wash a dog.*
Inu wa neko o mimasu.	*A dog sees a cat.*
Otōto wa ringo o tabemasu.	*The younger brother eats an apple.*
Okāsan wa tegami o kakimasu.	*Mother writes a letter.*
Otōsan wa shinbun o yomimasu.	*Father reads a newspaper.*
Inu wa mizu o nomimasu.	*The dog drinks water.*
Otōsan wa shinbun o kaimasu.	*Father buys a newspaper.*
Watashi wa Eigo o naraimasu.	*I learn the English language.*
Imōto wa pan o tsukurimasu.	*The younger sister makes bread.*

A Japanese verb may be translated into more than one verb in English, and vice versa. For instance, **kikimasu** may be translated as *hear*, *ask for* and *listen to* as follows.

Watashi wa tori no koe o kikimasu.	*I hear a bird's cry.*
Watashi wa hōkō o kikimasu.	*I ask for directions.*
Watashi wa ongaku o kikimasu.	*I listen to the music.*

When you learn a Japanese verb, care must be taken concerning its exact translation in English. For instance, **kikimasu** is a transitive verb, and its direct object is followed by **o**. But some of the equivalent English verbs *ask* and *listen* are not transitive verbs and they are followed by *for* and *to* respectively as may be seen above. That is, **kikimasu** may be translated as *hear/ask for/listen to* and not *hear/ask/listen*.

When you drink sake with other people, you do not pour your own drink. Pour your companions drinks, and they will return the favor.

That was quite straightforward, wasn't it? We now proceed to ask questions using **V•masu**-verbs. Just as with **desu,** we ask questions by putting the particle **ka** at the ends of statements.

Example

Anata wa ringo o tabemasu.	*You eat an apple.*
Anata wa ringo o tabemasu ka.	*Do you eat an apple?*

The next step is to ask questions such as "what do you eat?," "what do you drink?," and "what do you read?"

 For *what,* **nan** is used before a word starting with **n/t/d,** and **nani** is used before a word starting with any other letter.

Interrogative Pronoun

nani *what*

Examples

Kore wa hon desu ka.	*Is this a book?*
Kore wa nan *desu ka.*	*What is this?*

Kore wa Eigo no hon desu ka.	*Is this an English book?*
Kore wa nan *no hon desu ka.*	*What (kind of) book is this?*

Notice that **nan** comes before <u>desu</u> and <u>no</u>.

Anata wa ringo o kaimasu ka.	*Do you buy apples?*
Anata wa nani *o kaimasu ka.*	*What do you buy?*

Anata wa nani *o nomimasu ka.*	*What do you drink?*
Anata wa nani *o tabemasu ka.*	*What do you eat?*

Notice that **nani** comes before <u>o</u>.

You may add suffixes such as **-jin,** *people,* and **-go,** *language,* to produce **nani-jin,** *what nationality,* and **nani-go,** *what language.*

7.1. *Say the following sentences aloud in Japanese. Correct answers are recorded on the track for Exercise 7.1.*

1. I eat fish.

2. I drink milk.

3. I speak English.

4. I read newspapers.

5. I buy candy.

6. I listen to the music.

7. I learn Japanese.

7.2. 🔘 *Listen and write who does what in English.*

1. ____

2. ____

3. ____

4. ____

5. ____

6. ____

7. ____

7.3. Write either **nan** *or* **nani** *in the blanks and then translate the sentences into English.*

1. *Anata wa* _______________ *no niku o tabemasu ka.* <u>What meat do you eat?</u>

2. *Anata wa* _______________ *-go o hanashimasu ka.* ___________________________________

3. *Anata wa* _______________ *o nomimasu ka.* ___________________________________

7.4. Translate into English:

1. *Watashi wa terebi o mimasu.* ___________________________________

2. *Watashi to otōto wa Nihon-go o naraimasu.* ___________________________________

3. *Otōsan wa shinbun to zasshi o yomimasu.* ___________________________________

4. *Watashi-tachi wa ongaku o kikimasu.* ___________________________________

5. *Anata wa Nihon-go o hanashimasu ka.* ___________________________________

Lesson 7: Focus on Action: Verbs

6. *Anata wa nani o tabemasu ka.* _______________________________________

7. *Anata wa nan no hon o yomimasu ka.* _______________________________

8. *Anata wa nani o kaimasu ka.* _____________________________________

9. *Anata wa nani o tsukurimasu ka.* __________________________________

Translate into rōmaji:

10. We read Japanese books. ____

11. We learn the English language. ____________________________________

12. I listen to Japanese music. _______________________________________

13. Does your father drink sake? _____________________________________

14. What language do you speak? _____________________________________

15. What do you drink? ____

16. What (kind of) fruit do you eat? ___________________________________

17. What (kind of) book do you read? __________________________________

18. What movie do you watch? _______________________________________

FUTURE TENSE: I SHALL EAT STEAK, I SHALL DRINK WATER

There are basically three tenses of English verbs: present tense, future tense and past tense. The differences among these tenses are as follows. When a sentence describes what is happening *now*, it is in the present tense; when a sentence describes what *happened earlier*, it is in the past tense; and when the sentence describes what *will happen* in the future, it is in the future tense. So, "I *eat* an apple" is in the present tense; "I *ate* an apple" is in the past tense; and "I *shall eat* an apple" is in the future tense. So far we have been studying the present tense only.

In Japanese, **V•masu**-verbs have the same form for both the present and future tenses. (This is not the case for **desu**.) Hence, **watashi wa ringo o tabemasu** may be translated either as *I eat an apple* or *I shall eat an apple*. However, there is rarely any confusion as to which translation is to be chosen because the context/situation usually removes any ambiguity, as in the following conversation. Also the vocabulary, related to the future as shown below, may be included to indicate the future tense.

 *Nouns and Adverbs**

ashita *tomorrow*   **rainen** *next year*   **rai-shū** *next week*

 Conversation 1: What Will You Drink?

Tom and Hanako look at the show window of a restaurant to decide what to order.

Tom:	*(Hanako-san wa)* **nani o nomimasu ka.**	*What will you drink?*
Hanako:	*(Watashi wa)* **orenji-jūsu o nomimasu.**	*I'll drink orange juice.*
	(Tom-kun wa) **nani o nomimasu ka.**	*What will you drink?*
Tom:	*(Boku wa)* **tomato-jūsu o nomimasu.**	*I'll drink tomato juice.*
	(Anata wa) **nani o tabemasu ka.**	*What will you eat?*
Hanako:	*(Watashi wa)* **tenpura o tabemasu.**	*I'll eat tempura.*
Tom:	**Tenpura wa niku desu ka.**	*Is tempura meat*
	(Tenpura wa) **sakana desu ka.****	*or (is it) fish?*
Hanako:	*(Tenpura wa)* **sakana desu.**	*It is fish.*
Tom:	**Boku wa karēraisu to pan o tabemasu.**	*I'll eat Indian curry and bread.*

NEGATIVE STATEMENTS: I DO NOT EAT NOODLES

For the verbs ending with **masu,** you can make negative statements by changing **masu** into **masen.**

Examples

Watashi wa inu o araimasu.	*I wash a dog.*
Watashi wa inu o araimasen.	*I do not wash a dog.*
Otōto wa Eigo o hanashimasu.	*(My) younger brother speaks English.*
Otōto wa Eigo o hanashimasen.	*(My) younger brother does not speak English.*
Okāsan wa pan o tsukurimasu.	*Mother makes bread.*
Okāsan wa pan o tsukurimasen.	*Mother does not make bread.*

QUESTIONS AND ANSWERS

When a question is asked, you may answer it with **hai** + a positive verb (for a positive reply) or **iie** + a negative verb (for a negative reply).

***Ashita, rainen,** and **rai-shū** are defined as nouns in Japanese grammar.
When the same question is repeated with just one different noun, as in **tenpura wa niku desu ka. (tenpura wa) **sakana desu ka.,** the English equivalent is *is tempura meat or (is it) fish?* Similarly, **anata wa Hanako-san desu ka.** (anata wa) **Kazuko-san desu ka.** means *are you Hanako or (are you) Kazuko?*

A question is asked

Anata wa Nihon-go no hon o yomimasu ka.	Do you read Japanese books?

The reply is either

Hai yomimasu.	Yes, I do.
or	
Iie yomimasen.	No, I don't.

A question is asked

Anata wa Itaria-go o hanashimasu ka.	Do you speak Italian?

The reply is either

Hai hanashimasu.	Yes, I do.
or	
Iie hanashimasen.	No, I don't.

 ## Conversation 2: Do American Children Learn Japanese?

Hanako asks Tom about America.

Nouns

chiri geography	*kokugo* the national language	*sansū* arithmetic
kagaku science	*rekishi* history	*sūgaku* mathematics

Hanako:	*Amerika no kodomo-tachi wa Nihon-go o naraimasu ka.*	Do American children learn Japanese?
Tom:	*Iie naraimasen.*	No, they don't.
Hanako:	*(Amerika no kodomo-tachi wa) nani o naraimasu ka.*	What do they learn?
Tom:	*(America no kodomo-tachi wa) Eigo to Furansu-go to chiri to kagaku to sansū o naraimasu.*	They learn English, French, geography, science and arithmetic.
Hanako:	*Amerika-jin wa nani-go o hanashimasu ka.*	What language do Americans speak?
Tom:	*(Amerika-jin wa) Eigo o hanashimasu.*	They speak English.
Hanako:	*Amerika-jin wa nani o tabemasu ka.*	What do Americans eat?
Tom:	*(Amerika-jin wa) niku to yasai to pan o tabemasu.*	They eat meat, vegetables and bread.

EXERCISES

7.5. I shall ask questions about Conversation 1. When you hear a question, reply to it aloud in a full sentence in Japanese. Correct answers are recorded at the end of this exercise.

1. ____

2. ____

3. ____

4. ____

7.6. *Listen to the track for Exercise 7.1 again. After you listen to a sentence, convert it into a negative sentence and say it aloud. The correct answers are recorded on the track for Exercise 7.6.*

1. ____

2. ____

3. ____

4. ____

5. ____

6. ____

7. ____

7.7. Fill in the table below.

Meaning	Positive verb	Negative verb
read	*yomimasu*	*yomimasen*
	torimasu	
sell		
		okurimasen
	nomimasu	

7.8. *I shall talk about my younger sister. Answer the following questions as simply as possible in rōmaji, e.g.,* **hai tabemasu,** *yes, she does;* **iie tabemasen,** *no, she doesn't.*

1. **Watashi no imōto wa miruku o nomimasu ka.** _____________________________

2. **Watashi no imōto wa (o)-cha o nomimasu ka.** _____________________________

   Lesson 7: Focus on Action: Verbs

3. *Watashi no imōto wa shinbun o yomimasu ka.*_______________________________

4. *Watashi no imōto wa Nihon-go o naraimasu ka.* ______________________________

5. *Watashi no imōto wa terebi o mimasu ka.* ______________________________

6. *Watashi no imōto wa Eigo o hanashimasu ka.* ______________________________

7.9. Translate into English:

1. *Boku wa inu o araimasen.*_______________________________

2. *Onēsan wa niku o tabemasen.*_______________________________

3. *Okāsan wa kudamono o kaimasen.*_______________________________

4. *Imōto wa pan o tsukurimasen.* _______________________________

5. *Otōto wa otōsan no hon o yomimasen.* _______________________________

6. *Watashi wa Eigo o hanashimasen.* _______________________________

7. *Anata wa Doitsu-go o naraimasu ka. Iie naraimasen.* _______________________________

____

8. *Anata wa kore o tabemasu ka. Hai tabemasu.* _______________________________

____

Translate into rōmaji:

9. I do not write letters._______________________________

10. (My) mother does not drink milk. _______________________________

11. Makoto does not eat udon. _______________________________

12. Tom does not read newspapers. _______________________________

13. I do not listen to the music. _______________________________

14. I do not speak Japanese. ____

15. Are you going to buy this? No, I am not. ________________________________

____

16. Do you read this? Yes, I do. ____

JAPANESE CUSTOMS AND CULTURE

The School System

The Japanese school system consists of six years of elementary school from ages 7 to 13, three years of secondary school from ages 13 to 16, three years of high school from ages 16 to 19, and four years of university from ages 19 to 23. Elementary schools and secondary schools are compulsory, and enrollment and literacy rates are essentially 100 percent. There are also kindergartens for children of ages 4 to 7, technical colleges instead of high schools for those of ages 16 to 21, and junior colleges instead of universities for those of ages 19 to 21. More than 90 percent of secondary school graduates go to high schools.

Japanese society judges a person by the school he has attended, and his career greatly depends on the university from which he graduated. Because of this, the competition to get into a good university is fierce. To get into a good university, one has to get into a good high school, and to do that one has to first get into a good secondary school, etc. Even at as young as 10 years old, a child often has to go to a cram school after coming home from a regular school. He or she hardly has any other free time except to do homework from the school and the cram school.

Scholastic performance is judged only through written tests with multiple-choice questions rather than essay-type written tests; the results are figures ranking each student. Learning is done mainly by rote, and students are strictly controlled by the teachers.

English is taught from secondary school on, and a student must get passing grades in English, mathematics and Japanese on the university entrance exam. Once the student gets into a university, graduation is almost guaranteed, so he or she spends a good part of his or her time having a good time or working at a part-time job. The Japanese school year begins in April.

In Japan, coming of age occurs at 20; this is when one has the right to vote, smoke and drink alcohol.

A Brief Introduction to Japanese History

The Prehistoric Period (30,000 B.C.–300 A.D.)

Because Japan was connected to mainland Asia a long time ago, the original inhabitants of Japan came from the Asian continent. They worshipped natural objects and phenomena such as the sun, moon, mountains, trees, rocks, wind, storms, etc. They believed that those objects and phenomena were inhabited by gods who were the spirits of dead people. Around 8,000 B.C., the Ice Age ended, Japan became warmer, and the sea level started to rise. Between about 300 B.C. and 300 A.D., people started to cultivate rice. This led people to work together (such as for planting, harvesting, etc.) and they started to form groups called clans. Within clans, hierarchies developed, with powerful people becoming rulers, and others becoming commoners.

The Kofun Period (300–710)

Many clans appeared all over Japan during this period. In 538, Buddhism was introduced from Korea and it ignited fights among powerful clans. The Yamato clan established an imperial court, modeled after the centralized Chinese imperial court, around 600, under the empress Suiko*, to the south of Nara. To strengthen imperial power, the history of Japan from the day of its creation was compiled, listing emperors as the direct descendants of the gods who created Japan. The worshipping of ancestors was incorporated into this belief, and thus the Shinto religion was formed.

The Nara Period (710–794)

The empress Genmei built a magnificent capital in Nara in 710, and she instituted the system for the administration of taxes, censuses, land holdings, etc. The imperial court (headed by the empress) sponsored and practiced Buddhism—which led to much advanced Chinese culture and technology being brought into Japan—to support and enforce its political authority. Temples were built all over Japan to enforce imperial power. During this period, Buddhism became the state religion, and Buddhist culture (statues, paintings, etc.) flourished. (As strange as it may seem, Buddhist monks persuaded emperors that Shinto gods required salvation.)

The Heian Period (794–1185)

In 784, the emperor Kanmu decided to make a fresh start and moved the capital to a new location near Kyoto, to avoid infighting among nobles and clerics in Nara. After several misfortunes there, and for the convenience of transportation, in 794 he built a new capital in Kyoto, which also became the home of the imperial court until the middle of the nineteenth century. During this period, Chinese culture and the elegant courtly culture flourished among nobles. However, with no effective military system, the imperial court had difficulty in controlling the growing power of provincial warriors and the accumulation of land by some individuals. Samurai (warriors), who served and guarded nobles, began to derive more power.

The Medieval Period (1185–1600)

In 1185, Minamotono Yoritomo**, a samurai lord, defeated the imperial forces and appointed himself as Shōgun (the absolute military ruler), establishing a military government in Kamakura. From 1467 to 1568, known as the Sengoku Period (Period of Civil Wars), Japan was thrown into chaos by constant fighting among daimyō (local feudal lords), who ignored Shōgun and the imperial court. A movement towards national reunification gradually emerged out of violence.

*In Japanese history books, female imperial rulers are always referred to as "emperors" and the term "empresses" is used for wives and daughters of emperors. I have used "empress" here to emphasize that Suiko (and Genmei in the next paragraph) were female rulers. Although women ruled as "emperors" almost as often as men before 770, they essentially disappeared from the political scene after 770. It should also be noted that, throughout Japanese history, emperors/empresses have rarely ruled the country or fought wars themselves, having almost always delegated their powers to others.

**Japanese names are listed by family names followed by given names; for example, Hepburn Audrey.

The Edo Period (1600–1868)

In 1600, Tokugawa Ieyasu united Japan under his military rule and became Shōgun. He built a new capital in Edo, present day Tokyo, which he controlled directly, and he partitioned the rest of the country into 250 or so fiefs, giving them to the daimyō to govern. He made it quite clear that none of his daimyō could ever revolt against him by instituting "sankin kōtai." Sankin kōtai was a system in which a daimyō's family (wife and children) must live in Edo, while the daimyō must alternate his residence between Edo and his domain every other year. This prevented a daimyō from ever raising his army against Shōgun: he could have an army sufficient to raise rebellion when he was in his domain, but his family could be instantly captured if he did so. Also, the maintenance of his estate in Edo, and traveling between Edo and his domain in extravagant processions, exhausted 70 to 80 percent of a daimyō's income, so that he could not accumulate enough money to raise an army. Shōgun held very tight reins on everybody else also; he enforced status distinction among samurai, merchants, artisans and peasants, and he forbade Christianity and any contact with the Western world. The main characteristic of this period is that the society was dominated by samurai, relying heavily on taxes collected from peasants. Apart from samurai, people were very oppressed, although Japan was peaceful, and secluded from the outside world.

The Modern Period (1868–1945)

Ships from Russia, America and Europe started to arrive in Japan in search of trade. This set things in motion for young local samurai, who were very impressed with the advanced Western technology, to restore the emperor Meiji into power in 1868. They wanted to transform the feudal society into a strong nation, and they began an all-out effort to industrialize Japan in order to catch up with the West. They reformed the country in the Western way, socially, politically and economically. In 1889, the constitution was made and the parliament was established in the next year. Japan achieved industrial progress and military power: it defeated China in 1895 and Russia in 1905, and annexed Korea in 1910, emerging as the major power in East Asia. The years from 1868 to 1912 are known as The Meiji Period. The First World War (1914–1918) brought an economic boom to Japan. A coalition of right-wing politicians and army officers seized control of

The Heian Shrine, built in 1895 to commemorate the moving of the capital of Japan from Nara to Kyoto.

The Atomic Bomb Dome in The Peace Memorial Park, Hiroshima.

     Lesson 7: Focus on Action: Verbs

the country and led Japan into military expansion in central Asia. This led Japan to enter the Second World War in 1941.

The Contemporary Period (1945–Present)

Nuclear bombs were dropped on Hiroshima and Nagasaki in 1945, forcing Japan to surrender. The Allied Forces occupied Japan from 1945 to 1952, and they forced sweeping democratic reforms such as the renunciation of divinity by the emperor, a new constitution, and a new educational system. The post-war years saw Japan's recovery from defeat in the Second World War, and phenomenal economic growth, although this has changed somewhat since 1995.

The Peace Bell at The Peace Memorial Park, Hiroshima.

WOULD YOU LIKE TO _?

object o **V•masen ka** implies *Would you like to _?*

"Negative **V•masu**-verb + **ka**" produces an expression equivalent to "Would you like to _?" in English. This expression is used primarily in one-to-one conversation, and the subject, which is always the person to whom you are speaking, is usually dropped. (Japanese has no negative questions like *don't you eat an apple?, don't you watch TV?*, etc.)

Examples

Eiga o mimasen ka.	*Would you like to see a movie?*
Kore o yomimasen ka.	*Would you like to read this?*

Replies are

Hai mimasu/yomimasu.	*Yes, I would.*
Iie mimasen/yomimasen.	*No, I would not.*

When the expression **_masen ka** is used with respect to food or drinks, replies are a little tricky. Let us look at the following example in which someone suggests that you drink coffee.

Coffee is suggested

Kōhī o nomimasen ka.	*Would you like to drink coffee?*

Replies are

Hai nomimasu.	*Yes, I would.*
Iie nomimasen.	*No, I would not.*

In the example, coffee is suggested by a speaker without specifying who will provide it. For instance, when you are walking on a street with a friend, he may suggest having a coffee. In this situation, you do not know whether he is thinking of buying coffee for you or going Dutch. If that is the case, the above replies are appropriate. But, when it is obvious that he is offering you a coffee, such as when you are in his home, more polite replies are appropriate although the above replies are perfectly all right. You may recall from lesson 2 that **itadakimasu**, *thank you*, implies acceptance and gratitude when someone offers you something, and that is the phrase used in a positive reply for accepting the offer with gratitude. In the same way, a refusal with gratitude is used for refusing a kind offer as below.

Hai itadakimasu.	*Yes, thank you. (accepting with gratitude)*
Iie kekkō desu.	*No, thank you. (rejecting with gratitude)*

 ## Conversation 3: Would You Like to Watch a Video?

Hanako suggests that Tom watch a video with her. The following vocabulary appears in the conversation.

Personal Pronoun	Nouns	
Dizunī Disney	*manga* comics, cartoon	*bideo* video

Hanako:	*Bideo o mimasen ka.*	*Would you like to watch a video?*
Tom:	*(Bideo wa)* **nan no bideo desu ka.**	*What kind of video is it?*
Hanako:	*(Bideo wa)* **inu no eiga desu.**	*It's a movie of a dog.*
	(Eiga wa) **Dizunī no manga desu.**	*It's a Disney cartoon.*
	Eiga wa Eigo desu.	*The movie is in English.*
Tom:	*Hai mimasu.*	*Yes, I'll watch it.*

EXERCISES

7.10. *I shall suggest an activity to you. Write down what I have suggested in English.*

1. ____

2. ____

3. ____

4. ____

5. ____

7.11. *Say the following sentences aloud in Japanese. The correct answers are recorded on the track for Exercise 7.11.*

          Lesson 7: Focus on Action: Verbs

1. Would you like to drink?

2. Would you like to watch?

3. Would you like to buy?

4. Would you like to learn Japanese?

5. Would you like to eat chow mein?

7.12. Translate into English:

1. *Kore o mimasen ka.* ____

2. *Furansu-go o naraimasen ka.* _______________________________________

3. *Ongaku o kikimasen ka.* ____

4. *Nihon-go o hanashimasen ka.* _______________________________________

5. *Sushi o tabemasen ka.* ____

   Hai itadakimasu. ____

6. *Mizu o nomimasen ka.* ____

   Iie kekkō desu. ____

Translate into rōmaji:

7. Would you like to speak English? _____________________________________

8. Would you like to draw a picture? ____________________________________

9. Would you like to listen to Japanese music? ___________________________

10. Would you like to learn German? ____________________________________

11. Would you like to drink Japanese green tea? Yes, thank you. _____________

   ____

12. Would you like to take a photograph? No, thank you. __________________

   ____

When you ride on Japanese trains, you will be surprised to see that so many men are reading magazines, and you may conclude that Japanese men are very studious. Well, you are absolutely wrong! What they are reading are not magazines, filled with useful information; rather, they are reading **manga,** comics. Comics are very popular in Japan. You will see many young people reading comics, and flocking around comics sections in bookstores. These comics are astonishingly violent and sexually explicit: in them, it is common for women to be raped and otherwise physically violated. On a more positive note, many well known stories are also written in comics.

WRITING EXERCISE: HIRAGANA FOR *TA, CHI, TSU, TE* AND *TO*

Practice the five hiragana characters た, ち, つ, て *and* と.

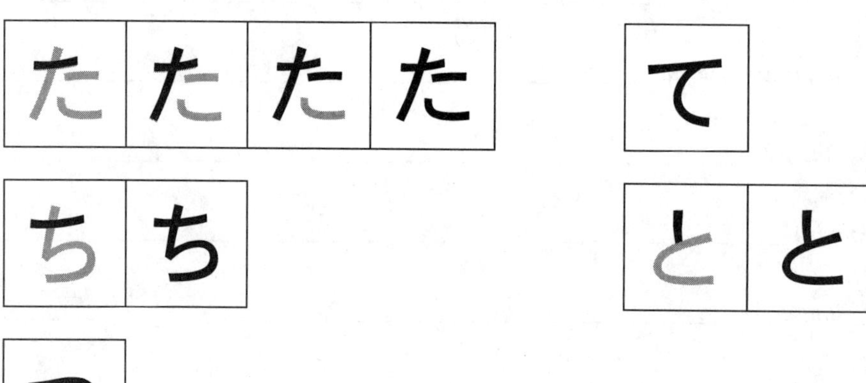

What you must remember from this lesson to proceed to the next lesson:
V•masu-verbs have the sentence structure _ **wa** _ **o** V•masu where
the particle **wa** follows the subject and
the particle **o** follows a direct object.
V•masen + ka implies Would you like to _ ?

     Lesson 7: Focus on Action: Verbs

The Mighty Little Words: Japanese Particles

In this lesson you will learn:

Speaking
To talk about how and where something is done
To ask how to say something in Japanese/English
To talk about doing things with others
To ask if your listener agrees
To make an exclamation

Grammar
To expand action sentences with the particles **de** and **to**
To use the particle **de** with the verb **desu**
To use the particles **ne** and **yo** at the ends of sentences
To understand word order in Japanese sentences

Using the **V•masu**-verbs you have learned in the previous lesson, you can say many simple sentences such as "I eat an apple," "I read a book," etc. You may note that the verbs in the previous lesson are verbs of doing (action verbs) and they are transitive verbs (they take direct objects).

In this lesson, you will learn to expand those action sentences by including locations of actions, with what instruments the actions are done, and how the actions are done. In other words, you will be able to say sentences such as "I eat an apple *in a kitchen*" to mention the *location* of the action of "eating," "I read a book *with my glasses*" to mention *with what instrument* the action of "reading" is done, and "I read a book *in Japanese*" to mention *how* the action of "reading" is done. All the above expansions to the basic action sentences are accomplished by using the particle **de** in Japanese. You will also learn the use of **de** with the verb **desu** to expand sentences.

In life, you cannot do everything by yourself. In fact, quite often you will be doing things with someone else, and you will learn the particle **to** to express that idea in this lesson. You will also learn the particles **yo** and **ne** which are placed at the ends of sentences.

THE PARTICLE *DE*

Some of the most useful tools we use for our actions are our bodies. For instance, we read *with our eyes,* we eat *with our mouths,* etc. Let us look the names of our body parts and some eating utensils which we use for the most enjoyable actions we do.

karada body

ashi leg	*me* eye	*hashi* chopsticks
atama head	*mimi* ear	*hōku* fork
hana nose	*onaka* stomach, abdomen, belly	*naifu* knife
kami hair	*te* hand	*supūn* spoon
kao face	*ude* arm	
kata shoulder	*yubi* finger	*basu* bus
kuchi mouth		

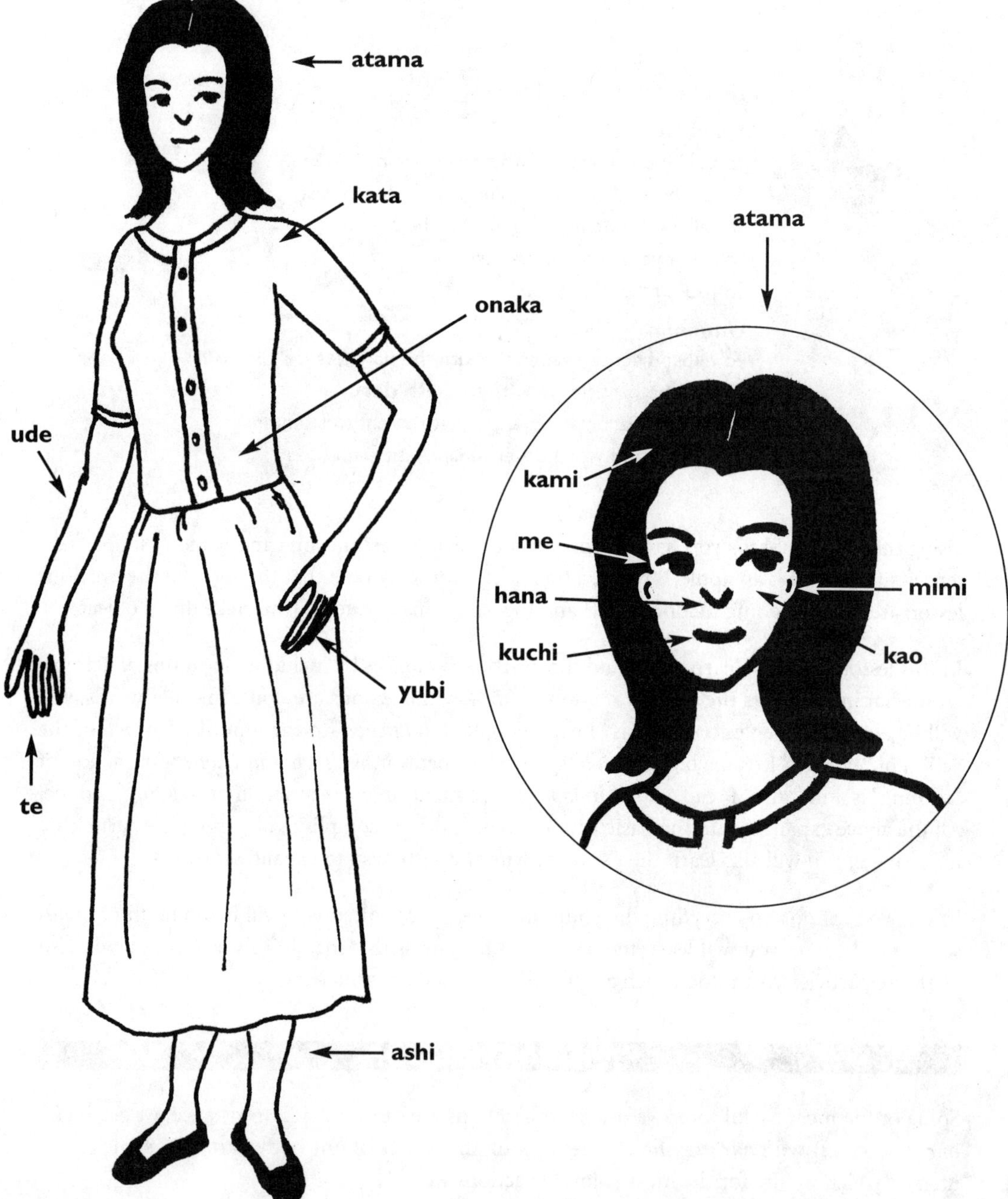

With What Instrument (or How) Do You Do That?

The particle **de** following a noun has two uses. One is to indicate "with what instrument something is done" or "how something is done." Translated according to context, it can mean *in/with/by*. This "with" should not be confused with the "with" of accompaniment (e.g., I go to school *with* Makoto).

Examples

Watashi wa inu o mizu de araimasu.	*I wash a dog* with *water. (with what?)*
Watashi wa inu o te de araimasu.	*I wash a dog* by *hand. (with what?)*
Otōsan wa tegami o pen de kakimasu.	*Father writes a letter* with *a pen. (with what?)*
Otōsan wa tegami o Eigo de kakimasu.	*Father writes a letter* in *English. (how?)*

 Conversation 1: Do You Eat with Chopsticks or a Fork?

Hanako offers Tom yakisoba.

Hanako:	*Yakisoba o tabemasen ka.*	*Would you like to eat yakisoba?*
Tom:	*Hai itadakimasu.*	*Yes, thank you.*
Hanako:	*(Anata wa yakisoba o) (o)hashi de tabemasu ka. Hōku de tabemasu ka.*	*Do you eat it with chopsticks or a fork?*
Tom:	*(Boku wa yakisoba o) hōku de tabemasu.*	*I will eat it with a fork.*
Hanako:	*(Anata wa) nani o (o)hashi de tabemasu ka.*	*What do you eat with chopsticks?*
Tom:	*(Boku wa) sakana o ((o)hashi de) tabemasu.*	*I eat fish.*

Where Do You Do That?

The second use of **de** is that of expressing "action in a place." Translated according to context, it can mean *in/at/on*.

Examples

Watashi wa inu o niwa de araimasu.	*I wash a dog* in *the garden.*
Watashi wa zasshi o basu de yomimasu.	*I read a magazine* on *a bus.*
Otōsan wa e o yama de kakimasu.	*Father draws a picture* at *a mountain.*

EXERCISES

8.1. I shall say a Japanese word for a body part. Write the number corresponding to the body part in the correct blank on the next page.

8.2. Say the following sentences aloud in Japanese. The correct answers are recorded on the track for Exercise 8.2.

1. I write a letter with (my) hand.____
   [not with a computer]
2. I write a letter in the garden.____

3. I write a letter with a pen. ____

4. I write a letter in English. ____

5. I eat steak in the kitchen.____

6. I eat steak with knife and fork. ____

   Lesson 8: The Mighty Little Words: Japanese Particles

8.3. 💿 *I shall ask questions about Conversation 1. When you hear a question, reply to it aloud in a full sentence in Japanese. Correct answers are recorded at the end of this exercise.*

1. ____

2. ____

8.4. Translate into English:

1. *Watashi wa udon o (o)hashi de tabemasu.* ___________________________________

2. *Onēsan wa Eigo no uta o rajio de kikimasu.* _________________________________

3. *Anata wa tegami o nan de kakimasu ka.* _____________________________________

4. *Otōsan wa hon o heya de yomimasu.* ____

5. *Watashi-tachi wa Eigo o gakkō de naraimasu.* _______________________________

____

6. *Okāsan wa kudamono o niwa de tsukurimasen.* _______________________________

____

7. *Ojīsan wa pan o doko de kaimasu ka.* _______________________________________

Translate into rōmaji:

8. Hanako washes a cat with water. ____

9. We eat meat with knife and fork. ____

10. Grandmother reads books with glasses. _____________________________________

11. Elephants eat bananas with (their) trunks (noses). __________________________

____

12. I do not write a letter in Japanese. _______________________________________

13. Do you learn music at school? _______________________________________

14. I do not speak Japanese at home. _______________________________________

Chopsticks and Eating Manners

A traditional Japanese meal consists of small servings of many different colorful dishes, all served together on your own tray. You may have ten or more small plates and bowls in front of you. Japanese use chopsticks to eat, and food is served in bite-sized pieces which you pick up with your chopsticks. You will never need to cut anything. If there is anything large, you can break it up with your chopsticks. Some bowls, such as soup bowls, have covers. You take the cover off and put it beside the bowl inside up; when you are finished with your meal, you put all the covers back on. You use one hand for holding chopsticks and the other hand for picking up bowls and plates (to bring the food close to your mouth) so that food does not drop out of the chopsticks before it is put into your mouth. You should never pull a plate toward you with chopsticks. When you eat soup, you put a soup bowl to your mouth and you are allowed to slurp while drinking it. When you eat fish, you pick the meat off the top side without breaking bones, and, when you are finished with that side, you flip the fish over to eat the other side. Fish bones and heads should be left in a neat orderly fashion. Chopsticks should not be dug into rice or any other food. It is regarded as very bad manners: sticking chopsticks into rice is done only when people offer rice to a deceased person at an altar! When you are not using them, you should rest the "eating end" of chopsticks on a plate or a chopsticks-rest.

Formal Japanese meal setting.

With a buffet style meal, there may be chopsticks on communal plates and bowls for serving. If there are not, you eat with one end of your chopsticks and pick food from communal serving plates with the other end.

One of the first things you will do, when you get friendly with a Japanese person, is to ask for a word in Japanese. It is a great way to get acquainted and, at the same time, you will learn new words.

De is used with the verb **desu** when you want to ask for words in Japanese. Let us consider **Kore wa nan desu ka,** *What is this?* By inserting **Nihon-go de,** *in Japanese,* you get **Kore wa Nihon-go de nan desu ka,** *What is this in Japanese?*

Similarly, let's consider **Kore wa RINGO desu,** *This is RINGO.* By inserting **Nihon-go de,** *in Japanese,* you get **Kore wa Nihon-go de RINGO desu,** *This is RINGO in Japanese.* By changing **Kore** with **APPLE,** you get **APPLE wa Nihon-go de RINGO desu,** *APPLE is RINGO in Japanese.*

 ## Conversation 2: What Is *Tokei* in English?

Hanako asks Tom what the following Japanese words are in English.

Nouns

sangurasu sunglasses	*tokei* watch	*undō-gutsu* sport shoes

Hanako:	*TOKEI wa Eigo de nan desu ka.*	*What is TOKEI in English?*
Tom:	*(TOKEI wa Eigo de) WATCH desu.*	*It's WATCH.*
Hanako:	*SANGURASU wa (Eigo de nan desu ka).*	*What about SANGURASU?*
Tom:	*(SANGURASU wa Eigo de) SUNGLASSES desu.*	*It's SUNGLASSES.*
Hanako:	*UNDŌ-GUTSU wa (Eigo de nan desu ka).*	*What about UNDŌ-GUTSU?*
Tom:	*UNDŌ-GUTSU wa (Eigo de) SPORT SHOES desu.*	*UNDŌ-GUTSU is SPORT SHOES.*

EXERCISES

8.5. *I shall describe myself. I want you to write who I am in rōmaji in the sentence below. I am one of the following: Amerika-jin, zō, saru, Nihon-jin, kuma, raion.*

1. *Anata wa* _________________________________ *desu.*

2. *Anata wa* _________________________________ *desu.*

3. *Anata wa* _________________________________ *desu.*

4. *Anata wa* _________________________________ *desu.*

5. *Anata wa* _________________________________ *desu.*

6. *Anata wa* _________________________________ *desu.*

8.6. Translate into English.

1. *Kore wa Nihon-go de nan desu ka.* _________________________________

2. *Kore wa Eigo de nan desu ka.* _________________________________

8.7. Make sentences by putting appropriate words in the blanks.

1. _________________________________ wa Nihon-go de MIZU desu.

2. ASHI wa Eigo de _________________________________ desu.

3. NEKO wa Eigo de _________________________________ desu.

4. DOG wa Nihon-go de _________________________________ desu.

5. _________________________________ wa Eigo de BOOK desu.

8.8.  *When you hear a question, reply to it aloud in a full sentence in Japanese. Correct answers are recorded at the end of this exercise.*

1. ____

2. ____

3. ____

4. ____

TOGETHER, WE SHALL OVERCOME: THE PARTICLE *TO*

When the particle **to** follows a person, it means *together/along with.*

Examples

Watashi wa eiga o Hanako-san to mimasu.	*I watch a movie with Hanako.*
Ranchi o watashi to tabemasen ka.	*Would you like to eat lunch with me?*

DO YOU AGREE WITH ME? OF COURSE!: THE PARTICLE *NE*

Quite often, you will hear **ne** at the end of a sentence. The particle **ne** at the end of a sentence solicits agreement from the listener. Translated according to context, it can mean *isn't it?, don't you?,* etc.

Examples

Are wa hon desu ne.	*That is a book, isn't it?*
Anata wa ringo o tabemasu ne.	*You will eat an apple, won't you?*
Are wa Eigo no sensei de wa arimasen ne.	*He is not the English teacher, is he?*

   Lesson 8: The Mighty Little Words: Japanese Particles

Yo at the ends of sentences alerts the listener to what the speaker is saying. It is very similar to the exclamation mark in English.

Examples

Are wa watashi-tachi no basu desu yo.	_That is our bus!_
Watashi-tachi wa gohan o tabemasu yo.	_We shall eat meals!_

Conversation 3: That's Kazuko, Isn't It?

Tom sees a familiar face and asks Hanako who she is.

Tom:	_Are wa Kazuko-san desu ne._	_That's Kazuko, isn't it?_
Hanako:	_Iie (are wa) Yōko-san desu yo._	_No, that's Yoko!_
	(Yōko-san wa) Kazuko-san no onēsan desu yo.	_Kazuko's elder sister!_
	(Yōko-san wa) watashi no onēsan no tomodachi desu.	_She is (my) elder sister's friend._

EXERCISES

_8.9._ _I shall say a sentence. I want you to convert it into a sentence which solicits an agreement from the listener. Say it after my sentence. The correct answers are recorded at the end of this exercise._

1. ____

2. ____

3. ____

4. ____

5. ____

_8.10._ _Listen to the track for Exercise 8.9 again. This time, I want you to say a sentence which alerts the listener. The correct answers are recorded on the track for Exercise 8.10._

1. ____

2. ____

3. ____

4. ____

5. ____

8.11. *Say the following sentences aloud in Japanese. The correct answers are recorded on the track for Exercise 8.11.*

1. I drink coffee with a friend. _______________________________________

2. I watch TV with my family. _______________________________________

3. I speak Japanese with my elder brother. _______________________________

4. I learn Japanese with my younger brother. _____________________________

5. I listen to the music with my mother. _________________________________

8.12. Translate into English:

1. **Watashi wa ongaku o Makoto-kun to kikimasu.** ______________________

   ____

2. **Sukiyaki o watashi-tachi to tabemasen ka.** __________________________

   ____

3. **Anata wa Eigo o dare to hanashimasu ka.** ___________________________

   ____

4. **Anata wa Hanako-san desu ne.** ______________________________________

5. **Are wa boku-tachi no basu desu yo.** _________________________________

Translate into rōmaji:

6. What do you make with Makoto? ____

7. Would you like to watch a video with me? ______________________________

     Lesson 8: The Mighty Little Words: Japanese Particles

8. I shall not speak with Hanako. ____

9. That is the hospital, isn't it?____

10. This is mine! ____

THE ORDER OF WORDS IN JAPANESE SENTENCES

The particles may be separated into three categories, depending on where they appear in sentences, as follows.

1. **Ka, ne, yo:** They are placed at the ends of sentences after the verbs, meaning *?, isn't it?, !.*

2. **To, ka, no:** They are put between words, meaning *and, or,* and in the case of **no,** possessive, "origin of," or *of/for/in/on* (see page 45). They always stay between words.

3. **Wa, o, de, to, (ni, ga, e, kara):** They describe and follow nouns/pronouns: they make a noun/pronoun the subject, the object, the adverb clause, etc. A "noun/pronoun + its particle" may be put anywhere in a sentence before a verb.

Note that **ka** appears in two different locations for two different purposes in sentences: one for questions at the ends of sentences, and another to mean *or* between words. Note also that **to** appears in two different locations: one between nouns/pronouns meaning *and* and another after a noun/pronoun meaning *with.*

Verbs always come either at the ends of sentences or just before **ka/ne/yo** placed at the ends.

Complements, which are not followed by any particle, must come before the verb **desu.**

Hence the following sentences are equivalent.

Anata wa inu o niwa de araimasu ka.   *Do you wash the dog in the garden?*
Anata wa niwa de inu o araimasu ka.
Inu o anata wa niwa de araimasu ka.
Inu o niwa de anata wa araimasu ka.
Niwa de anata wa inu o araimasu ka.
Niwa de inu o anata wa araimasu ka.

To make learning easier, we will stick basically to the sentence structure **SUBJECT + OBJECT + OTHERS + V·MASU-VERB + KA/NE/YO.** That is, we shall write **Anata wa inu o niwa de araimasu ka,** rather than any other forms shown above.

Note also that the following sentences are equivalent.

APPLE wa Nihon-go de RINGO desu yo. *APPLE is RINGO in Japanese!*
Nihon-go de APPLE wa RINGO desu yo.

You can see that the verb **desu** always comes before the particle **yo (/ka/ne),** and the complement (**RINGO** in the above sentences), which is not followed by any particle, comes before **desu**. The "noun/pronoun + its particle"s (**APPLE wa** and **Nihon-go de**) may interchange between themselves. Just as with **V•masu**-verbs, we keep basically to the sentence structure **SUBJECT + OTHERS + COMPLEMENT + DESU + KA/NE/YO.**

The following examples show you that "noun/pronoun + **to/ka/no** + noun/pronoun" is treated as one unit (**to/ka/no,** *and/or/_* of category 2 above).

Examples

Watashi wa inu to neko *o araimasu.*   *I wash the dog and the cat.*
Inu to neko *o watashi wa araimasu.*

Watashi wa otōsan no hon *o yomimasen.*   *I do not read (my) father's book.*
Otōsan no hon *o watashi wa yomimasen.*

Watashi wa terebi o Hanako-san ka Makoto-kun *to mimasu.*
Hanako-san ka Makoto-kun *to watashi wa terebi o mimasu.*   *I watch TV with either Hanako or Makoto.*

EXERCISES

8.13. Rewrite the following sentences in as many ways as you can.

1. *Tom-kun wa Nihon-go to Eigo o hanashimasu yo.* ___________________________

____

____

2. **Watashi wa Hanako-san to ranchi o tabemasu.** _______________________________

____

____

3. **Anata no namae wa Hanako-san desu ka.** ___________________________________

____

____

Practice the five hiragana characters な，に，ぬ，ね and の.

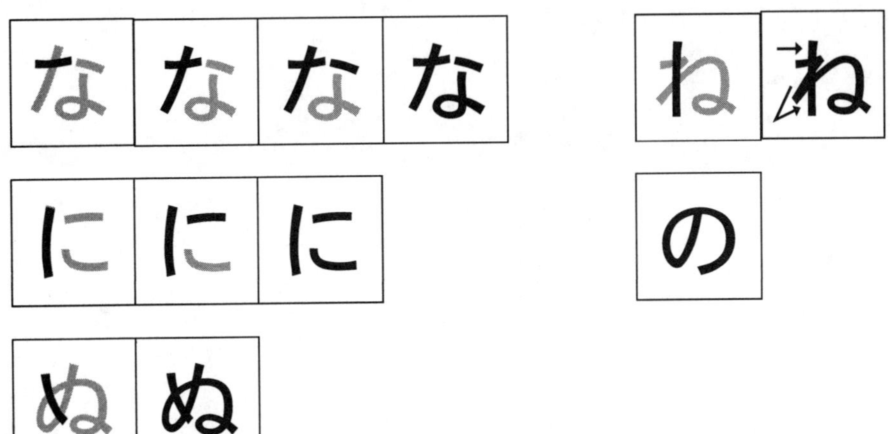

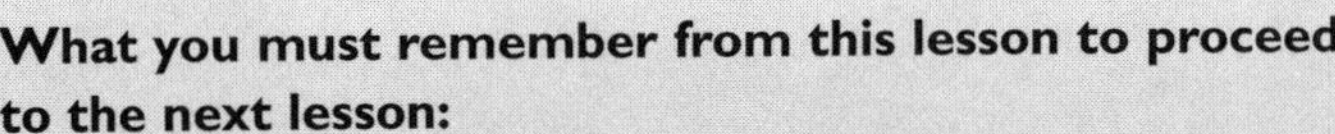

What you must remember from this lesson to proceed to the next lesson:

The particle **de** with **V•masu**-verbs indicates "with what instrument something is done" or "how something is done." Translated according to context, it can mean *in/with/by*. It also indicates the "place of the action." Translated according to context, it can mean *at/in/on*.

9 Numbers, Dates and Times

In this lesson you will learn:

Speaking
To tell someone your telephone number
To ask how much something is
To tell and ask the date
To tell and ask the time

Grammar
To understand the suffixes associated with numbers

By now, you are able to communicate fairly well with Japanese people, and you have developed friendships with some of them. You may even have met somebody you are fairly eager to spend time with, or, if not, there may be someone who is eager to ask you out to do something together. To make any kind of arrangement with anybody, you need to learn to express dates and times.

In this lesson, you will learn the Japanese number system, how to count money and how to express dates and times to get you ready for that big day. You will also learn some suffixes which go with the numbers.

NUMBERS

I am very pleased to tell you that Japanese uses the same numerical characters as those of the West. So if you could not understand the price a shop clerk tells you, you could always hand him a piece of paper to write it down. Similarly, if you could not tell the time and date you want your friend to meet you, you could always write it on a piece of paper. It is better to be sure of the time and date for an important event, such as inviting out the friend on whom you have a secret crush. After all, there is not much point in going to a restaurant at the wrong time or on the wrong day. The date is written in year/month/day format, and the time is written as hour:minute. That is, 23 April 2004 is written as 2004/04/23 and 25 minutes after 11 o'clock is written as 11:25. Japanese uses the 24-hour system for timetables, for example for trains and buses.

How to Express a Number

Let us look at the basic numbers listed below.

Numbers

zero	0	*roku*	6	*hyaku*	100
ichi	1	*nana / shichi**	7	*sen*	1,000
ni	2	*hachi*	8	*man*	10,000
san	3	*kyū/ ku**	9	*jū-man*	100,000
*yon / shi**	4	*jū*	10	*hyaku-man*	1,000,000
go	5				

The Japanese number system is similar to the English number system. For instance, *2,457* is expressed as **2 sen** *(thousand)* + **4 hyaku** *(hundred)* + **5 jū** *(ten)* + **7**. The **2, 4** and **5** are called multipliers and the **7** is called the last digit.

A number is expressed as:**

multiplier -man + multiplier -sen
+ multiplier -hyaku + multiplier -jū + the last digit

Some numbers go through phonetic changes when **hyaku** and **sen** are combined with multipliers: they are **sanbyaku**, *300*, **roppyaku**, *600*, **happyaku**, *800*, **sanzen**, *3000* and **hassen**, *8000*. The multiplier **ichi**, *1*, is used only for **ichi-man**, *10,000*, and not used for **sen**, *1,000*, **hyaku**, *100*, and **jū**, *10*. Hence *11,111* is **ichi-man sen hyaku jū ichi**. You are now able to produce any number from 1 to 1,000,000 in Japanese.

Examples

5,263   go-sen ni-hyaku roku-jū san

7,928   nana-sen kyū-hyaku ni-jū hachi

EXERCISES

9.1. Say the numbers from 1 to 10, and then 100, 1,000, and 10,000 aloud. The correct answers are recorded on the track for Exercise 9.1.

9.2. I shall tell you some Japanese telephone numbers. Write them down. Japanese telephone numbers are expressed as "number for the area code – number for the exchange – number." The numbers are said individually; **no** is used for hyphens and **ban**, number, is put at the end; 2 and 5 are pronounced as **nī** and **gō** when describing telephone numbers.

1. _072-856-7211_

2. ___________________________

3. ___________________________

*Note that 4, 7 and 9 have two forms in Japanese.

Note that **shi, *4,* **shichi,** *7,* and **ku,** *9,* are not used as multipliers (they are used only for the last digit).

          Lesson 9: Numbers, Dates and Times

9.3. Translate into English:

1. *ni-sen nana-hyaku san-jū ni* _______________________________

2. *san-man yon-sen go-hyaku roku-jū hachi* _______________________

3. *yon-sen kyū-hyaku hachi-jū ichi* ____________________________

Translate into rōmaji:

4. 735 ____

5. 5,241 ____

6. 9,726 ____

MONEY

The most important suffix that is put after a number is the suffix **-en,** which tells an amount of money. **_-en,** written also as **¥_,** is translated as _ *yen.* For example, **ni-hyaku-en,** ¥200, means *200 yen.*

Let us try to make the sentence *How much is this?* Consider **kore wa ni-hyaku-en desu,** *this is 200 yen.* By replacing **ni-hyaku-en** with **ikura,** *how much,* and putting **ka** at the end, we get **kore wa ikura desu ka,** *how much is this?*

The pronoun **ikura*** is used to indicate *how much.*

Area where you pay for your shopping purchases.

Japanese paper money.

***Ikura** is defined as a number (noun) in Japanese grammar. I have defined it as a pronoun in accordance with English grammar.

Japanese coins.

 **Conversation 1: How Much Is This?**

Tom goes shopping.

Tom:	*Kore wa ikura desu ka.*	*How much is this?*
Clerk:	*(Kore wa) go-hyaku kyū-jū-en desu.*	*It's 590 yen.*
Tom:	*Kore wa (ikura desu ka).*	*How about this?*
Clerk:	*(Kore wa) roppyaku san-jū-en desu.*	*It's 630 yen.*
Tom:	*Kore o kudasai.*	*May I have this please?*

DATES

Months

It is very easy to express months in Japanese. You just put the suffix **-gatsu** after a number to indicate the month, as you can see from the table below. **Yon**, *4*, **nana**, *7*, and **kyū**, *9*, are not used to indicate the months; instead, the alternate forms of 4, 7, and 9 (**shi, shichi** and **ku,** respectively) are used. We shall write numbers associated with the month, day, hour and minutes without hyphens. That is, instead of **jū-ni**, *12*, **jūni** is used to write the numerical part of **jūni-gatsu,** *December;* instead of **san-jū-ichi**, *31*, **sanjūichi** is used to write the numerical part of **sanjūichi-nichi,** *31st;* etc.

ichi-gatsu January	*go-gatsu* May	*ku-gatsu* September
ni-gatsu February	*roku-gatsu* June	*jū-gatsu* October
san-gatsu March	*shichi-gatsu* July	*jūichi-gatsu* November
shi-gatsu April	*hachi-gatsu* August	*jūni-gatsu* December

Days of the Month

Days of the month are slightly more complicated, and you must memorize the 1st to the 10th of the month. The suffix **-nichi** is put after the numbers to obtain the rest of the days of the month except those of the 14th, 20th and 24th.

🔘 **Days of the Month**

tsuitachi	1st	*jūichi-nichi*	11th	*nijūichi-nichi*	21st
futsuka	2nd	*jūni-nichi*	12th	*nijūni-nichi*	22nd
mikka	3rd	*jūsan-nichi*	13th	*nijūsan-nichi*	23rd
yokka	4th	*jūyokka**	14th	*nijūyokka**	24th
itsuka	5th	*jūgo-nichi*	15th	*nijūgo-nichi*	25th
muika	6th	*jūroku-nichi*	16th	*nijūroku-nichi*	26th
nanoka	7th	*jūshichi-nichi**	17th	*nijūshichi-nichi**	27th
yōka	8th	*jūhachi-nichi*	18th	*nijūhachi-nichi*	28th
kokonoka	9th	*jūku-nichi**	19th	*nijūku-nichi**	29th
tōka	10th	*hatsuka*	20th	*sanjū-nichi*	30th
				sanjūichi-nichi	31st

Days of the Week

You must memorize the days of the week since they don't follow any rules except that they all carry the suffix **-yōbi**.

🔘 **Days of the Week**

nichi-yōbi Sunday	*sui-yōbi* Wednesday	*do-yōbi* Saturday
getsu-yōbi Monday	*moku-yōbi* Thursday	
ka-yōbi Tuesday	*kin-yōbi* Friday	

How to Tell a Date

Japanese expresses a date in the order of the year, followed by the month, followed by the day of the month, followed by the day of the week, and it is written as year/month/day of the month/day of the week. The suffix **–nen,** *year,* is put after a number for the year.

Examples

Sen kyū-hyaku kyū-jū kyū-nen go-gatsu nanoka getsu-yōbi	*Monday 7 May 1999*
Ni-sen ichi-nen san-gatsu itsuka sui-yōbi	*Wednesday 5 March 2001*

*Note that **shi**, *4*, **nana**, *7*, and **kyū**, *9*, are not used to indicate the days of the month.

The suffixes associated with dates are summarized below.

Suffixes

-gatsu is put after a number to tell the month.
-nen is put after a number to tell the year.
-nichi is put after some numbers to tell the day of the month.
-yōbi denotes the day of the week.

EXERCISES

9.4. *You have asked a shop clerk* **kore wa ikura desu ka,** how much is it? *Listen for the replies. Write down the amount you hear in English.*

1. _______________ yen   4. _______________ yen

2. _______________ yen   5. _______________ yen

3. _______________ yen

9.5. *I shall tell you the birthday for each of Hanako's family members. Write down the date for each of her family members in English. The Japanese word for birthday is* **(o)tanjōbi/bāsudē.**

1. Father's birthday is ____.

2. Mother's birthday is ____.

A pair of Hina dolls to celebrate the festival for girls.

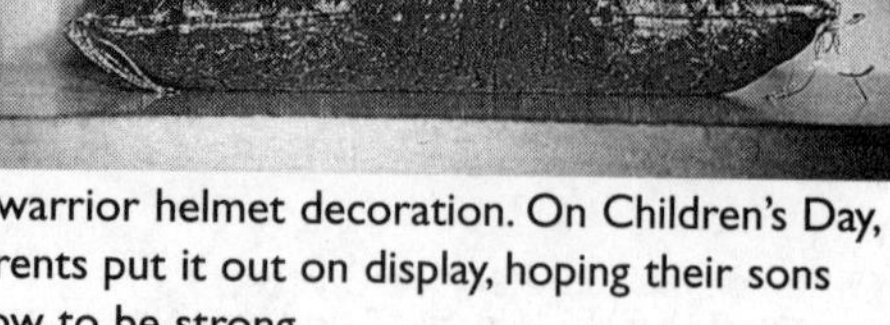

A warrior helmet decoration. On Children's Day, parents put it out on display, hoping their sons grow to be strong.

Tanabata Festival: decorations on a street.

3. The elder sister's birthday is ____.

4. Hanako's birthday is ____.

5. The younger sister's birthday is ____.

9.6. *Say the following special dates in Japanese. The correct answers are recorded on the track for Exercise 9.6.*

1. 1 January ((**O**)**shōgatsu,** *New Year's Day*)

2. 3 March (**Hinamatsuri,** *The Festival of Dolls,* regarded as festival for girls)

3. 5 May (**Kodomo no hi,** *Children's Day,* regarded as festival for boys)

4. 7 July (**Tanabata,** *The Festival of Stars,* celebration of the annual tryst of stars Altair and Vega, separated by the Milky Way)

5. 25 December (**Kurisumasu,** *Christmas*)

6. 31 December (**Ōmisoka,** *New Year's Eve*)

Now, write and then say complete sentences to state the date with its special festivity. The correct answers are recorded on the track for Exercise 9.6.

7. **Ichigatsu tsuitachi wa** (*o*)**shōgatsu desu.** *January 1 is New Year's Day.*

8. ____

9. ____

10. ____

11.____

12.____

9.7. Translate into English:

1. *Ni-sen ni-nen san-gatsu itsuka sui-yōbi* _____________________________

2. *Ni-sen-nen roku-gatsu nijūgo-nichi getsu-yōbi*

____

3. *Sen kyū-hyaku hachi-jū ichi-nen san-gatsu futsuka do-yōbi*

____

4. *Sen nana-hyaku ni-jū roku-nen hachi-gatsu jūku-nichi nichi-yōbi*

____

Translate into rōmaji:

5. Saturday 14 February 2004 _______________________________________

6. Wednesday 28 October 1579 ______________________________________

7. Sunday 5 July 1400 ____

8. Monday 1 January 2001 ____

TIME OF DAY

By now, you are able to make arrangements for a particular day and week. You now have to learn to express the time of day so that you don't mess up that big day of yours by arriving too late.

Hours

Hours are obtained by just putting the suffix **-ji** after the numbers, except for **yo-ji,** *four o'clock,* which has gone through a phonetic change (from **yon-ji**).

ichi-ji	*1 o'clock*	*go-ji*	*5 o'clock*	*ku-ji**	*9 o'clock*
ni-ji	*2 o'clock*	*roku-ji*	*6 o'clock*	*jū-ji*	*10 o'clock*
san-ji	*3 o'clock*	*shichi-ji**	*7 o'clock*	*jūichi-ji*	*11 o'clock*
*yo-ji**	*4 o'clock*	*hachi-ji*	*8 o'clock*	*jūni-ji*	*12 o'clock*

*Note that **shi**, *4,* **nana**, *7,* and **kyū**, *9,* are not used to indicate hours.

     Lesson 9: Numbers, Dates and Times

The minutes table is shown below. To obtain 2 to 9 minutes, add **-pun** or **-fun** after the numbers. **Ip-pun,** *1 minute,* and **jup-pun,** *10 minutes,* have gone through phonetic changes. Notice that there are two forms each for *6 minutes,* and *8 minutes,* and they are both used interchangeably.

ip-pun	*1 minute*	*go-fun*	*5 minutes*	*hachi-fun*	*8 minutes*
ni-fun	*2 minutes*	*roku-fun*	*6 minutes*	*hap-pun*	*8 minutes*
san-pun	*3 minutes*	*rop-pun*	*6 minutes*	*kyū-fun**	*9 minutes*
*yon-fun**	*4 minutes*	*nana-fun**	*7 minutes*	*jup-pun*	*10 minutes*

When you put **jū,** *10,* **nijū,** *20,* **sanjū,** *30,* **yonjū,** *40,* and **gojū,** *50* before 1 to 9 minutes of the above table, you can obtain *11 minutes, 12 minutes, 59 minutes,* and so on. You obtain *20, 30, 40, 50* and *60 minutes* by putting **ni,** *2,* **san,** *3,* **yon,** *4,* **go,** *5,* and **roku,** *6,* in front of **jup-pun,** *10 minutes*; they are **nijup-pun, sanjup-pun, yonjup-pun, gojup-pun** and **rokujup-pun** respectively.

Putting 10 in front of 1, 2, 3 and 4 minutes, you get:		*Putting 20 in front of 1, 2, 3 and 4 minutes, you get:*	
jū-ip-pun	*11 minutes*	*nijū-ip-pun*	*21 minutes*
jū-ni-fun	*12 minutes*	*nijū-ni-fun*	*22 minutes*
jū-san-pun	*13 minutes*	*nijū-san-fun*	*23 minutes*
jū-yon-fun	*14 minutes*	*nijū-yon-fun*	*24 minutes*

Putting 30, 40 and 50 in front of 1 minute, you get:		*Putting 50 in front of 5 and 6 minutes, you get:*	
sanjū-ip-pun	*31 minutes*	*gojū-go-pun*	*55 minutes*
yonjū-ip-fun	*41 minutes*	*gojū-roku-fun*	*56 minutes*
gojū-ip-pun	*51 minutes*	*gojū-rop-pun*	*56 minutes*

How to Tell the Time

In Japanese you tell the time by telling the hour followed by the minute, and it is written as hour:minute.

Examples	
ni-ji jūgo-fun	*2:15*
ku-ji sanjūgo-fun	*9:35*

Japanese has expressions such as *before/after* the hour (e.g., *before/after* 3 o'clock) just as in English. In these cases, **mae/sugi,** *before/after,* is put after the hour to indicate *before* or *after* as follows.

Examples	
san-ji mae	*before 3 o'clock*
san-ji sugi	*after 3 o'clock*

*Note that **shi,** *4,* **shichi,** *7,* and **ku,** *9,* are not used to indicate minutes.

Japanese has expressions such as *to/past* the hour (e.g., 5 minutes *to/past* 3 o'clock) just as in English. In these cases, **mae/sugi** is put after the minutes to indicate *to* or *past*.

Examples

san-ji go-fun mae	*5 minutes to 3 o'clock*
san-ji go-fun sugi	*5 minutes past 3 o'clock*

Although there is no special word for a *quarter* of an hour, Japanese has **han** for *half past* and it is put after the hour. So 9:30 may be expressed in the following ways.

ku-ji sanjup-pun	*9:30*
ku-ji sanjup-pun sugi	*30 minutes past 9 o'clock*
ku-ji han	*half past 9*

Gozen and **gogo** are used for A.M. and P.M., and they come before the hour.

Examples

gogo ni-ji jūgo-fun	*2:15* P.M.
gozen ku-ji sanjūgo-fun	*9:35* A.M.

The suffixes and nouns which are associated with time are collected below.

Suffixes	Nouns
han half past hour	*gogo* P.M.
mae before/to hour/minutes	*gozen* A.M.
sugi after/past hour/minutes	

-fun/pun is put after a number to tell minutes, and it is translated as minutes.
-ji is put after a number to tell the hour, and it is translated as o'clock.

HOW TO ASK THE DATE AND TIME

The prefix **nan-**, *what,* is put before **nen, gatsu, nichi, yōbi, ji** and **fun** to obtain the following expressions.

nan-nen what year?	*nan-ji* what time?, what hour?
nan-gatsu what month?	*nan-fun* how many minutes?
nan-nichi what day of the month?	
nan-yōbi what day of the week?	

The date and time may be asked using the following vocabulary.

Nouns and Adverbs*

ima at this moment	*kyō* today

*Ima and **kyō** are defined as nouns in Japanese. I have defined them as nouns and adverbs in accordance with English grammar.

          Lesson 9: Numbers, Dates and Times

Examples

Kyō wa nan-gatsu nan-nichi desu ka.	*What day (month and day) is it today?*
(kyō wa) san-gatsu hatsuka desu.	*It's the 20th of March.*
San-gatsu mikka wa nan-yōbi desu ka.	*What day of the week is the 3rd of March?*
Ima (wa) nan-ji desu ka.	*What time is it now?*
(Ima wa) san-ji desu.	*It is 3 o'clock.*

 Conversation 2: What Day Is It Today?

Tom asks the date and time.

Tom:	*Kyō wa nan-gatsu nan-nichi desu ka.*	*What day is it today?*
Hanako:	*(Kyō wa) go-gatsu mikka desu.*	*It is the 3rd of May.*
Tom:	*(Kyō wa) nan-yōbi desu ka.*	*What day of the week is it?*
Hanako:	*(Kyō wa) sui-yōbi desu.*	*It's a Wednesday.*
Tom:	*Ima (wa) nan-ji desu ka.*	*What time is it now?*
Hanako:	*(Ima wa) jūni-ji yonjūgo-fun sugi desu.*	*It's 45 minutes past 12.*

OTHER SUFFIXES ASSOCIATED WITH NUMBERS

One of the more difficult features of the Japanese number system is the concept of classifiers, namely special words which are attached after numbers to show to which categories of objects they belong. For instance, in the English language, you talk of "two *sheets* of paper" (rather than "two papers"), "three *cups* of water" (rather than "three waters") or "two *pieces* of cake." The words *sheet, cup* and *piece* are called classifiers because they classify the category of things, namely papers, liquid and "sliced objects" respectively. In the Japanese number system, most articles must be described in terms of classifiers. The following vocabulary lists the classifiers associated with counting animals, just to illustrate a few of the many classifiers that exist in Japanese.

Suffixes

-hiki is put after a number to count animals such as dogs, tigers, rabbits*, fish and insects.

-tō is put after a number to count animals such as whales, cows and horses.

-nin is put after a number to count people.

-wa is put after a number to count animals such as rabbits*, and birds such as ducks and chickens.

It should be also pointed out that classifiers go through some phonetic changes when they are combined with some numbers (e.g., **ichi-hiki** becomes **ippiki**). You will see the following suffixes, -**ban** and -**mai,** as we continue.

Suffixes

-ban is put after a number to tell the order. For example, ichi-ban means number one; ni-ban means number two; etc.

-mai is put after a number to count thin flat objects such as stamps, papers, tickets, plates, blankets, etc.

*Note that rabbits are counted with both -**hiki** and -**wa.**

Kippu-uriba sign.

Train tickets.

Numbers are not followed by any particle.

Examples

Kippu o san-mai kudasai.	*May I have three tickets please?*
Okāsan wa sakana o ni-hiki kaimasu.	*Mother buys two fish.*

Conversation 3: What Time Is It Now?

Tom buys a train ticket at a station using the following vocabulary.

Nouns		Particle	Suffix
densha electric train	*sen* (train) line	*made* until, till	*-sen* line _
purattohōmu platform	*tsuri* change		

Tom:	*Sumimasen. Ima (wa) nan-ji desu ka.*	*Excuse me. What time is it now?*
Clerk:	*(Ima wa) hachi-ji nijūgo-fun sugi desu.*	*It is 25 past 8.*
Tom:	*(Kippu o) Seto made ichi-mai kudasai.*	*May I have 1 ticket to Seto please?*
	(Kippu wa) ikura desu ka.	*How much is it?*
Clerk:	*(Kippu wa) yon-hyaku hachi-jū-en desu.*	*It is ¥480.*
	Tom puts money on the money-receiving tray.	
Tom:	*(Kore wa) sen-en desu.*	*This is ¥1,000.*
Clerk:	*(O)tsuri * wa go-hyaku ni-jū-en desu.*	*The change is ¥520.*
Tom:	*Densha wa nan-ji desu ka.*	*What time is the (electric) train?*
Clerk:	*(Densha wa) ku-ji go-fun desu.*	*It's at 9:05.*
Tom:	*Purattohōmu wa doko desu ka.*	*Where is the platform?*
Clerk:	*(Purattohōmu wa) ni-ban sen desu.*	*It's the (train) line number 2.*

*See honorific speech in "Japanese Customs and Culture" on page 96.

9.8. Write down in English the times I shall tell you.

1. ____

2. ____

3. ____

4. ____

5. ____

6. ____

9.9. Say the following times aloud in Japanese. The correct answers are recorded on the track for Exercise 9.9.

1. 2:15

2. 4:30

3. 6:00

4. 8:40

5. 10:20

6. 12:00

9.10. Translate the times into English:

1. *jūichi-ji nijūgo-fun sugi*____

2. *ku-ji jūnana-fun mae* ____

3. *gogo roku-ji sanjup-pun* ____

4. *go-ji han* ____

Tell the times in rōmaji:

5. 1:15 P.M.

6. 12:30 P.M.

7. 6:45 A.M.

8. 7:23 P.M.

9.11.   *I shall ask some questions about Conversation 3. Reply to each question aloud in Japanese. The correct answers are recorded at the end of this exercise.*

1. ____

2. ____

3. ____

4. ____

5. ____

6. ____

JAPANESE CUSTOMS AND CULTURE

Choice of Japanese Speech Style

There are four levels of speech style in Japanese: polite, plain, honorific and rude. Their differences are listed below.

Polite Speech

Polite speech is used in formal situations, such as when you speak in public, in business, while shopping, and to strangers or superiors. It is characterized by the use of the polite verbal forms **desu** and **V•masu.**

When you talk to another person, the speech style is determined by the status of the person to whom you are talking, and by the degree of familiarity between you. When he is of equal or higher status than you are, or when he and you are not very familiar with each other, you use the polite speech style. The speakers' relative status is determined by a combination of factors, such as age (an older person is regarded as being superior to you), gender (a male is regarded as being superior to a female), rank, social status and favors done or owed. Observance of status hierarchy is particularly strict within an in-group situation.

In the reverse case, where you are of a higher status, you have a choice of using plain speech or polite speech. The choice depends partly on how great the status difference is, and partly on your personal preference.

When you talk to a stranger, you use the polite speech style unless there is an obvious difference in age or social status, as reflected in dress, manner, occupation, or gender, for example.

Women are usually expected to use the polite speech style more often than men. Women are not as likely as men to speak in the plain speech style to people of lower status; they restrict the use of plain speech to immediate family members, close friends and children.

      Lesson 9: Numbers, Dates and Times

In this book, you will learn polite speech since that is the speech style you should use: it is safer to be polite than plain, and honorific speech is not called for on the part of a foreign speaker.

Plain Speech

The plain speech style is used in informal, everyday situations among family, friends, equals, or when addressing children. For example, if you replace **desu** with **da** in a polite-style sentence, it will become a plain-style sentence: **kore wa inu da** is a plain form of **kore wa inu desu**, *this is a dog*. Similarly, by changing the endings of **V•masu**-verbs, you may convert polite-style **V•masu**-verb sentences into plain-style sentences. For example, **mizu o nomu** is a plain form of (**watashi wa**) **mizu o nomimasu**.

Honorific Speech

You use honorific speech when you want to express your respect for the person to whom you are speaking, or about whom you are speaking. For instance, if you were a clerk in a shop, you would use honorific speech to a customer so that you may make a sale; also, if you were talking to your teacher or supervisor, you would use honorific speech. There are two ways (Methods 1 and 2 below) to show your respect for others.

METHOD 1: Besides using polite speech, you may show your respect for the person to whom you are speaking, or about whom you are speaking, by exalting him by using honorific nouns, pronouns, verbs, adjectives, adverbs and conjunctions when referring to him and anything directly associated with him, such as his family, house and possessions.

The most common form of expressing your respect for the person to whom, or about whom, you are speaking is by prefixing **o** or **go** to nouns and adjectives, referring to the person or a thing belonging to him.

Example

Kore wa boku no tegami desu.	*This is my letter.*
Kore wa sensei no (o)tegami desu.	*This is the teacher's letter.*

In some words those honorific prefixes have become so common that they have lost their honorific meaning and are thought of as a part of words. For instance, (**o**)**cha** is almost always used to mean *tea* and its plain form **cha** is rarely used. Not every noun or adjective takes an honorific prefix and there is no specific rule as to whether a word is prefixed by **o** or **go**. For example, you may prefix **o** on **ringo**, *apple*, but **banana**, *banana*, does not take any honorific prefix. It is only through hearing and reading that you can learn which particular word may take an honorific prefix **o** or **go**; hence, you should not try to make honorific words up by yourself until you have reached a more advanced level of proficiency in the language.

Another common way of expressing your respect for the person to whom you are speaking, or about whom you are speaking, is to add -**san** to his family, as shown below.

Example

Kore wa anata no imōto-san desu ka.	*Is this your younger sister?*
Hai kore wa watashi no imōto desu.	*Yes, this is (my) younger sister.*

METHOD 2: You may show your respect by using humble terms for yourself by depreciating yourself and your belongings.

Expressing deeper respect for the other person creates a greater distance between you both, and, unless you are advanced in Japanese, you should not try to use honorific speech.

Rude Speech

Rude speech may be used toward inferiors, or as insults, and you should obviously avoid it.

Practice the five hiragana characters は， ひ， ふ， へ and ほ.

 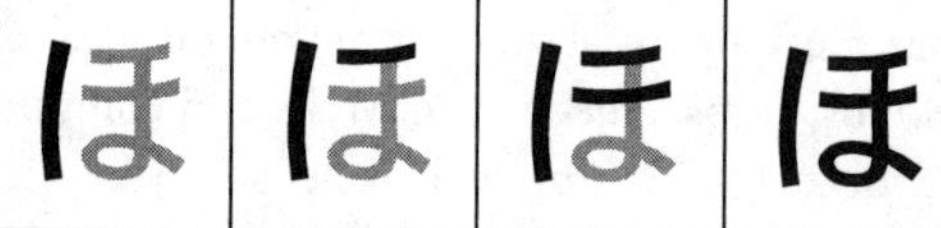

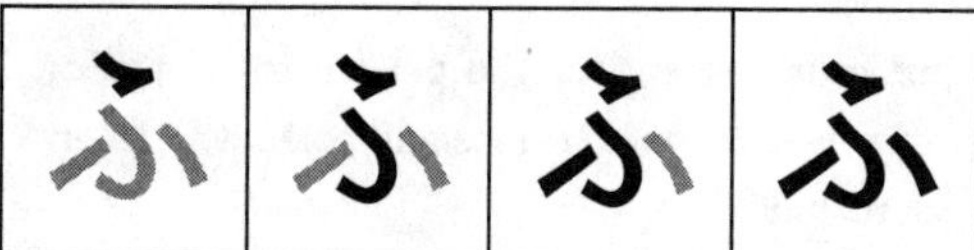

> **What you must remember from this lesson to proceed to the next lesson:**
>
> A number is expressed as: multiplier-**man** + multiplier-**sen** + multiplier-**hyaku** + multiplier-**jū** + the last digit.
>
> A date is expressed in the order of the year, followed by the month, followed by the day of the month, followed by the day of the week: number-**nen** + number-**gatsu** + the day of the month + the day of the week (-**yōbi**).
>
> Time is expressed by telling the hour followed by the minute: number-**ji** + number-**pun/fun**.
>
> **O/go** is put in front of some nouns, adjectives and verbs to show respect for the person to whom, or about whom, you are speaking.

10 I Do That, Too!

In this lesson you will learn:

Speaking

To talk about daily routines and habits

To talk about people doing the same things as others

To talk about people doing several things

To express to whom or for whom something is done

To ask somebody to join you in an activity

Grammar

To understand the role of the particles **mo** and **ni**

To use more transitive verbs

To expand basic sentence structure to indicate time of action

To understand the difference between specific time and general time in time expression

In the previous lesson, you learned to express dates and times. Although they are fairly straightforward, you had to memorize many words. Don't worry too much about them if you cannot remember them all. At least you know by now whether your friend is talking about dates and times or not, and usually that is enough to go on. After all, your friend can write the date and time of your meeting on a piece of paper if needed: a date is written as year/month/day and the time is written as hour:minutes, just as in English.

Since you are now able to arrange a date and a time, you can now ask any friend of your desire to go out with you. But, it is very frightening to ask him/her out for the first time. After all, a rejection is hard to overcome. However, I have a better suggestion: why don't you ask him/her to join you in whatever you are doing? That way you don't have to feel too rejected if he/she refuses; after all, he/she may not like the activity you suggested but may still like your company. For that purpose, you will learn to say sentences such as "Would you also like to watch TV?" and "Would you also like to drink coffee?" when you are watching TV or drinking coffee.

Since you have just learned to express time in the previous lesson, I am going to expand the basic sentence structure to include time of action in this lesson. You will learn to say sentences such as "I eat breakfast *at 7 o'clock,*" "I shall learn English *in the summer,*" etc.

You will also learn to place other people in your obligation. In other words, you will learn to express indirect objects so that you may say sentences such as "I buy this *for you,*" "I shall lend this *to you,*" etc.

You will also learn more transitive verbs in this lesson in order to increase your speaking power.

"""

The particle **mo** corresponds to *also/too*. It replaces the particle **wa** or **ga** (which is discussed later) if it refers to a subject and it replaces **o** if it refers to a direct object. But if it refers to a noun followed by a particle **de** or **ni/e** (which is discussed later), **mo** follows that particle. In other words, **mo** is placed strictly after the word to which it refers.

Examples

Watashi wa *hon o yomimasu.*	*I read a book.*
Otōsan mo *hon o yomimasu.*	*Father also reads a book (as well as I).*
Otōsan wa hon o yomimasu.	*Father reads a book.*
Otōsan wa zasshi mo *yomimasu.*	*Father reads a magazine also (as well as a book).*
Kore wa *hon desu.*	*This is a book.*
Are mo *hon desu.*	*That also is a book.*
Watashi wa hon o watashi no heya de *yomimasu.*	*I read a book in my room.*
Watashi wa hon o ima de mo *yomimasu.*	*I read a book in the living room also (as well as in my room).*

When, in a succession of nouns, each is followed by **mo,** a convenient translation is *both _ and _.*

Examples

Imōto mo *onēsan* mo *hon o yomimasu.*	*Both younger sister and older sister read books.*
Neko wa sakana mo *niku* mo *tabemasu.*	*The cat eats both fish and meat.*

For the negative verbs, **_ mo _ mo** is translated as *neither _ nor _.*

Examples

Imōto mo *onēsan* mo *hon o yomimasen.*	*Neither the younger sister nor the older sister reads books.*
Usagi wa sakana mo *niku* mo *tabemasen.*	*A rabbit eats neither fish nor meat.*

 **Conversation 1: My Father Speaks French, Too**

Hanako is drinking coffee and asks Tom if he'd also like some coffee. Then Hanako asks Tom about his parents' skill in the Japanese language.

Hanako:	*Anata mo* kōhī o nomimasen ka.*	*Would you also like to drink coffee?*
Tom:	*Hai (boku mo kōhī o) nomimasu.*	*Yes, I would.*

***Anata mo** is put in the sentence to emphasize that the meaning is *you too.*

Hanako:	*Anata no otōsan to okāsan wa Nihon-go o hanashimasu ka.*	Do your father and mother speak Japanese?
Tom:	*Hai (Boku no) otōsan mo okāsan mo (Nihon-go o) hanashimasu.*	Yes, both (my) father and (my) mother speak Japanese.
	(Boku no) otōsan wa Furansu-go mo hanashimasu.	My father speaks French too.
Hanako:	*Watashi no onēsan mo Furansu-go o hanashimasu.*	My elder sister also speaks French.

THIS VERY MOMENT IS IMPORTANT: THE PARTICLE *NI* AFTER "SPECIFIC TIME"

The time expressions may be separated into three different categories, namely, "specific time," "general time" and "relative time."

"Specific time" is defined as the time that may be indicated as a point on a clock, calendar, and so on (e.g., 1 o'clock, March 25). "Relative time" is defined as the time which depends on when "now" is, such as last month, next year and tomorrow (e.g., last month is April if it is May now, and it means July if it is August now). "General time" is defined as the time referred in general such as everyday, morning and spring.

Now, we are going to expand our sentences by including the specific time of actions ("I eat breakfast *at 7 o'clock*," "We watch TV *at 9 o'clock*," and so on).

The time expression is put at the beginning of a sentence or just after a subject (so far, after **wa**), and it must be followed by **ni**, *at/in/on*, if it indicates "specific time."

Examples

Hachi-ji ni watashi wa terebi o mimasu.	*At 8 o'clock, I watch TV.*
Watashi wa hachi-ji ni terebi o mimasu.	*I watch TV at 8 o'clock.*
Ku-gatsu ni watashi-tachi wa Nihon-go o naraimasu.	*In September, we shall learn Japanese.*
Ku-ji ni mo watashi wa kōhī o nomimasu.*	*I drink coffee at 9 o'clock also (as well as at 8 o'clock).*

SEASONS: TIME "IN GENERAL"

You do not put any particle after the time expression if you refer to it in general. Although they are not followed by **ni**, *at/on/in* must be substituted when you translate them into English.

The following is a list of times and seasons which are referred to in general.

*See the previous section.

Nouns

asa morning	*ban* evening	*haru* spring	*aki* autumn
hiru afternoon	*yoru* night	*natsu* summer	*fuyu* winter

Examples

Natsu watashi-tachi wa Eigo o naraimasu.	*In summer, we will learn English.*
Watashi-tachi wa natsu Eigo o naraimasu.	*We will learn English in summer.*
Yoru anata wa terebi o mimasu ka.	*Do you watch TV at night?*

THIS IS FOR YOU!: THE PARTICLE *NI* AFTER AN INDIRECT OBJECT

There are two types of verbs of doing (verbs of action): transitive verbs and intransitive verbs. A transitive verb may have a direct object and an indirect object. A direct object is the person/thing/matter to which the verb directs its action. An indirect object is the person/thing "for" or "to whom" the action is taking place, and, most cases, the words "to" or "for" can be inserted before it, if they are not already. Let us consider the following two sentences.

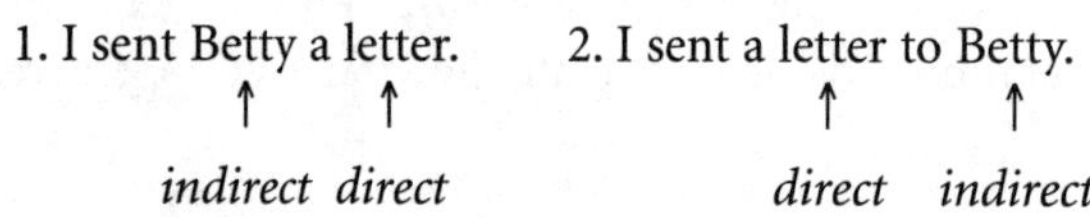

The sentences 1 and 2 have the same meaning, but in different forms. *Letter* is "*what* I sent" and therefore it is the direct object; *Betty* is "*to whom* the letter is sent" and therefore it is the indirect object.

For Japanese transitive verbs, indirect objects must be followed by **ni.**

An indirect object, which may be preceeded by *to* or *for* in English, must be followed by **ni** in Japanese. In other words, you must have Japanese sentences in the form of example sentence 2 (above), and not example sentence 1.

Examples

Watashi wa tegami o ojīsan ni kakimasu.	*I write a letter to (my) grandfather.*
Okāsan wa purezento o obāsan ni kaimasu.	*Mother buys a present for grandmother.*
Okāsan wa purezento o ojīsan ni mo kaimasu.	*Mother buys a present for grandfather also (as well as for grandmother).*

 ## Conversation 2: I Am Sending This to America

Tom is at the post office.

Nouns

funabin surface mail	*kōkūbin* air mail	*gōkei* total

Dōmo arigatō gozaimasu is a very polite phrase meaning *Thank you very much.*

Tom:	*Sumimasen.*	Excuse me.
	(Boku wa) kore o Amerika ni okurimasu.	I am sending this to America.
	(Kitte wa) ikura desu ka.	How much is it?
Clerk:	*(Tegami wa) kōkūbin desu ka.*	Is it air mail?
	(Tegami wa) funabin desu ka.	Or surface mail?
Tom:	*(Tegami wa) kōkūbin desu.*	It's air mail.
Clerk:	*(Kōkūbin wa) hyaku jū-en desu.*	It is ¥110.
Tom:	*Kore wa ikura desu ka.*	How much is this?
Clerk:	*Kore mo Amerika desu ka.*	Is this also to America?
Tom:	*Hai sō desu.*	Yes, it is.
Clerk:	*Kore mo hyaku jū-en desu.*	This also is ¥110.
Tom:	*Hyaku jū-en no kitte o jū-mai kudasai.*	May I have ten ¥110 stamps please?
	Gōkei (wa) sen hyaku-en desu ka.	Is the total ¥1,100?
Clerk:	*Hai sō desu.*	Yes, it is.
Tom:	*(Kore wa) sen hyaku-en desu.*	This is ¥1,100.
Clerk:	*Dōmo arigatō gozaimasu.*	Thank you very much.

Post office board listing all services, such as banking, insurance and ordinary mailing services.

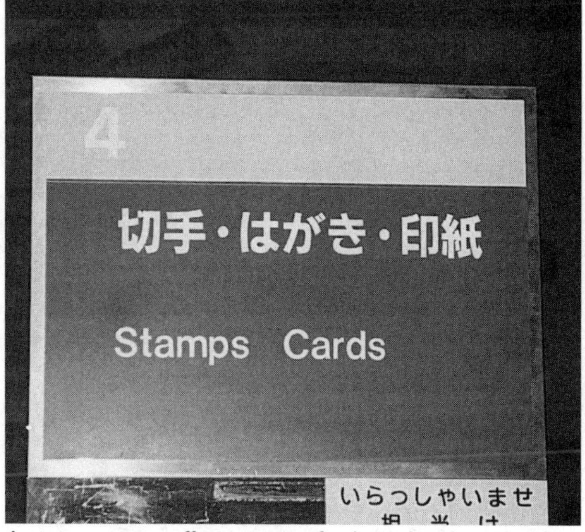

A sign at a post office counter for kitte, hagaki and inshi (little stamps you attach to forms to show that you have paid fees, taxes, etc. when you apply for visas or other official documents).

Addressing Letters and Post Cards

In Japan, *hagaki* (plain post cards) are very widely used. You write the addresses and names of both the sender and the receiver on the front of the post card: larger characters are used for the

receiver and smaller characters for the sender. All messages are written on the back of the post card. Also special post cards are issued every year for the New Year celebration and Summer Season greetings. (During the hottest time in August, people send summer greeting cards to others to inquire after their health.)

On an envelope, the address and the name of the receiver are written in front while the sender's address and name are written on the back with smaller characters.

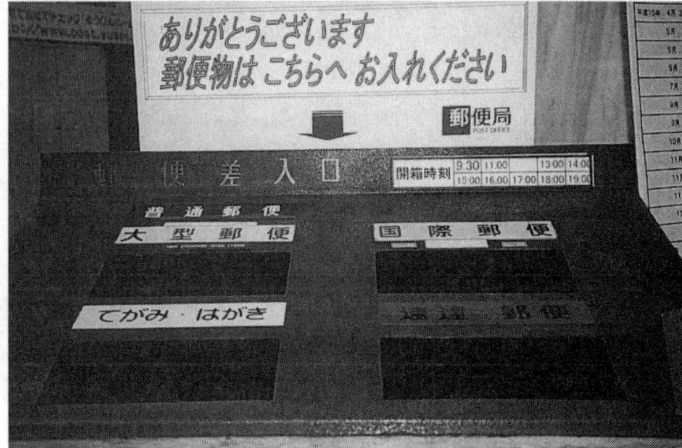

Mailbox inside a post office.

Japanese post offices are marked with 〒. They have banking services such as savings accounts and money transfers, and insurance services such as life insurance and automobile insurance, as well as the usual postal services. You must go to the counter marked はがき・切手 for stamps, post cards, aerogrammes and the other usual postal services.

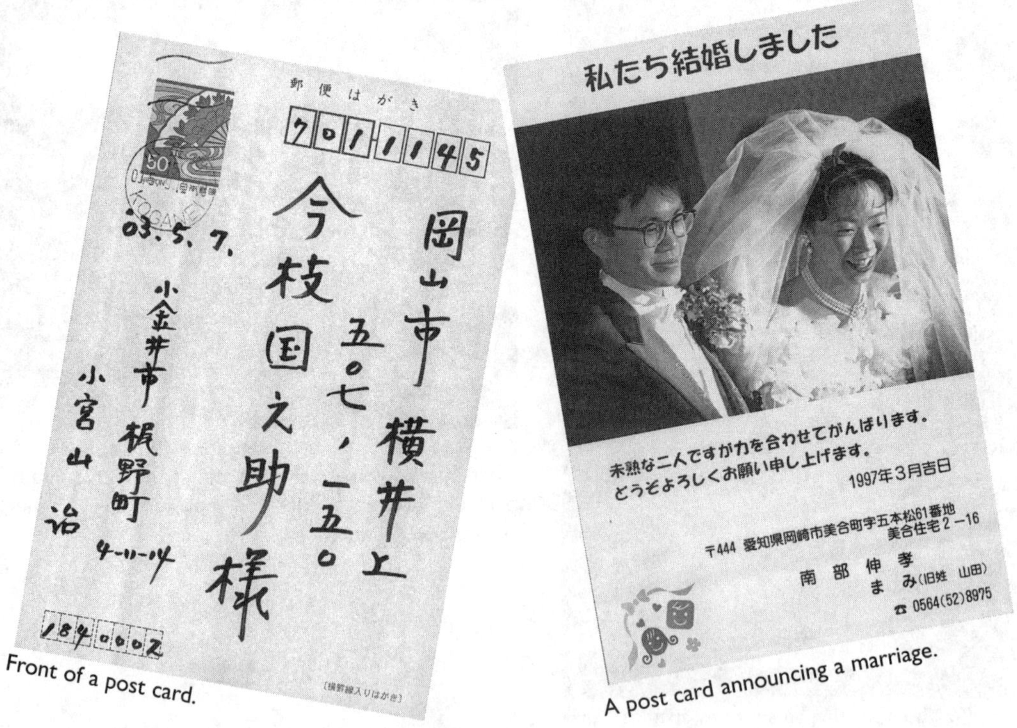

Front of a post card.

A post card announcing a marriage.

　　　　　Lesson 10: I Do That, Too!

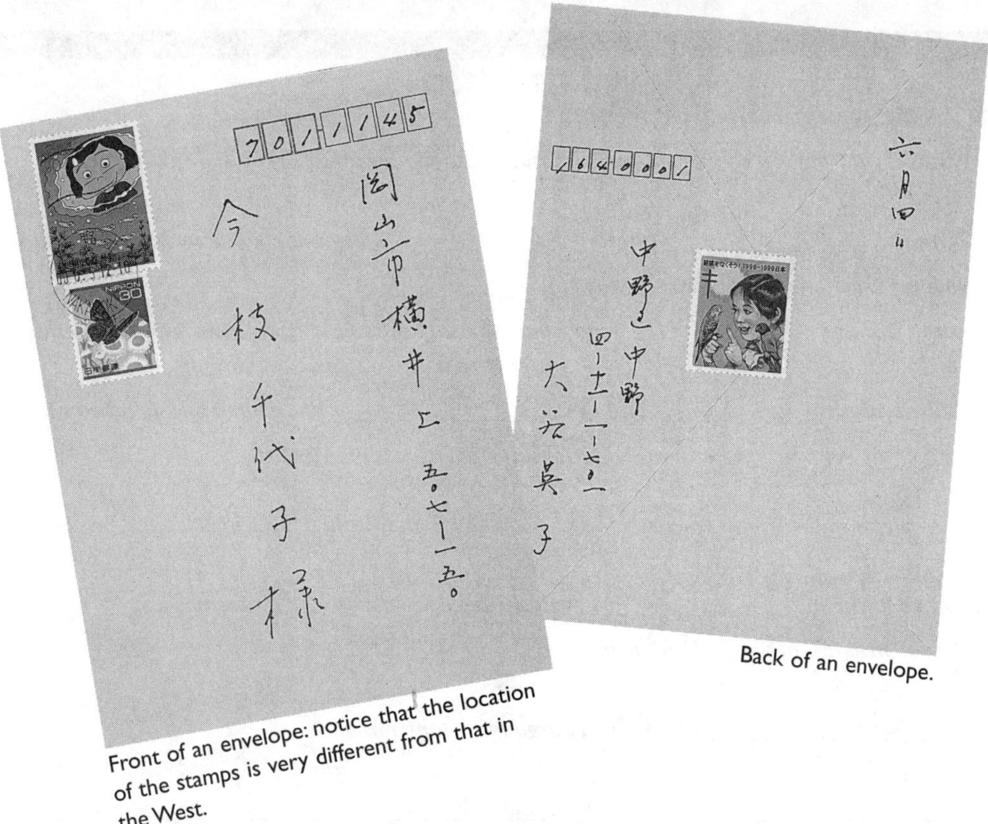

Front of an envelope: notice that the location of the stamps is very different from that in the West.

Back of an envelope.

 **Conversation 3: What Time Do You Eat Breakfast?**

Hanako asks Tom about his daily eating habits. The following vocabulary lists daily meals.

Nouns

asa-gohan *breakfast*	**ranchi** *lunch*	**gohan** *meal, boiled rice*
ban-gohan *dinner*	**hiru-gohan** *lunch*	

Hanako:	*Nan-ji ni (anata wa)* **asa-gohan o tabemasu ka.**	*What time do you eat (your) breakfast?*
Tom:	*Asa no shichi-ji han ni (boku wa asa-gohan o)* **tabemasu.**	*I eat at 7:30 in the morning.*
Hanako:	*(Anata wa)* **nani o** *(asa-gohan ni)* **tabemasu ka.**	*What do you eat?*
Tom:	*(Boku wa asa-gohan ni)* **pan o tabemasu.**	*I eat breads.*
	(Boku wa) **kōhī mo nomimasu.**	*I drink coffee too.*
Hanako:	*Nan-ji ni (anata wa)* **ban-gohan o tabemasu ka.**	*What time do you eat (your) dinner?*
Tom:	*Roku-ji ni (boku-tachi wa ban-gohan o)* **tabemasu.**	*We eat at 6 o'clock.*
Hanako:	*Yoru (anata wa)* **hon o yomimasu ka.**	*Do you read books at night?*
Tom:	*Hai yomimasu.*	*Yes, I do.*
	(Yoru boku wa) **terebi mo mimasu.**	*I watch TV too.*

10.1. Make two sentences into one sentence.

1. *Watashi wa tegami o kōkūbin de okurimasu. Imōto mo tegami o kōkūbin de okurimasu.*

   Watashi _________________ imōto _________________ tegami o kōkūbin de okurimasu.
   Both my sister and I send letters by airmail.

2. *Ashita watashi wa ban-gohan o ie de tabemasen. Ashita otōto mo ban-gohan o ie de tabemasen.*

   Ashita watashi _________________ otōto _________________ ban-gohan o ie de tabemasen.
   Neither my younger brother nor I will eat dinner at home tomorrow.

*10.2. Write **ni** in the blanks wherever it is needed, and then translate the sentences into English.*

1. *Asa no hachi-ji _________________ watashi-tachi wa asa-gohan o tabemasu.*
   We eat breakfast at 8 o'clock in the morning.

2. *Kyō _________________ otōsan wa ban-gohan o tabemasen.*

   ____

3. *Yoru _________________ watashi-tachi wa terebi o mimasu.*

   ____

4. *Okāsan wa obasan _________________ tegami o kakimasu.*

   ____

5. *Natsu _________________ otōsan wa ie o urimasu.*

   ____

10.3. 🔘 *I shall ask questions about Conversation 2. Reply to each question aloud in Japanese. The correct answers are recorded at the end of this exercise.*

1. ____

2. ____

3. ____

     Lesson 10: I Do That, Too!

4. ____

5. ____

10.4. 💿 *I shall ask some questions about Conversation 3. Reply to each question aloud in Japanese. Correct answers are recorded at the end of this exercise.*

1. ____

2. ____

3. ____

4. ____

10.5. Translate into English:

1. *Watashi wa mizu o nomimasu.* ___________________________________

   Imōto mo mizu o nomimasu. ____________________________________

2. *Okāsan mo otōsan mo hon o heya de yomimasu.*

____

3. *Ashita anata mo watashi-tachi to bideo o mimasen ka.*

____

4. *Yoru watashi-tachi wa tegami o tomodachi ni kakimasu.*

____

5. *Ichi-ji ni Igirisu-jin wa ranchi o tabemasu.*

____

6. *Ku-gatsu ni watashi-tachi wa kuruma o kaimasu.*

____

7. *Kyō watashi-tachi wa Eigo o Amerika-jin ni gakkō de hanashimasu.*

____

8. Hanako does not read French books.

____

Makoto also does not read French books.

____

9. In December, we send presents to (our) grandfather and grandmother.

____

10. I speak both English and Japanese.

____

11. Neither (my) father nor (my) mother speaks English.

____

12. At twelve o'clock, we listen to Japanese music on the radio.

____

13. In spring, we will grow (make) vegetables in the garden.

____

14. In the evening, we watch TV.

____

MORE TRANSITIVE VERBS

Let us look at more transitive verbs below in order to increase your speaking power. They have the sentence structure **_ wa _ o V•masu,** as did the verbs you learned in lesson 7.

Verbs (Transitive)

atsumemasu *collect*	**wasuremasu** *forget*
erabimasu *choose*	**yamemasu** *resign from, cease, stop*
kaeshimasu *return (things borrowed)*	
karimasu *borrow*	**agemasu** *give (to somebody)*
kashimasu *lend*	**kuremasu** *give (to me)*
machimasu *wait for*	
manekimasu *invite*	**hakimasu** *put on (footwear, trousers, for example)*
misemasu *show*	**kaburimasu** *put on (hat, for example)*
nakushimasu *lose*	**kimasu** *put on (dress, for example)*
tomemasu *stop (vehicles)*	

You may notice that the verb *wait* is followed by *for* in English. The Japanese equivalent **machi-masu** is a transitive verb and is preceeded by **o**. Similarly, the verb *resign* is followed by *from* in English. The Japanese equivalent **yamemasu** is a transitive verb and is also preceded by **o**.

You may notice that the verb *give* has two distinct words in Japanese. **Agemasu** is used when the receiver is not the speaker and **kuremasu** is used when the receiver *is* the speaker.

You may notice that there are three different words for *put on* (clothing on a body) in Japanese. You use **kaburimasu** for *put on* on the head, **kimasu** for *put on* above the waist and below the head, and **hakimasu** for *put on* below the waist. The following vocabulary lists some clothing that you may put on your body.

Nouns

bōshi hat	*kōto* coat	*sūtsu* suit
burausu blouse	*kutsu* shoe	*wanpīsu* one-piece dress
doresu dress	*kutsushita* sock, stocking	*zubon* trousers, pants
fuku clothes, clothing	*sētā* sweater	
kimono kimono	*sukāto* skirt	

Examples

Boku wa kuruma o koko de tomemasu.	*I stop (my) car here.*
Watashi wa kore o anata ni agemasu.	*I give you this. (I give this to you.)*
Anata wa kore o watashi ni kuremasu ka.	*Will you give me this?*
Ashita watashi wa kore o anata ni kaeshimasu.	*Tomorrow, I will return you this. (Tomorrow, I wil return this to you.)*
Ku-ji kara Itaria no eiga o terebi de misemasu.	*From 9 o'clock, they will show an Italian movie on TV.*
Ku-gatsu ni rekishi no sensei wa gakkō o yamemasu.	*In September, the history teacher resigns from the school.*
Hachi-ji ni watashi wa anata o eki de machimasu.	*At 8 o'clock, I'll wait for you at the station.*

EXERCISES

10.6. *I shall tell you the things I do. I want you to say after me that you too do the things I do. You may check your replies against the correct answers recorded at the end of this exercise. Then, translate what you have said into English.*

1. ____

2. ____

3. ____

4. ____

10.7. Make two sentences into one sentence by putting rōmaji words in the blanks.

1. Obāsan wa kimono o kimasu. Obāsan wa fuku mo kimasu.

   Obāsan wa kimono ________________ *fuku* ________________ *kimasu.*

10.8. Translate into English:

1. Watashi wa kore o karimasu. ______________________________

2. Haru sensei wa gakkō o yamemasu. ________________________

3. Natsu okāsan wa obāsan o Nihon ni manekimasu. ________________

____

4. Otōsan wa kuruma o doko de tomemasu ka. ____________________

____

5. Anata wa fuyu bōshi o kaburimasu ka. ________________________

____

6. Betty-san o basu-sutoppu de machimasen ka. ____________________

____

Translate into rōmaji:

7. My younger brother and I invite Robert to our house.

____

8. My elder sister collects hats. ________________________________

9. I shall not forget you. ______________________________________

10. In winter, do you put on a coat? ____________________________

11. I shall not show (my) painting to (my) father.

____

12. Would you like to put on my shoes? ___________________________

Japanese people always wore kimono until the end of the Second World War. Because women's kimono require skill to put on, young women go to special schools just to learn how to wear them nowadays. There are kimono-dressers who dress people for fees. Because kimono constrain movements, with heavy belts and tight wraps around the legs, most women wear Western dress nowadays, and kimono are worn only on special ceremonial occasions such as weddings, graduations, etc. Those kimono are made of pure silk, and long-sleeved kimono, worn by young unmarried women, can cost ¥300,000 or more—sometimes even more than ¥1,000,000.

WRITING EXERCISE: HIRAGANA FOR *MA, MI, MU, ME* AND *MO*

Practice the five hiragana characters ま， み， む， め and も.

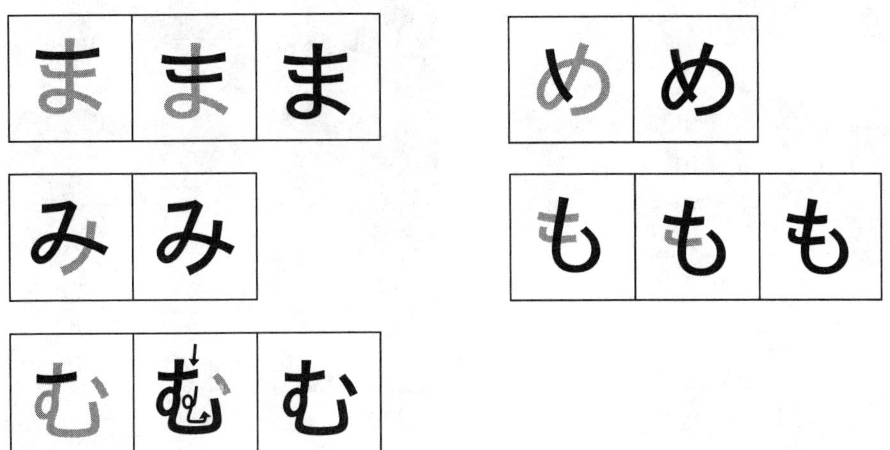

What you must remember from this lesson to proceed to the next lesson:

The particle **mo**, *also/too,* replaces **wa** if it refers to a subject and it replaces **o** if it refers to a direct object, but it is placed after the "noun + particle (**de** or **ni**)" if it refers to that noun.

The time expression is put at the beginning of a sentence or just after a subject. If it indicates "specific time," it must be followed by **ni**, *at/in/on,* and if it indicates "general time," it is used without any particle after it.

The particle **ni**, *to/for,* is used to show a direction of attention or interest.

Kimono.

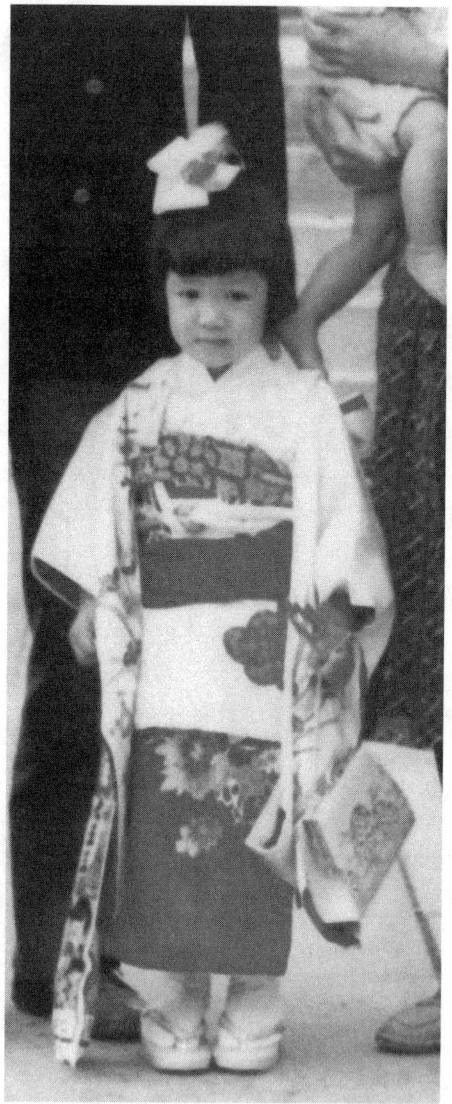

A little girl dressed in a kimono.

Lesson 10: I Do That, Too!

Would You Like to Go to a Movie with Me?

In the previous lesson, you learned to use the particles **mo** and **ni**.

In this lesson, you are going back to the pursuit of a busy social schedule with full vigor. You have found out that the person of your desire likes to join you in whatever you are doing. It is now time for you to ask him/her out! In this lesson, you are going to learn to do this, not with gestures and a piece of paper, but with eloquence and class just as if you were Japanese. You are going to say sentences such as "Would you like to go to a movie on Saturday?" and "Would you like to come to my home on Sunday?" With your charm and the command of the Japanese language, I'd bet that nobody could say no to you. Let's proceed!

VERBS OF MOTION

I Shall Go Places

In this lesson, you are going to learn verbs of motion such as *go, come,* etc. Let us look at the following vocabulary which lists the verbs of motion.

 **Verbs (Intransitive)**

demasu go out	*ikimasu go*	*kimasu come*
hairimasu come in, enter, join, get in	*kaerimasu return*	*orimasu get off*

The verbs of motion are intransitive verbs (verbs which may not have direct objects) and they have the sentence structure

subject wa place e/kara V•masu.

The particle **wa** follows the subject,
the particle **e/kara** follows the "place" of motion *to/from* and
the verb of motion **V•masu** is placed at the end of the sentence.

It should be noted that **e** is translated as *to* in the sense of motion toward a "place" and, it should not be confused with that of giving "to" which requires **ni** as shown in the previous lesson.

Let us look at the vocabulary which lists the places you are likely to go regularly.

Nouns

shōgakkō primary school	*kaisha* company	*jugyō* lecture
chūgakkō secondary school	*kōjō* factory	*kurasu* (lecture) class
juku cram school		
kōkō high school	*kaigi* meeting	*kissaten* coffee shop
kōgyō-daigaku technical college	*shigoto* work	*furo* bath
daigaku university, college		

Some typical sentences using the verbs of motion are as follows.

Examples

Watashi wa Amerika e otōsan to ikimasu.	*I go to America with (my) father.*
Otōsan wa koko e kimasu.	*Father will come here.*
Onēsan wa daigaku e hairimasu.	*(My) elder sister enters a university.*
Otōsan wa kaisha kara kaerimasu.	*Father returns from work (company).*
Obāsan wa basu kara orimasu.	*Grandmother gets off (from) the bus.*

You can make the above sentences more complete by including the time and the methods of transportation. The following vocabulary lists vehicles of transportation.

Nouns

fune ship, boat	*kisha* train	*takushī* taxi
hikōki airplane	*kuruma* car	*torakku* truck
jidōsha automobile	*ōtobai* motorcycle	
jitensha bicycle	*sukūtā* scooter	

Examples

Natsu watashi-tachi wa gakkō e jitensha de ikimasu.	*In summer, we go to school by bicycle.*
Hachi-gatsu ni Tom-kun wa Amerika kara hikōki de kaerimasu.	*In August, Tom will return from America by airplane.*
Ku-ji ni otōsan wa koko e kuruma de kimasu.	*(My) father will come here by (his) car at 9 o'clock.*

Asking Someone Out for Lunch

You may be wondering what happened to all that talk of your asking a friend out for a date. Don't worry: I haven't forgotten it! Let's talk about going to an "event" such as a party, lunch, meeting, lecture, or date.

When you are going to an "event," and not to a "place," **ni** follows the event and is translated as *to*. An "event" should not be followed by **e**.

Finally, you are able to ask that big question as in the examples below.

Examples

Kissaten ni ikimasen ka.	*Would you like to go to a coffee shop?*
Ban-gohan ni kimasen ka.	*Would you like to come to dinner?*
Watashi wa Nihon-go no jugyō ni ikimasu.	*I shall go to a Japanese lecture.*
Do-yōbi ni eiga ni ikimasen ka.	*Would you like to go to a movie on Saturday?*

WHAT BEGINS MUST END

Japanese use expressions **furo ni hairimasu,** *come in to a bath,* and **furo kara demasu,** *go out from a bath,* for the place of "take a bath" and "finish a bath" since their way of cleaning involves getting into and out from a bathtub.

Examples

Watashi wa yoru furo ni hairimasu.	*I take a bath at night.*
Otōsan wa furo kara demasu.	*Father finishes (his) bath.*

Likewise, when you are making an arrangement for a party or a meeting, it is often required to tell the other person when the event will start and when it will end. In this case, you use the expression **A kara B made,** implying *from A to B.* **A kara B made** may be used also to denote locations.

Examples

ku-ji kara jū-ji made	*from 9 o'clock till 10 o'clock*
Ōsaka kara Tōkyō made	*from Osaka to Tokyo*

You have learned three different particles meaning *to* and their differences are listed as follows, while **kara** always implies *from.*

Particles

e is used as *to* in the sense of motion toward a "place."

made is used as *to* in the sense of *until.*

ni is used as *to* in the sense of motion toward an "event" and direction of attention or interest.

kara *from*

MAKING A TELEPHONE CALL

You are now able to ask a friend out eloquently. In fact, you are eloquent enough to talk on the telephone.

When you talk to a person on the telephone, you always say **moshi-moshi** for *Hello!* The person on the other line will reply **moshi-moshi,** *Hello!,* back also. **Moshi-moshi** is used *only* on the telephone.

A public telephone: you can use either coins or a pre-paid telephone card.

Machine from which you may buy telephone cards.

Telephone cards.

 Conversation 1: Would You Like to Come to My Birthday Party?

Hanako phones Tom to invite him to her birthday party, using the following vocabulary.

Nouns

bāsudē birthday	*hima free, time to spare*	*pātī* party*

Tom:	*Moshi-moshi.*	*Hello!*
Hanako:	*Moshi-moshi. (Anata wa) Tom-kun desu ka.*	*Hello! Is that (Are you) Tom?*
Tom:	*Hai (boku wa Tom desu). Hanako-san Konbanwa.*	*Yes. Good evening Hanako.*
Hanako:	*Konbanwa.*	*Good evening.*
	San-gatsu nijūichi-nichi no hiru (ni) anata wa hima desu ka.	*Are you free in the afternoon of March 21st?*
Tom:	*(San-gatsu nijūichi-nichi wa) nan-yōbi desu ka.*	*What day of the week is it?*
Hanako:	*(San-gatsu nijūichi-nichi wa) do-yōbi desu.*	*It's a Saturday.*
Tom:	*(Boku wa) hima desu.*	*I'm free.*
Hanako:	*San-gatsu nijūichi-nichi wa watashi no bāsudē desu.*	*March 21st is my birthday.*
	Bāsudē pātī ni kimasen ka.	*Would you like to come to (my) birthday party?*
Tom:	*Hai (Boku wa bāsudē pātī ni) ikimasu.*	*Yes, I would.*
	(Bāsudē pātī wa) nan-ji kara nan-ji made desu ka.	*From what time to what time is it?*
Hanako:	*(Bāsudē pātī wa) jūni-ji kara yo-ji made desu.*	*It's from 12 o'clock to 4 o'clock.*

*Lately, many foreign words (mostly English words) have become Japanese. In order to make the sounds as close as possible to the original English sounds, new syllables such as **ti** are introduced into Japanese.

        Lesson 11: Would You Like to Go to a Movie With Me?

 **Conversation 2: Is He Coming by Airplane?**

Tom meets Hanako on his way to a post office.

Tom:	*Hanako-san Konnichiwa.*	*Good afternoon, Hanako.*
Hanako:	*Tom-kun Konnichiwa. (O)genki desu ka.*	*Good afternoon, Tom. How are you?*
Tom:	*Hai genki desu. (O)genki desu ka.*	*I am fine. How are you?*
Hanako:	*Hai okagesama de. (Anata wa) doko e ikimasu ka.*	*I am fine, thank you. Where are you going?*
Tom:	*(Boku wa) yūbinkyoku e ikimasu.*	*I am going to the post office.*
	(Boku wa) tegami o ojīsan ni okurimasu.	*I am sending a letter to (my) grandfather.*
Hanako:	*(Anata wa) tegami o Nihon-go de ojīsan ni kakimasu ka.*	*Do you write letters to (your) grandfather in Japanese?*
Tom:	*Iie (boku wa tegami o) Eigo de kakimasu.*	*No, I write in English.*
	Ojīsan wa Nihon-go o yomimasen.	*(My) grandfather does not read Japanese.*
	Haru ojīsan wa Nihon e kimasu.	*In spring, (my) grandfather is coming to Japan.*
Hanako:	*(Ojīsan wa Nihon e) hikōki de kimasu ka.*	*Is he coming by airplane?*
Tom:	*Hai (ojīsan wa Nihon e hikōki de kimasu).*	*Yes.*
Hanako:	*Ojīsan wa Nihon-go o hanashimasu ka.*	*Does (your) grandfather speak Japanese?*
Tom:	*Iie hanashimasen.*	*No, he doesn't.*
Hanako:	*Watashi wa Eigo o naraimasu.*	*I shall learn English.*
	(Watashi wa) Eigo o ojīsan ni hanashimasu.	*I shall speak English to (your) grandfather.*
	Dewa mata. Sayōnara.	*See you. Good-bye.*
Tom:	*Sayōnara.*	*Good-bye.*

EXERCISES

11.1. *I shall invite you for activities. Write down what they are in English.*

1. ____

2. ____

3. ____

4. ____

5. ____

6. ____ Mailbox.

11.2. 🎧 *I shall tell you the places my family goes. Answer the questions in rōmaji.*

1. Otōsan wa doko e kisha de ikimasu ka. ___________________________________

2. Okāsan wa sūpāmāketto e nan de ikimasu ka. ___________________________

   ____

3. Imōto wa gakkō e basu de ikimasu ka. ________________________________

   ____

4. Onēsan wa doko e ikimasu ka. _______________________________________

11.3. *Circle the words that make sense in the blank for the sentence* Watashi wa __ ni ikimasu.

pikunikku (picnic) konsāto (concert) otōsan no kaisha Eigo no jugyō ranchi yama Tōkyō

11.4. *Make sentences by joining each phrase on the left to the correct phrase on the right.*

1. Ichi-gatsu kara go-gatsu made •   • watashi wa kisha de ikimasu.

2. Tōkyō kara Ōsaka made   •   • otōto wa terebi o mimasu.

3. Asa kara yoru made   •   • otōsan wa gaikoku e ikimasu.

Now translate the complete sentences into English.

1. ____

2. ____

3. ____

11.5. 🎧 *I shall ask some questions about Conversation 1. Reply to each question aloud in Japanese. Correct answers are recorded at the end of this exercise.*

1. ____

2. ____

3. ____

4. ____

5. ____

11.6. ⊙ *I shall ask some questions about Conversation 2. Reply to each question aloud in Japanese. Correct answers are recorded at the end of this exercise.*

1. ____

2. ____

3. ____

4. ____

5. ____

7. ____

8. ____

11.7. Translate into English:

1. *Ichi-gatsu ni Betty-san wa Amerika e kaerimasu.*

____

2. *Anata wa doko e kisha de ikimasu ka.*_______________________

3. *Onēsan mo basu kara orimasu.*_______________________

4. *Otōto mo watashi mo gakkō e kuruma de ikimasen.*

____

5. *Haru ni ojīsan wa Nihon e fune de kimasu.*

____

6. *Kissaten ni hairimasen ka.* _______________________

Translate into rōmaji:

7. Father comes out of (goes out from) a bath.

____

8. I go to school at 8 o'clock in the morning.

____

9. In September, I shall go to America by airplane.

____

10. Tom will not go back (return) to America in summer.

____

11. My younger brother does not enter kindergarten in September.

____

12. Would you like to come to a party?

____

When you are invited to a Japanese home, you may notice that the lady of the house rarely joins you in the conversation, especially if you are a guest of the man of the house. Instead, she stays in the kitchen preparing dishes to serve. It is usual for only the man of the house to eat with the guest.

Japanese people like to wear uniforms to show their affiliation to their groups. Students wear kindergarten, school or university uniforms; factory, company, restaurant, department store, hospital, train, bus and taxi employees wear their individual uniforms.

Secondary school uniform.

WRITING EXERCISE: HIRAGANA FOR YA, YU AND YO

Practice the three hiragana characters や, ゆ *and* よ.

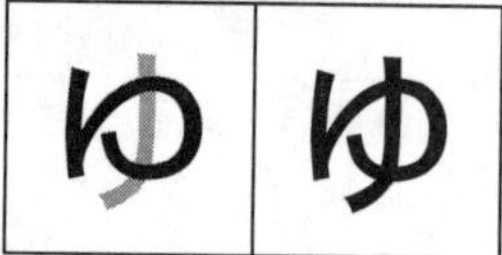

What you must remember from this lesson to proceed to the next lesson:

The verbs of motion have the sentence structure ___ **wa** ___ **e/kara/ni V•masu.**

I Do This, I Do That, I Do Everything!

In this lesson you will learn:

Speaking
To talk about people's interests and hobbies, such as sports
To ask for favors
To attract someone's attention in order to ask a question or a favor
To express decisions

Grammar
To use the verb **shimasu**

In the previous lesson, you learned the verbs of motion such as *go* and *come,* and you are now able to ask a friend out eloquently. Well, you may spend the whole time with him/her just watching a movie together, but sooner or later, you will want to do other things with him/her as well. If you want to do other activities with him/her, you need to find out first what he/she likes to do. Also, you need to find out his/her preferences on the restaurants, food, etc.

In this lesson, you are going to learn to do all the things mentioned above with the single most versatile **V•masu**-verb **shimasu,** *do.* This is the verb you use to find out what someone does. You use it to ask questions such as "Do you cook?" and "Do you drive?". But that's not all. You will be surprised to learn that you can make many verbs using the single verb **shimasu** combined with some nouns. That is, you will be able to say sentences such as "Do you cook fish?," "Do you drive a car?" and "Do you play tennis?". You will also learn very useful, and yet very simple, expressions using **shimasu,** like asking for a favor as well as stating a decision on what to do, what to eat, what to see, etc. This lesson is one of the most rewarding lessons you will find in this book and all you need to learn is the single following verb.

Verb (Transitive)

shimasu do

I STUDY, I COOK, I TRAVEL

subject wa **object** o shimasu

Shimasu, *do,* is a very useful transitive verb; it has the sentence structure _ **wa** _ **o shimasu,** just like other transitive verbs. The following nouns may be used as direct objects for **shimasu.**

Nouns

aisatsu greeting	*kaimono* shopping	*sōji** cleaning
amimono knitting	*kekkon*** marriage	*tetsudai* help
*benkyō** study	*ryokō** travel	*unten** driving
*deito*** date	*ryōri** cooking	*yakusoku** promise
hanashi talk, conversation	*sentaku** laundry	

Unlike the English language where the verb *do* emphasizes actions (e.g., I *do* greet, I *do* study, etc.), there is no such emphasis with **shimasu**. **Shimasu** just converts some nouns (direct objects of **shimasu**) into single verbs, so to speak. Hence, "noun + **o** + **shimasu**" may be translated as single verbs as follows.

aisatsu o shimasu means *greet* rather than *do greet*.
benkyō o shimasu means *study* rather than *do study*.
amimono o shimasu means *knit* rather than *do knit*.

Examples

Okāsan wa amimono o shimasu.	*Mother knits.*
Otōsan wa ryokō o shimasu.	*The father travels.*
Anata wa nani o shimasu ka.	*What do you do?*
Ryōri o shimasen ka.	*Would you like to cook?*
*Otōsan wa aisatsu o sensei ni*** shimasu.*	*The father greets the teacher.*

When the direct objects are sports, such as those listed below, **shimasu** may be translated according to context.

Nouns

supōtsu sports	*suiei* swimming	*tenisu* tennis
jūdō judo	*sumō* sumo wrestling	*yakyū* baseball
karate karate	*taisō* gymnastics	

Examples

karate o shimasu	*practice karate*
tenisu o shimasu	*play tennis*
suiei o shimasu	*swim*
yakyū o shimasen	*do not play baseball*

Some nouns may be expanded with **no** and used with shimasu *as shown below.*

ryōri	*cooking*
sakana no ryōri	*cooking of fish*
sakana no ryōri o shimasu	*(I) cook fish*
hanashi	*talk*
Kanada no hanashi	*talk about (on) Canada*
Kanada no hanashi o shimasu	*(I) talk about (on) Canada*

*, **(See page 126.)
***Note that **sensei** is an indirect object in the Japanese sentence and so it is followed by **ni.**

 Conversation 1: What Are You Doing Next Week?

Hanako tells Tom about the Golden-Week holiday, using the following vocabulary.

Nouns	Adverb
Gōruden-uīku Golden-Week	_itsu*_ when
yasumi holiday	

Hanako:	_Raishū wa Gōruden-uīku desu. Daigaku wa yasumi desu._	Next week is Golden-Week. Colleges are on holiday.
Tom:	_(Yasumi wa) itsu kara itsu made desu ka._	From when to when is it?
Hanako:	_(Yasumi wa) getsu-yōbi kara kin-yōbi made desu._	From Monday to Friday.
Tom:	_Raishū (anata wa) nani o shimasu ka._	What are you doing next week?
Hanako:	_(Watashi-tachi wa) ryokō o shimasu._	We are going to travel.
	(Watashi-tachi wa) ojīsan to obāsan no ie e ikimasu.	We are going to (our) grandfather and grandmother's house.
Tom:	_(Anata wa) nani o ojīsan to obāsan no ie de shimasu ka._	What do you do at (your) grandfather and grandmother's house?
Hanako:	_Okāsan to obāsan wa ryōri o shimasu._	(My) mother and (my) grandmother cook.
	Watashi wa tetsudai o shimasu.	I help (them).
Tom:	_Anata wa benkyō o shimasu ka._	Do you study?
Hanako:	_Iie shimasen._	No, I don't.

JAPANESE CUSTOMS AND CULTURE

Holidays

A working person usually has three one-week holidays per year. They are New Year's Holiday (around New Year's Day), "Golden-Week" (a string of national holidays from April 29 to May 5) and O-Bon (around August 13–August 16). Because everyone, except in service industries, is on holiday at the same time, trains, planes, expressways and tourist spots are packed during these holidays. New Year's Holiday and O-Bon are times to visit one's parents.

A summer festival.

*__Itsu__ is defined as a pronoun in Japanese grammar. I have defined it as an adverb in accordance with English grammar.

A summer festival.

Fireworks during a summer festival.

Mountain in Kyoto: huge bonfires are lit on August 16 to send the spirits of the dead back, after their short visits.

O-Bon is a Buddhist festival to commemorate deceased family members. According to Japanese tradition, spirits of the deceased wander in space not far from home, usually for thirty-three years, after the bodies die; they return once a year for a short visit, arriving on the evening of August 13 and returning to the spirit world on August 16. On the night of the thirteenth, small welcoming fires or lanterns are lit in front of homes so that spirits will not get lost. Food is put out on the family altar in little dishes for them. People usually go back to their ancestral homes to welcome the spirits with other living relatives and to visit cemeteries. On the last day of O-Bon, send-off fires are lit in the same places where welcoming fires burned a few days before. In some areas, lanterns and food offered to the spirits are taken to rivers or the sea to float away.

EXERCISES

12.1. *I shall tell you about things Hanako's elder sister does on Saturdays. Answer the questions in rōmaji.*

1. *Asa hachi-ji ni onēsan wa nani o shimasu ka.*

____

2. *Asa onēsan wa sentaku to sōji o shimasu ka.*

____

　　　　Lesson 12: I Do This, I Do That, I Do Everything!

3. *Hiru onēsan wa nani o shimasu ka.* ________________________________

4. *Ban onēsan wa nani o shimasu ka.* ________________________________

12.2. *Translate into English:*

1. *ryokō o shimasu* ________________________________

2. *sentaku o shimasu* ________________________________

3. *sumō o shimasen* ________________________________

4. *Natsu onēsan wa tenisu o shimasu.* ________________________________

5. *Yoru okāsan wa amimono mo shimasu.* ________________________________

6. *Anata wa nani o shimasu ka.* ________________________________

7. *Onīsan wa yakyū o shimasen.* ________________________________

8. *Watashi wa kuruma no unten o shimasen.* ________________________________

Translate into rōmaji:

9. promise ________________________________

10. do gymnastics ________________________________

11. do not play tennis ________________________________

12. In August, we travel by car. ________________________________

13. Does your father cook? ________________________________

14. What do you do at school? ________________________________

15. Do you study on Sundays too? ________________________________

16. I clean my room. ________________________________

Sumō wrestling is one of the most popular spectator sports in Japan. Two huge men, wearing only loin cloths, push each other in a small ring covered with sand. The rule for winning is very simple. One has to push the opponent out of the ring, or, get any part of his body, except the soles of the feet, to touch the ground.

Verbs: Noun + *Shimasu*

Some "noun + **shimasu**" structures may become single verbs, and those nouns are marked with * or ** in the list of vocabulary on page 122. In this expression, the nouns cannot be extended with **no**.

Examples

ryokō shimasu	*travel*
kekkon shimasu	*marry*
unten shimasu	*drive*
benkyō shimasu	*study*

A "noun (marked with * on page 122) + **shimasu**" has the sentence structure

subject **wa** **object** **o** **noun + *shimasu***

Examples

Watashi wa Nihon-go o benkyō shimasu.	*I study Japanese.*
Watashi wa sētā o sentaku shimasu.	*I wash (my) sweater.*

Although *to travel* does not take a direct object in English, **ryokō shimasu** follows **o** and should be translated according to context.

Although *to date* and *to marry* may be transitive verbs in English (we may say "I date Betty" and "I marry Betty" in English), the equivalent **deito shimasu**, *to date*, and **kekkon shimasu**, *to marry*, are not transitive verbs in Japanese. You must use expressions such as "I date *with* Betty" and "I marry *with* Betty" in Japanese. Hence, **deito shimasu** and **kekkon shimasu** must follow the particle **to**, *together/along with* (and not **o**).

Examples

Watashi-tachi wa Kyōto o ryokō shimasu.	*We travel in Kyoto.*
Watashi wa Betty-san to deito shimasu.	*I date Betty.*
Kazuko-san wa Amerika-jin to kekkon shimasu.	*Kazuko marries an American.*

The sentence structure _ **wa** _ **o** "noun + **shimasu**" gives more information than the sentence structure _ **wa** _ **o shimasu** as can be seen from the examples below.

Examples

Watashi wa unten o shimasu.	*I drive.*
Watashi wa kuruma o unten shimasu.	*I drive a car.*

　　　　Lesson 12: I Do This, I Do That, I Do Everything!

<table>
<tr><td>Watashi wa ryokō o shimasu.</td><td>I travel.</td></tr>
<tr><td>Watashi wa Nihon o ryokō shimasu.</td><td>I travel in Japan.</td></tr>
</table>

You may note that the following sentences have the same meaning. In the examples below, **Nihon-go no benkyō**, *study of Japanese*, and **sētā no sentaku**, *laundry of the sweater*, are treated as nouns (see the previous section).

Examples

<table>
<tr><td>Watashi wa Nihon-go o benkyō shimasu.</td><td>I study Japanese.</td></tr>
<tr><td>Watashi wa Nihon-go no benkyō o shimasu.</td><td>I study Japanese.</td></tr>
<tr><td></td><td></td></tr>
<tr><td>Watashi wa sētā o sentaku shimasu.</td><td>I wash (my) sweater.</td></tr>
<tr><td>Watashi wa sētā no sentaku o shimasu.</td><td>I wash (my) sweater.</td></tr>
</table>

Conversation 2: What Will You Do This Saturday?

Tom asks Makoto what he's doing on Saturday, because he wants to get together with him.

Tom:	*Do-yōbi no asa (anata wa) nani o shimasu ka.*	*What will you do on Saturday morning?*
Makoto:	*(Boku wa) tenisu o Kazuko-san to shimasu.*	*I'll play tennis with Kazuko.*
Tom:	*Gogo (anata wa) nani o shimasu ka.*	*What will you do in the afternoon?*
Makoto:	*(Boku wa) Hiroshi-kun-tachi* to yakkū o shimasu.*	*I'll play baseball with Hiroshi and the guys.*
Tom:	*Ban (anata wa) nani o shimasu ka.*	*What will you do in the evening?*
Makoto:	*(Boku wa) Eigo o benkyō shimasu.*	*I'll study English.*
Tom:	*Boku no uchi e kimasen ka.*	*Would you like to come to my house?*
	(Boku wa anata no) Eigo no benkyō no tetsudai o shimasu yo.	*I'll help you with your study of English!*

EXERCISES

*12.3. Rewrite the sentences with "noun + o + **shimasu**" to become sentences with "noun + **shimasu**."*

1. *Watashi wa niwa no sōji o shimasu.*

Watashi wa niwa o sōji shimasu

2. *Ojisan wa torakku no unten o shimasu.*

Ojisan wa ____

3. *Okāsan wa yasai no ryōri o shimasu.*

Okāsan wa ____

4. *Onēsan wa Eigo no benkyō o shimasu.*

Onēsan wa ____

*Just as **watashi-tachi,** *we,* implies *I and others,* **Hiroshi-kun-tachi** implies *Hiroshi and his friends.*

12.4. Translate into English:

1. *Watashi wa kore o ryōri shimasu.* _______________________________________

2. *Watashi wa sore o yakusoku shimasu.* _____________________________________

3. *Betty-san wa kuruma o unten shimasen.* ___________________________________

4. *Hachi-gatsu ni watashi-tachi wa kekkon shimasu.*

____

Translate into rōmaji:

5. In fall, I shall travel in America. ____

6. I cook steak for lunch. ____

7. In spring, I clean the garden. ____

8. Does Tom study Japanese? ____

12.5.   *I shall ask some questions about Conversation 2. Reply to each question aloud in Japanese. Correct answers are recorded at the end of this exercise.*

1. ____

2. ____

3. ____

JAPANESE CUSTOMS AND CULTURE

Marriage, Women and the "Ie" System

The Prehistoric, Kofun and Nara Period (30,000 B.C.–794 A.D.)

Women seem to have had considerable political and religious power at the beginning of Japanese history. According to the earliest record of Japan in a Chinese document, Himiko, probably a shamaness (a medicine woman who can converse with gods), ruled the Japanese political confederation around the third century A.D. The earliest Japanese history, written in 712 A.D., lists a goddess as the principal creator of Japan, and several women ruled Japan as empresses in the seventh and eighth centuries.

The Heian Period (794–1185)

Before and during much of the Heian Period, people married within their households (cousins, and so on). Until at least the eleventh century, it was customary for a husband to move in with his wife's family, or to live separately and visit her on mutually arranged nights in her home. Women's partners were decided by their parents. Society treated men and women equally: women could be the heads of households, they could inherit family property, etc. Among the nobles (court aristocracy of the ruling elite), some women had several husbands, just as some men had several wives. But, an aristocratic woman had to conduct herself with discretion since her child had to be recognized by her husband (not necessarily the father) for her child to have his social rank. Aristocratic women were very literate and many women writers appeared during this period. Among the aristocracy, parents strived to marry their daughters to men belonging to the more powerful families, to advance themselves or their sons in high society. The Fujiwara family (614–1160) came to control the imperial court by marrying Fujiwara women to emperors whenever possible. The Fujiwara men controlled the imperial court by "being appointed" as regents to emperors who were too young, too old, or too ill to govern the country. During this period between 614 and 1160, very few emperors' mothers were from outside the Fujiwara family. Around the end of the Heian Period, the samurai (warriors) class started the practice of sending a bride to join her husband's family.

The Medieval Period (1185–1600)

By the late twelfth century, the samurai class became the ruling elite. Constant danger of war made it practical for the ablest person in a samurai household to be in charge of the family to consolidate and defend land against enemies. This led samurai families to adopt the "ie" system, that is the system in which the power of a household was concentrated in the hands of the ablest man, usually the father. The eldest son inherited the family's property and the title of the head of the family, with total power to name the next head, to eject unilaterally any family member, and to control and administer the family estate. Hence, in a samurai household, it became very important to produce a male heir. At the same time, a marriage became a military alliance between two families, resulting in breaking away from the traditional marriage within a close group, and requiring a match-maker to arrange a marriage to ensure an appropriate match. Since a marriage was a military alliance of two totally unrelated families, the marriage ceremony came to be performed to formalize the alliance and to introduce all the members of the families. After the marriage, a wife moved in with her husband's family. The samurai household often included the family of younger brothers and other relatives (the parents and the families of the brothers of the head of the household). A wife was expected to be monogamous, with great stigma attached to her adultery, while a husband took many women outside the marriage without stigma. The influence of Buddhism and Confucianism, which regarded women as inferior to men, had been creeping into Japanese society gradually, and it reflected and reinforced a shift towards men-centered family structure in the samurai class. People of other classes continued as before with nightly visits and many liasons.

The Edo Period (1600–1868)

In 1600, Tokugawa Ieyasu united Japan under his military rule, and he appointed himself as Shōgun. Social order during this period was characterized by the feudalistic concepts of lord and vassal, master and employee, land owner and peasant. A samurai served a daimyō (a local feudal lord), who in turn served Shōgun, with unswerving allegiance. In return, Shōgun granted a fief to a daimyō, who in turn granted a samurai land or rice, peace, and security. The right to daimyō's, or Shōgun's, favor was inherited by the heir upon the death of the old samurai. The right to become a samurai became something inherited also: if one were not born into a samurai family, one could not become a samurai. Only the samurai had the exclusive right to own and wear swords. The "ie" system filtered down to all the classes by the middle of the Edo Period: an eldest son inherited the family fortune and his father's occupation, while other sons were doomed to bachelorhood, making livings by working for their eldest brother. It established the social status within a family. The practice of arranged marriages in the samurai class also filtered down to the rest of the population. Also, each marriage had to be approved by a government official and the appropriateness of the match had to be confirmed beforehand, thus keeping firm the status quo of the samurai class. The samurai had absolute power during this period, and peasants (people other than samurai, aristocrats, merchants and artisans) rented land from samurai and were often very poor due to the heavy taxes. With this social atmosphere, the position of women sank lower and lower with the help of the influence of Confucianism. A daughter, particularly in a samurai family, was married off at a very young age to an ally or an enemy in order to strengthen the family. A woman was to obey her parents until her marriage, then her husband and his family, and, in old age, her sons. She could not become the head of the family; she could not take any official role in the imperial court (except as a lady in waiting) or military government; a woman could not inherit the family property. A husband had total control over his wife and her property; a husband could get a divorce for any reason he wanted, while a wife could obtain a divorce only if she was abandoned or her husband had committed a heinous crime. A wife's adultery was punished by death, while a wealthy man could maintain concubines outside or inside his home to ensure the male line. Women were, in general, necessarily very discreet in their speech and acts.

The Modern Period (1868–1945)

After the collapse of the Tokugawa government, Japan started modernization and industrialization under the emperor Meiji. Although people were allowed to choose their professions now, the former samurai class continued to have privileges and lowly citizens remained

A wedding photograph.

     Lesson 12: I Do This, I Do That, I Do Everything!

lowly. Universal primary education was introduced, but girls were educated to become good homemakers. Even so, many women started to enter the labor market. The industrialization brought mobility to people, resulting in rural people moving to cities. It also brought long-distance arranged marriages with more parental authority. In the Civil Code of 1898, the "ie" system was legalized, and it became the law for marriages to be conducted under that system. That is, a marriage required the agreement between the heads of the two households involved, rather than between the man and the woman. Also, under this law, a wife lost legal right to engage in property transactions, management of her property came under her husband's control, and only the wife had the duty of chastity. Feminist movements, started in 1911 or so for things such as voting rights, fizzled away by the early 1930s when right-wing militaristic sentiments surged. During the Second World War, the government mobilized single women into a labor force while married women were kept at home to produce more soldiers. The male-centered society continued as the social norm throughout this period.

The Contemporary Period (1945–Present)

After Japan's defeat in the Second World War, a new constitution was enforced by the United States in 1947. It is essentially written along the same lines as the American legal system, giving

A wedding photograph.

equal rights to all in political, economical and social matters, eliminating the "ie" system. Under this constitution, for example, a husband and a wife have equal rights in divorce, and a wife may negotiate a contract without her husband's consent. People (men at least eighteen years old and women at least sixteen) may now marry without the consent of their parents, and "love marriages" have been increasing rapidly. An "arranged marriage" became a way of introducing a suitable couple by a go-between who checks the individuals' backgrounds thoroughly. In the past, a husband and a wife had totally different social circles, but they have started to spend more social time together. A wife has great authority in the house: she controls the family budget and makes most of the decisions regarding the children. A husband usually does not do any house chores even if a wife works outside.

In order to defend themselves against samurai, many martial arts (karate, jūdō) were developed by farmers and tradesmen. Deprived of owning weapons, they used simple sticks, mental preparedness and their bodies.

When **shimasu** is combined with **onegai,** *appeal/wish,* it may mean many things. **Onegai shimasu,** which literally means *do wish* or *do appeal,* is a very useful expression to attract someone's attention and ask a favor; it means *I beg you* or *Please do such and such.*

Onegai shimasu is used in the following situations:

1. When calling a clerk in a store or a waiter in a restaurant for service.

   Onegai shimasu. Excuse me.

2. Ordering food in a restaurant.

   Sutēki onegai shimasu. May I have a steak please?

3. When you don't understand the amount the salesperson said, you can ask the person to write it down, by handing over a pencil and paper and saying the following:

   Onegai shimasu. Please (write it down).

4. When submitting bills or papers at a bank, a post office or a hospital.

   Onegai shimasu. Please look after this.

5. When you wish to tell the elevator operator to which floor you want to go.

   Go-kai onegai shimasu. Fifth floor please.

6. When telling a taxi driver your destination.

   Eki onegai shimasu. Could you take me to the train station please?

7. When you ask for somebody.

   Betty-san onegai shimasu. May I speak to Betty please?

Note that the phrases are used in one-to-one conversations, and the direct objects of the verb **onegai shimasu** (**go-kai, eki,** etc.) are not followed by **o.**

Nouns

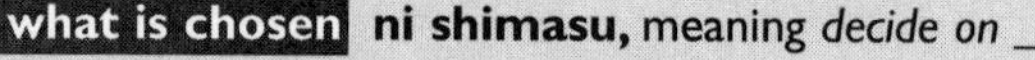

(o)negai appeal, wish   *go-kai* fifth floor

I AM IN CHARGE: I CHOOSE

If you want to say that one *decides* to choose something, you use the sentence structure

> what is chosen **ni shimasu,** meaning *decide on _.*

It is an abbreviation of the sentence structure

> subject **wa** topic **wa** what is chosen **ni shimasu.**

The first **wa** follows the person making the choice, the second **wa** follows the topic under discussion, and **ni** follows what is chosen.

You will need this vocabulary word to state decisions on what to eat!

Noun

tabemono food

Examples

Sushi ni shimasu.	*Decide on sushi.*
Are ni shimasu.	*Decide on that.*

Watashi wa tabemono wa sushi ni shimasu.	*I shall have sushi. (I decide on sushi for food.)*
Anata wa tabemono wa nani ni shimasu ka.	*What will you eat? (What do you decide on for food?)*

Conversation 3: Which Restaurant Should We Go To?

Tom and Hanako go to a restaurant.

Tom:	*(Boku-tachi wa)* **resutoran wa doko ni shimasu ka.**	*To which restaurant do we go? (Where do we decide on for a restaurant?)*
Hanako:	*(Watashi-tachi wa resutoran wa)* **Edo ni shimasen ka**	*Would you like to go to Edo? (Would you like to decide on Edo?)*

Tom and Hanako arrive at Edo restaurant.

Tom:	*(Anata wa)* **tabemono wa nani ni shimasu ka.**	*What will you have for food?*
Hanako:	*(Watashi wa tabemono wa)* **yakisoba ni shimasu.**	*I'll have yakisoba.*
	Anata wa (tabemono wa nani ni shimasu ka).	*How about you?*

A menu at a restaurant.

Tom:	*Boku wa (tabemono wa)* **tonkatsu ni shimasu.**	*I'll have a pork cutlet.*
	(Anata wa) **nomimono wa** *(nani ni shimasu ka).*	*How about the drinks?*
Hanako:	*(Watashi wa nomimono wa)* **miruku ni shimasu.**	*I'll have milk.*
	Anata wa *(nomimono wa nani ni shimasu ka).*	*How about you?*
Tom:	*Boku wa (nomimono wa)* **orenji-jūsu ni shimasu.**	*I'll have orange juice.*

EXERCISES

12.6. Join each question on the left with a correct reply on the right.

Dore ni shimasu ka. •   • *Koko ni shimasu.*

Doko ni shimasu ka. •   • *Kore ni shimasu.*

Nan ni shimasu ka. •

12.7. Translate into English:

1. **Byōin onegai shimasu.** (in a taxi) _______________________________

2. **Tom-kun onegai shimasu** (on a telephone)_______________________________

3. *(Watashi-tachi wa)* **kudamono wa nani ni shimasu ka.** _______________

____

4. **Doko no (o)tera ni shimasu ka.**_______________________________

5. **Dare no ie ni shimasu ka.** _______________________________

Translate into rōmaji:

6. Could you take me to the Tokyo zoo please?

____

7. May I speak to the English teacher please?

____

8. What do we decide on for a present for Hanako?

____

9. On whom do we decide? ____

10. Where do we decide on for travelling?

____

12.8. 🔘 *I shall ask some questions about Conversation 3. Reply to each question aloud in Japanese. Correct answers are recorded at the end of this exercise.*

1. ____

2. ____

3. ____

4. ____

WRITING EXERCISE: HIRAGANA FOR *RA, RI, RU, RE* AND *RO*

Practice the five hiragana characters ら， り， る， れ and ろ.

What you must remember from this lesson to proceed
to the next lesson:

Shimasu has the sentence structure __ **wa** __ **o shimasu.**

Some "noun + **shimasu**" constructions have the sentence structure __ **wa** __ **o** "noun + **shimasu.**"

The expression **onegai shimasu** is used to attract someone's attention and ask for a favor.

The expression __ **ni shimasu** implies *decide on* __.

13

The Apple Is Delicious

In the previous lesson, you learned the transitive verb **shimasu,** *do,* which more or less concludes transitive verbs. You are now able to make any sentence which uses a transitive verb, with all the frills. For example, you are capable of saying fairly complex sentences such as "In August, I shall travel to America with my older brother," or "Tomorrow, I shall make chairs in the garden." You have also learned some intransitive verbs in the previous lessons: **desu** and the verbs of motion.

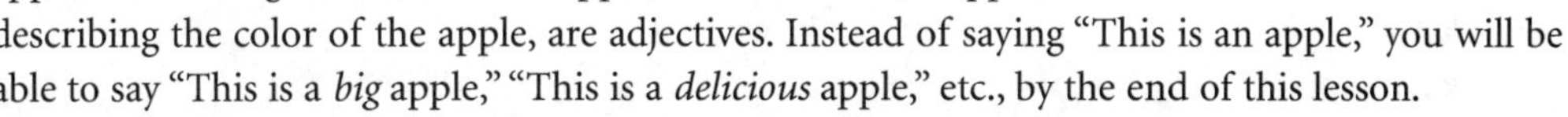

In this lesson, you are going to learn something different. You are going to learn adjectives. So, let me quickly jog your memory about adjectives. Adjectives describe nouns by adding size, color, number and other qualities to them. For example, *big* of *"big apple,"* describing the size of the apple, and *red* of *"red* apple," describing the color of the apple, are adjectives. Instead of saying "This is an apple," you will be able to say "This is a *big* apple," "This is a *delicious* apple," etc., by the end of this lesson.

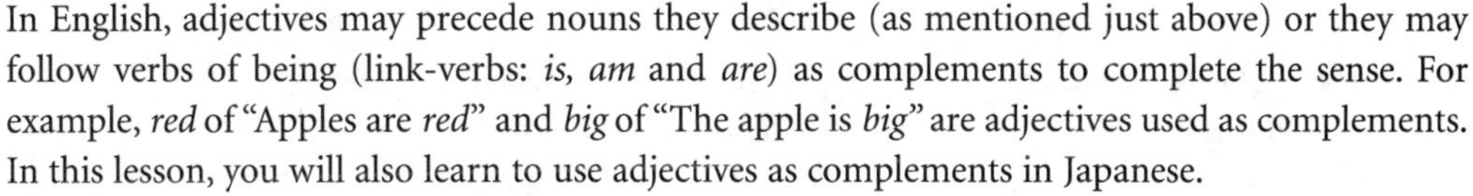

In English, adjectives may precede nouns they describe (as mentioned just above) or they may follow verbs of being (link-verbs: *is, am* and *are*) as complements to complete the sense. For example, *red* of "Apples are *red*" and *big* of "The apple is *big*" are adjectives used as complements. In this lesson, you will also learn to use adjectives as complements in Japanese.

Adjectives are very useful tools for small talk such as "It is warm today," "It is big," and "This is delicious." Although the sentence "The apple is delicious" may not sound interesting to you, it uses the same sentence structure as "Your eyes are beautiful." Wouldn't it be nice if you could say a sentence such as "Your eyes are beautiful" to that special person? Changing a boring sentence, such as "The apple is delicious," into an exciting sentence, such as "Your eyes are beautiful," is what you must do by yourself. The important thing about learning is not what you have learned, but how you use it.

Let us look at the sampling of Japanese adjectives below. You may notice that the adjectives on the righthand side have contrary meanings to those of the lefthand side. You may also notice that the adjectives listed below end with _i; these adjectives are called **i**-adjectives for that reason.

 **I-Adjectives**

atatakai warm	*suzushii cool* (temperature)
atsui hot (temperature)	*samui cold* (temperature)
atsui hot (of touch)	*tsumetai cold* (of touch)
atsui thick (of flat things)	*usui thin* (of flat things)
futoi thick (of cylindrical things), *fat*	*hosoi thin* (of cylindrical things)
hiroi spacious	*semai limited* (space)
kawaii cute	*minikui ugly*
kowai frightful, frightening	*yasashii gentle*
muzukashii difficult	*yasashii easy*
nagai long	*mijikai short* (length)
oishii delicious, tasty	*mazui unsavory* (taste)
ōkii big, large	*chiisai small, little*
omoi heavy	*karui light* (weight)
omoshiroi interesting, amusing	*tsumaranai boring*
takai expensive	*yasui cheap*
takai high, tall	*hikui low, short* (height)
yoi/ii good	*warui bad*

Japanese adjectives describe nouns, and they precede them, just as in English.

Examples

omoi hon	*heavy book*
takai kudamono	*expensive fruit*
chiisai akai kuruma	*small red car*

Kore wa mijikai enpitsu desu.	*This is a short pencil.*
Koko wa ōkii ie desu.	*This is a big house.*
Otōsan wa ōkii kuruma o kaimasu.	*Father buys a big car.*

The negative **i**-adjectives (*not* big, *not* delicious, etc.) are obtained by changing _i to **_ku nai.** You should notice that Japanese adjectives conjugate (change their endings), just like Japanese verbs.

Examples

ōkii ringo	*a big apple*
ōkiku nai ringo	*a not big apple*

oishii ringo	*a delicious apple*
oishiku nai ringo	*a not delicious apple*

It should be noted that **ii,** *good,* is an irregular adjective (it does not conjugate); conjugatable **yoi,** *good,* is used for its conjugate.

Example

ii hon	*a good book*
yokunai hon	*a not good book*

I-adjectives which do not have contrary **i**-adjectives are listed below. Some (not all) colors are also **i**-adjectives and they are listed below also.

I-Adjectives

abunai dangerous	*kurushii* hard (full of suffering)	*tanoshii* enjoyable
isogashii busy	*mezurashii* unusual, rare	*urusai* noisy
kitanai dirty	*sabishii* lonely	

akai red	*chairoi* brown	*kuroi* black
aoi blue	*kiiroi* yellow	*shiroi* white

HOW MANY SETS OF "THIS" AND "THAT" ARE THERE IN JAPANESE?

Nouns

hi day	*hito* person

There are very many words meaning "this" and "that" in the Japanese language and we have one more set to learn to make them complete. Corresponding to the demonstrative adjectives in "*this* book," "*that* station," "*that* person (over there)" and "*which* apple" are **kono, sono, ano** and **dono.** As you will expect from what you have learned of **kore, sore, are** and **dore** (as well as **koko, soko, asoko** and **doko**), the adjective **kono** describes a thing/person/place near a speaker, **sono** describes a thing/person/place near a listener, **ano** describes a thing/person/place away from both a speaker and a listener, and **dono** is an interrogative adjective meaning *which.* They are placed before the nouns they describe.

Demonstrative Adjectives*

kono this	*sono* that	*ano* that (over there)	*dono* which

Examples

kono hon	*this book (near the speaker)*
sono enpitsu	*that pencil (near the listener)*
ano (o)tera	*that temple (away from the speaker and the listener)*
dono ringo	*which apple*

*I have defined **kono, sono, ano** and **dono** as demonstrative adjectives, in accordance with English grammar. Although they qualify nouns, just as adjectives, they do not conjugate (Japanese adjectives conjugate). And, in Japanese grammar they are defined as belonging to a group called **rentaishi,** a set of words which qualify nouns but do not conjugate as adjectives.

If both a demonstrative adjective and an ordinary adjective describe a noun, the ordinary adjective follows the demonstrative adjective.

Examples

ano ōkii hito	*that big person (over there)*
kono chiisai inu	*this small dog*

Kono ōkii tsukue wa sensei no tsukue desu.	*This big desk is the teacher's desk.*
Ano omoshiroi hito wa boku no ojīsan desu.	*That interesting person is my grandfather.*

It should be noted that **kore, sore, are** and **dore** (and **koko, soko, asoko** and **doko**) are pronouns: they are used instead of nouns and they always stand by themselves. **Kono, sono, ano** and **dono** are adjectives: they describe nouns and they are placed before the nouns they describe.

Examples

Ano hito *wa Hanako-san desu.*	*That person is Hanako.*
Are *wa Hanako-san desu.*	*That is Hanako.*
Sono ringo *o kudasai.*	*May I have that apple please?*
Sore *o kudasai.*	*May I have that please?*
Anata wa **kono hon** *o yomimasu ka.*	*Do you read this book?*
Anata wa **kore** *o yomimasu ka.*	*Do you read this?*
Anata wa **dono hon** *o yomimasu ka.*	*Which book do you read?*
Anata wa **dore** *o yomimasu ka.*	*Which do you read?*

You may have realized by now that, when two people are talking, a speaker may ask a listener **kore wa nan desu ka,** *what is this (near me)?,* meaning something near the speaker. The listener then answers with **sore wa pen desu,** *that (near you) is a pen,* since the pen is closer to the speaker than to the listener, and whenever they are talking about a thing/place/person away from them both, **are/asoko/ano-hito** is used.

Note that **kore/koko/kono-hito, sore/soko/sono-hito** and **are/asoko/ano-hito** are used not only for tangible sense, but they are also used in referring to both intangible and temporal sense. For example, once a speaker mentions a thing/place/person, it may be referred to as **kore/koko/kono-hito** in the rest of his conversation, and it is translated as *it/he/she.* The listener refers to it by **sore/soko/sono-hito,** and it is translated as *it/he/she.* In the same argument, **are/asoko/ano-hito** is used to refer to a thing/place/person somehow far away from them both, in an intangible or a temporal sense, and it is translated as *it/he/she.* Hence, **ano hito** and **are, sono ringo** and **sore, kono hon** and **kore,** and **dono hon** and **dore** in the examples above may be translated as *she, that/it, this/it* and *which* respectively.

EXERCISES

13.1. *I shall say an English adjective word. Say the corresponding Japanese word after me. The correct answers are recorded at the end of this exercise.*

  Lesson 13: The Apple Is Delicious

1. _______________________________________

2. _______________________________________

3. _______________________________________

4. _______________________________________

5. _______________________________________

6. _______________________________________

7. _______________________________________

13.2. Use lines to join each adjective on the left with the adjective on the right which has the opposite meaning.

atatakai •	• *nagai*
futoi •	• *oishii*
kawaii •	• *ōkii*
hiroi •	• *omoi*
muzukashii •	• *yasui*
hikui •	• *yoi*
mazui •	• *samui*
takai •	• *tsumaranai*
atsui •	• *suzushii*
chiisai •	• *hosoi*
warui •	• *atsui*
mijikai •	• *yasashii*
omoshiroi •	• *semai*
karui •	• *takai*
usui •	• *minikui*

13.3. Convert the following phrases to read "not ___."

1. *isogashii hito* _________ *isogashiku nai hito* _______________________

2. *mezurashii tori* _______________________________________

3. *sabishii (o)tera* _______________________________________

4. *urusai inu* ____

5. *tanoshii hi* ____

6. *akai ringo* ____

*13.4. Replace the following two words with one rōmaji word such as **kore**, **koko**, etc.*

1. *kono hito* __________ *kochira* _______________________

2. *ano tabemono* _______________________________________

3. *ano gakkō* ____

4. *kono kissaten* _______________________________________

5. *ano kaisha* ____

6. *sono kisha* ____

13.5. Translate into English:

1. *aoi me* ____

2. *ōkii sutēki* ____

3. *kono inu* ____

4. *kowaku nai sensei* ___________________________________

5. *samuku nai hi* _______________________________________

6. **Otōsan wa kaisha e kono kuroi kuruma de ikimasu.**

____

7. **Natsu watashi to otōto wa yasashii Nihon-go o naraimasu.**

____

8. **Anata wa muzukashii hon o gakkō de yomimasu ka.**

____

     Lesson 13: The Apple Is Delicious

9. *Ano inu wa ōkii niku o tabemasen.*

____

10. *Kore wa omoshiroku nai hon desu yo.*

____

11. *Anata no onēsan wa warui onēsan de wa arimasen.*

____

12. *Watashi wa kono akaku nai ringo mo kaimasu.*

____

Translate into rōmaji:

13. cold water ____

14. big person ____

15. tasteless meal _____________________________________

16. that (over there) child _______________________________

17. not interesting movie _________________________________

18. This is a long train. __________________________________
19. That person (over there) is our school teacher.

____

20. I do not drink warm (not cold) water.

____

21. My dog is not a black dog. ______________________________
22. My younger sister does not read this difficult book.

____

23. Which book will you read? _______________________________

24. Which movie do we watch?_________________________________

Let us look at the following two sentences with the adjective *big*.

1. This is a *big* apple.

2. The apple is *big*.

The *big* in the sentence 1 is an adjective which describes and preceeds the noun *apple* and we have discussed it in the previous section. The *big* in the sentence 2 is an adjective used as the complement of the sentence, which you are going to study now.

I-adjectives may be used as complements, just as English adjectives are.

akai desu to be red,
sabishii desu to be lonely, and
atatakai desu to be warm.

The sentences which use **i**-adjectives as complements have the structure

subject wa i-adjective desu.

Examples

Ringo wa akai desu.	*The apple is red.*
Sono inu wa kowai desu.	*That dog is frightening.*
Gaijin wa mezurashii desu.	*The foreigner is unusual.*
Koko wa kitanai desu.	*This place is dirty.*
Watashi wa atsui desu.	*I am hot.*

Let us now look at the following two sentences.

1. *This is red.* Kore wa akai desu.

2. *This is a book.* Kore wa hon desu.

There is no great difference grammatically between the sentences "This is red" and "This is a book" in English. The negative statements are obtained by putting *not* after the verb *is* for both sentences in English ("this is *not* red" and "this is *not* a book"). But the Japanese i-adjectives are very different from English adjectives: they conjugate (change forms), as you have seen for negative adjectives.

The negative statement of subject wa __i desu is

subject wa __ku nai desu (or __ku arimasen).

To negate the sentence which has an **i**-adjective as its complement, the **i**-adjective conjugates while the verb **desu** remains the same. Hence the negative statements for sentences 1 and 2 above are as follows.

1. *This is* not *red.*   *Kore wa akaku* nai *desu.*
   (adjective **akai** conjugates while **desu** remains unchanged)

2. *This is* not *a book.*   *Kore wa hon* de wa arimasen.
   (verb **desu** conjugates)

The form for the Japanese sentence 1, which has an adjective for its complement, differs from that of the Japanese sentence 2, which has a noun for its complement. The following examples show sentences which have adjectives for their complements.

Examples

Boku no heya wa hiroi desu.	*My room is spacious.*
Boku no heya wa hiroku nai *desu.*	*My room is not spacious.*
Kono hon wa omoshiroi desu.	*This book is interesting.*
Kono hon wa omoshiroku nai *desu.*	*This book is not interesting.*
Amerika-jin wa mezurashii desu.	*An American is unusual.*
Amerika-jin wa mezurashiku nai *desu.*	*An American is not unusual.*

EXERCISES

13.6. 💿 *I shall say a statement. I want you to say the corresponding negative statement after me. You may check your replies against the correct answers recorded at the end of this exercise.*

1. ____

2. ____

3. ____

4. ____

5. ____

13.7. Translate into English:

1. *Kono natsu wa atsui desu ne.* ___________________________________

2. *Betty-san no inu wa kitanai desu.* ___________________________________

3. *Kono kudamono wa yasui desu yo.* ___________________________________

4. *Umi no mizu wa tsumetai desu ne.* ___________________________________

5. *Nihon-jin wa mezurashiku nai desu.* ___________________________________

6. *Ano yama wa abunaku nai desu ka.* ___________________________________

7. *Nihon-go wa yasashiku nai desu.* ___________________________________

Translate into rōmaji:

8. Canada is cold. ___________________________________

9. This is unusual. ___________________________________

10. Is Britain interesting? ___________________________________

11. Is the school enjoyable? ___________________________________

12. My umbrella is not black. ___________________________________

13. I am not lonely at night. ___________________________________

14. This book is not interesting! ___________________________________

NA-ADJECTIVES*

So far, you have learned **i**-adjectives. In this section, you are going to learn the other type of adjective: **na**-adjectives. As you can see from the list of **na**-adjectives below, **na**-adjectives end with **na**.

Na-*Adjectives*

baka na foolish, stupid	*rikō na* clever
benri na convenient	*rippa na* splendid
fuben na inconvenient	*romanchikku na* romantic
genki na healthy, hearty	*shinsetsu na* kind
hansamu na handsome	*shizuka na* quiet, peaceful
hen na strange, suspicious	*taisetsu na* precious
kirei na beautiful, clean	*yūmei na* famous

Na-adjectives precede the nouns and pronouns they describe, just as **i**-adjectives do.

Examples

shinsetsu na hito	*kind person*
hen na hito	*strange person*

*They are defined as adjective verbs in Japanese grammar, but I have defined them as adjectives in accordance with English grammar.

     Lesson 13: The Apple Is Delicious

 The negative **na**-adjectives (*not* splendid, *not* beautiful, etc.) are obtained by changing **na** to **de (wa) nai.**

genki na *hito*	*a healthy person*
genki de nai *hito*	*a not healthy person*

shinsetsu na *hito*	*a kind person*
shinsetsu de nai *hito*	*a not kind person*

 ## Conversation 1: He's a Cute Dog, Isn't He?

Hanako meets Tom, walking his dog.

Nouns	**Na-***Adjective*
dakkusufundo dachshund	*pittari na perfectly fit*
kaeri return	

Hanako:	*(Sore wa) kawaii inu desu ne.*	*He is a cute dog, isn't he?*
	(Sore wa) anata no inu desu ka.	*Is he your dog?*
Tom:	*Hai sō desu.*	*Yes, he is.*
Hanako:	*(Inu no) ashi wa mijikai desu ne.*	*The legs are short, aren't they?*
Tom:	*Kono inu wa dakkusufundo desu yo.*	*He (This dog) is a dachshund!*
	Dakkusufundo no ashi wa mijikai desu yo.	*A dachshund's legs are short!*
Hanako:	*(Inu no) me wa ōkii desu ne.*	*His (The dog's) eyes are big, aren't they?*
	(Inu no) mimi wa nagai desu ne.	*His (The dog's) ears are long, aren't they?*
	(Inu no) namae wa nan desu ka.	*What is his (the dog's) name?*
Tom:	*(Inu no namae wa) Cute desu.*	*It's Cute.*
Hanako:	*(Inu no namae wa) kawaii namae desu ne.*	*It's a cute name, isn't it?*
Tom:	*CUTE wa Nihon-go de KAWAII desu.*	*CUTE is KAWAII in Japanese.*
Hanako:	*(Cute wa) kono inu ni pittari na namae desu ne.*	*It's a perfectly fit name (for this dog), isn't it?*

NA-ADJECTIVES AS COMPLEMENTS

 **Na** must be dropped when **na**-adjectives are used as complements.

Ano hito wa hen desu.	*He is odd.*
Watashi wa genki desu.	*I am healthy.*

You may notice that the greeting **(o)genki desu ka** is the abbreviation and honorific speech for **anata wa genki desu ka,** meaning *are you healthy?* The reply **hai genki desu** is the abbreviation of **hai watashi wa genki desu,** meaning *yes, I am healthy.*

 The negative of "**na**-adjective (without **na**) + **desu**" is obtained by changing **desu** into **de wa arimasen.** For **na**-adjectives, the verb **desu** conjugates, while the **na**-adjectives do not.

Examples

Ano hito wa shinsetsu desu.	*He is kind.*
Ano hito wa shinsetsu de wa arimasen.	*He is not kind.*
Koko wa shizuka desu.	*This (place) is quiet.*
Koko wa shizuka de wa arimasen.	*This (place) is not quiet.*

 ## Conversation 2: Is He Noisy at Night?

Tom and Hanako continue the conversation on Cute using the following vocabulary.

Verb (Transitive)	Noun
miokurimasu see (a person) off	*kaeri return*

Tom:	*Cute wa rikō desu yo.*	*Cute is clever!*
	Asa (Cute wa) boku o basu-sutoppu made miokurimasu.	*In the morning, he sees me off to the bus stop.*
	Gogo (Cute wa) boku no kaeri o basu-sutoppu de machimasu.	*In the afternoon, he waits for my return at the bus stop.*
	Cute wa boku no taisetsu na inu desu.	*Cute is my precious dog.*
Hanako:	*Cute wa genki desu ne.*	*Cute is energetic, isn't he?*
	Yoru Cute wa urusai desu ka.	*Is he noisy at night?*
Tom:	*Iie (yoru Cute wa) shizuka desu.*	*No, he is quiet.*

EXERCISES

13.8. Convert the following phrases to read "not ___" and then translate them into English.

1. *shinsetsu na hito*   *shinsetsu de nai hito*   *not a kind person*

2. *genki na inu*

3. *yūmei na (o)tera*

4. *kirei na ie*

5. *taisetsu na hon*

 Lesson 13: The Apple Is Delicious

13.9. 🔘 *Answer the following questions in full sentences in rōmaji.*

1. *Tom-kun wa ōkii desu ka. (Tom-kun wa) chiisai desu ka.*

____

2. *Tom-kun wa genki desu ka.* ___________________________

3. *Tom-kun wa baka desu ka.* ___*Iie Tom-kun wa baka de wa arimasen. Tom-kun wa rikō desu.*___

4. *Hanako-san wa dare desu ka.* __________________________

5. *Hanako-san wa shinsetsu desu ka.* ______________________

6. *Hanako-san wa urusai desu ka.* ________________________

7. *Hanako-san wa kirei desu ka.* _________________________

13.10. Translate into English:

1. *shizuka na (o)tera* __________________________________

2. *hansamu na hito* ___________________________________

3. *Tarō wa genki na neko desu.* __________________________

4. *Kore wa otōsan no taisetsu na hon desu.* ________________

5. *Ano hen na hito wa dare desu ka.* _____________________

6. *Koko wa benri desu ka.* ______________________________

7. *Kono inu wa baka de wa arimasen.* _____________________

8. *Ano hito wa yūmei de wa arimasen.* ____________________

9. *Kazuko-san wa romanchikku desu.* _____________________

Translate into rōmaji:

10. healthy cat ______________________________________

11. beautiful eyes _____________________________________

12. not kind person ____

13. This is a famous picture. _______________________________________

14. That is a healthy child. ____

15. Is Bob kind? ____

16. You are beautiful. ____

17. Cheap houses are not convenient. _________________________________

18. That person is not clever. _______________________________________

13.11. 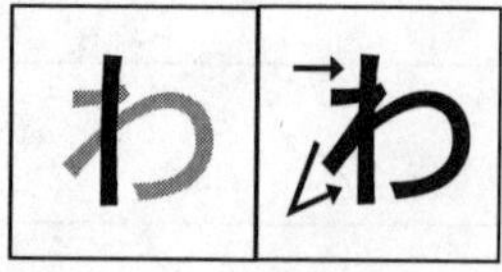 *I shall ask some questions about Conversations 1 and 2. Reply to each question aloud in Japanese. Correct answers are recorded at the end of this exercise.*

1. ____

2. ____

3. ____

4. ____

5. *Iie* ____

6. ____

7. ____

8. ____

9. *Iie* ____

WRITING EXERCISE: HIRAGANA FOR *WA, WO* AND *N*

Practice the three hiragana characters わ, を *and* ん.

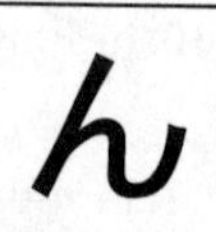

     Lesson 13: The Apple Is Delicious

**What you must remember from this lesson to proceed
to the next lesson:**

Adjectives describe and precede nouns and pronouns.

Negative **i**-adjectives are obtained by changing _**i** into _ **ku nai.**

Negative **na**-adjectives are obtained by changing **na** into **de (wa) nai.**

I-adjectives are used as complements in the sentence structure _ **wa _i
desu.** (_ **wa _ku nai desu** is used for negative statements.)

Na-adjectives are used as complements in the sentence structure _ **wa na**-
adjective (without **na**) **desu.** (_ **wa na**-adjective (without **na**) **de wa
arimasen** is used for negative statements.)

Kono/sono/ano/dono, *this/that/that-over-there/which,* are demonstrative
adjectives.

14

What Kinds of Things Do You Like?

In this lesson you will learn:

Speaking
To talk about likes, dislikes, interests and skills of people
To express desires of "wanting things"
To ask more complex questions
To say how you are feeling physically

Grammar
To understand and use more adjectives

In the previous lesson, you have learned some adjectives; you can now describe things in more detail. Instead of saying "This is an apple," you are now able to say "This is a *big* apple," "This is a *delicious* apple," "This is a *red* apple," and so on. Adjectives are extremely useful in making small talk too. If you say a single adjective such as **kawaii,** *cute,* **oishii,** *delicious,* etc., your feeling is conveyed without the rest of the sentence. Well, making small talk is not all you can do with adjectives; in fact, you can use adjectives to make real headway in your relationships with others.

In this lesson, you will learn new adjectives which may be used to find out what someone else likes. In other words, you will learn to say sentences such as "Do you like apples?," or "Do you like tennis?" There's not much point in asking him/her out to play tennis if he/she doesn't like tennis. You will also learn to compliment that special person with sentences such as "You are good at Japanese," "You are good at tennis," etc. Well, even if you haven't found anyone special yet, nobody dislikes hearing compliments! It is the easiest way to be noticed or liked. You will also learn to say the ultimate sentence, "I love you." Isn't it exciting? So let's continue on with more adjectives!

SUKI NA AND KIRAI NA

Let us study the following **na**-adjectives.

Na-*Adjectives*

suki na likable	*kirai na* detestable, dislikable

Let's consider **suki na** and **kirai na** to describe nouns. The literal English translations for **suki na ringo** and **kirai na ringo** are *a likable apple* and *a dislikable apple* which are not quite appropriate translations in English. The most appropriate English translations for them are *the apple that somebody likes* and *the apple that somebody dislikes.*

Suki na kudamono wa ringo desu.	*The fruit that somebody likes is apples.*
Ninjin wa kirai na yasai desu.	*The carrots are vegetables that somebody dislikes.*

Since the above sentences do not state the person *who* likes apples or *who* dislikes carrots, it is assumed that the speaker is talking about himself. Hence the above sentences imply *I like apples* and *I dislike carrots.*

The negative adjectives for **suki na** and **kirai na** are obtained just as for other **na**-adjectives: **na** is replaced by **de (wa) nai.**

Examples

suki de (wa) nai tabemono	*the food that somebody doesn't like (not a likable food)*
kirai de (wa) nai sensei	*the teacher that somebody does not dislike (not a dislikable teacher)*

Yoru watashi wa suki de (wa) nai hon o yomimasu.   *At night, I read the book that I do not like.*

I Like Apples

Now, let us consider the adjectives **suki na** and **kirai na** as complements. Just as for other **na**-adjectives, **na** must be dropped—**suki desu,** *to be likable,* and **kirai desu,** *to be dislikable*—but they use a different sentence structure from other adjectives we have learned in the previous lesson.

Suki/kirai na is used as a complement in the sentence structure

subject **ga suki/kirai desu.**

Ga follows the subject and **suki/kirai desu** is translated as *to be likable/dislikable.*

Examples

Ringo ga suki desu.	*Apples are likable,* implying *I like apples.*
Tenisu ga kirai desu.	*Tennis is dislikable,* implying *I dislike tennis.*

We have learned in lesson 12, on page 132, that _wa may be used to express a topic in a sentence and may be translated as *as for _.* Let us put **watashi wa** in the sentence **ringo ga suki desu:** **watashi wa ringo ga suki desu.** The literal translation is *as for me, apples are likable,* but of course, *I like apples* is a more appropriate translation in English.

It is easier to think of it in these terms: that **suki/kirai desu** uses the sentence structure

(English subject) **wa** **(English object)** **ga suki/kirai desu.**

Wa follows an indirect subject (topic) in Japanese and **ga** follows a grammatical subject in Japanese.

Watashi wa tenisu ga suki desu. — *I like tennis.*
Watashi wa ninjin ga kirai desu. — *I dislike carrots.*
Anata wa nani ga suki desu ka. — *What do you like?*

The negative of **suki/kirai desu** is **suki/kirai de wa arimasen,** just as for other **na**-adjectives.

Example

Betty-san wa ringo ga suki de wa arimasen. — *Betty does not like apples.*

Let us consider the sentence **watashi wa ringo ga suki desu,** *I like apples,* and let us insert **kudamono wa,** *as for fruit,* in the sentence. Then, we get **watashi wa kudamono wa ringo ga suki desu,** *as for fruit, I like apples.* Of course, *I like apples for fruit* may be a more appropriate translation in English.

Although **watashi wa _ ga suki desu** is usually translated as *I like _,* (**watashi wa**) **anata ga suki desu,** when spoken to a member of the opposite sex, it becomes a very strong statement and is interpreted as *I love you* and not *I like you.* Now you know what to say when you are in love!

I AM GOOD AT A LOT OF THINGS

Let us look at another set of **na**-adjectives.

Na-Adjectives

jōzu na good (at a particular skill such as a sport, language, etc.)
heta na bad (at a particular skill such as a sport, language, etc.)

Just as for other **na**-adjectives, negative adjectives are obtained by replacing **na** with **de (wa) nai.**

Examples

jōzu na e — *a good picture*
jōzu de (wa) nai e — *a bad (not good) picture*
Ano jōzu na e wa sensei no e desu. — *That good picture is the teacher's picture.*

When **jōzu na** and **heta na** are used as complements, **na** must be dropped, just as for other **na**-adjectives: **jōzu desu,** *to be good* (at a skill), and **heta desu,** *to be bad* (at a skill). **Jōzu/heta desu** uses the same expression as **suki/kirai desu.** The negative of **jōzu/heta desu** is obtained by changing **desu** into **de wa arimasen,** just as for other **na**-adjectives.

Examples

Ojīsan wa Nihon-go ga jōzu desu. — *Grandfather is good at the Japanese language.*
Boku wa tenisu ga jōzu de wa arimasen. — *I am not good at tennis.*

I WANT STEAK

I-Adjective

hoshii desirable

Now, let us look at **i**-adjective **hoshii,** *desirable.* It conjugates just as any other **i**-adjective: the negative of **hoshii** is **hoshiku nai.**

Examples

hoshii hon	*the book that somebody wants (a desirable book)*
hoshiku nai hon	*the book that somebody doesn't want (not a desirable book)*
Hoshii kudamono wa ichigo desu.	*I want strawberries. (The fruit that somebody wants is strawberries.)*

Hoshii desu, *to be desirable/wanted,* is used in the same sentence structure as **suki/kirai desu** to express "wanting something" and its negative tense is obtained just as any other "**i**-adjective + **desu**": **hoshiku nai desu.**

Examples

Watashi wa akai fuku ga hoshii desu.	*I want a red dress.*
Watashi wa asa-gohan ga hoshiku nai desu.	*I don't want breakfast.*
Anata wa nani ga hoshii desu ka.	*What do you want?*

QUESTIONS AND REPLIES

The replies for _ **wa** _ **ga** "adjective + **desu**" **ka** are

hai "adjective + **desu**" or **iie** negative of "adjective + **desu**."

A question is asked

Anata wa ringo ga suki desu ka.	*Do you like apples?*

Replies are

Hai suki desu.	*Yes, I do.*
Iie suki de wa arimasen.	*No, I don't.*

A question is asked

Anata wa kore ga hoshii desu ka.	*Do you want this?*

Replies are

Hai hoshii desu.	*Yes, I do.*
Iie hoshiku nai desu.	*No, I don't.*

 **Conversation 1: What Kinds of Movies Do You Like?**

Tom tries to find out what Hanako likes.

Tom:	(*Anata wa*) **eiga ga suki desu ka.**	*Do you like movies?*
Hanako:	*Hai suki desu.*	*Yes, I do.*
Tom:	(*Anata wa*) **nan no eiga ga suki desu ka.**	*What kinds of movies do you like?*
Hanako:	(*Watashi wa*) **romanchikku na eiga ga suki desu.**	*I like romantic movies.*

Tom:	*(Anata wa)* **tabemono wa nani ga suki desu ka.**	*What foods do you like? (As for food, what do you like?)*
Hanako:	*(Watashi wa tabemono wa)* **yakisoba ga suki desu.**	*I like yakisoba.*
Tom:	*(Anata wa)* **nomimono wa nani ga suki desu ka.**	*What drinks do you like? (As for drink, what do you like?)*
Hanako:	*(Watashi wa nomimono wa)* **orenji-jūsu ga suki desu.**	*I like orange juice.*
Tom:	*(Anata wa)* **dono sensei ga suki desu ka.**	*Which teacher do you like?*
Hanako:	*(Watashi wa)* **rekishi no sensei ga suki desu.**	*I like the history teacher.*

Samurai movies are very popular in Japan and they are watched by people of all ages and walks of life. The most popular storyline is the revenge of the death of a samurai's lord who died by foul play. It epitomizes the honor and duty of a samurai. The samurai who avenged his lord's death was a man of honor while he who shrunk from that obligation was regarded as beneath contempt in old times. A remake of such a famous samurai story, "Chūshingura," in which 46 samurai avenge their master, is still produced and played on TV during each New Year holiday season. Another popular story line is about a very high ranking samurai, disguised as a commoner, who fights "bad guys" who oppress ordinary people, just like Zorro in Western movies. These samurai movies emphasize the value of loyalty to one's lord, honor, humility, self control, living in harmony with nature and nonviolence. But the movies are almost always very violent because "bad guys" force a peace-loving hero into taking action to defend himself and others. All these qualities mentioned above are still very much valued by Japanese people.

EXERCISES

14.1. *Say the following sentences using the sentence structure __ wa __ ga __ desu (or de wa arimasen). The correct answers are recorded on the track for Exercise 14.1.*

Say that you like following things:

1. apple ____

2. tempura ____

Say that you dislike the following things:

3. carrot ____

4. milk ____

Say that you are good at the following things:

5. tennis ____

6. English ____

Say that you are not good at the following things:

7. swimming ____

8. Japanese ____

Say that you want the following things:

9. steak ____

10. TV ____

14.2. *I shall describe Tom's elder brother. Answer the following questions in rōmaji.*

1. **Onīsan wa nan no supōtsu o shimasu ka.** ____

2. **Onīsan wa jūdō ga jōzu desu ka.** _Iie_ ____

3. **Onīsan wa sumō ga suki desu ka.** ____

14.3. *Translate into English:*

1. **suki na hito** ____

2. **hoshii hon** ____

3. **kirai de wa nai sensei** ____

4. **hoshiku nai gohan** ____

5. **Ringo wa suki na kudamono desu.** ____

6. **Watashi wa Eigo ga heta desu.** ____

7. **Anata wa dare ga suki desu ka.** ____

8. *Watashi wa kirai na hon o gakkō de yomimasu.*

____

9. *Ano zō wa anata no banana ga hoshii desu.*

____

10. *Anata no otōsan wa yama no e ga jōzu desu ne.*

____

11. *Boku wa karate ga heta de wa arimasen.*

____

12. *Watashi wa gakkō ga kirai de wa arimasen.*

____

13. *Anata wa mizu ga hoshii desu ka. Hai hoshii desu.*

____

Translate into rōmaji:

14. the teacher whom somebody dislikes _______________________

15. bad English ____

16. not good Japanese ____

17. the drink that somebody doesn't want _____________________

18. Hanako speaks good English. ______________________________

19. I buy the picture (which) I want. ________________________

20. I like Japanese people. __________________________________

21. For dinner, I want a big steak. __________________________

22. I am bad at English._______________________________________

23. Whom do you like? ____

24. I do not dislike Hanako. ____

25. I do not want these fruits. ____

26. Do you like udon? No, I don't. ____

I HAVE A HEADACHE!

Let us look at another set of **i**-adjectives **itai**, *painful*, and **kayui**, *itchy*. They use the same sentence structure as **suki/kirai** to describe physical conditions.

I-Adjectives

itai painful	*kayui* itchy

Examples

Watashi wa atama ga itai desu.	*I have a headache. (As for me, the head is painful.)*
Watashi wa ashi ga kayui desu.	*My legs are itchy. (As for me, the legs are itchy.)*

HANAKO HAS BEAUTIFUL EYES

The same expression as **suki/kirai desu** may be used to describe people (and animated subjects), using the following vocabulary.

Nouns / I-Adjectives

Nouns	I-Adjectives	
se height, stature	*chiisai* quiet (sound, voice)	*ōkii* loud (sound, voice)

Examples

Hanako-san wa me ga ōkii desu.	*Hanako has big eyes. (As for Hanako, the eyes are big.)*
Amerika-jin wa se ga takai desu.	*Americans are tall. (As for Americans, the heights are big.)*
Makoto-kun wa koe ga chiisai desu.	*Makoto has a quiet voice. (As for Makoto, the voice is quiet.)*

The above sentences are equivalent to the following sentences.

Hanako-san no me wa ōkii desu.	*Hanako's eyes are big.*
Amerika-jin no se wa takai desu.	*Americans are tall. (Americans' heights are big.)*
Makoto-kun no koe wa chiisai desu.	*Makoto's voice is quiet.*

Conversation 2: You Are Good at Tennis, Aren't You?

Tom flatters Makoto's tennis skill.

Tom:	(Anata wa) **tenisu ga jōzu desu ne.**	*You are good at tennis, aren't you?*
Makoto:	(Boku wa tenisu ga) **heta desu yo.**	*I am bad!*
	Tarō-kun wa tenisu ga jōzu desu yo.	*Taro is good at tennis!*
Tom:	**Tarō-kun wa ude ga nagai desu.**	*Taro has long arms.*
	(Tarō-kun wa) **ashi mo nagai desu yo.**	*He has long legs too!*

14.4. 🔘 *I shall describe myself. Write down what you think I am in rōmaji.*

1. *Anata wa* _______________________________ *desu.*

2. *Anata wa* _______________________________ *desu.*

3. *Anata wa* _______________________________ *desu.*

4. *Anata wa* _______________________________ *desu.*

14.5. Translate into English:

1. *Watashi wa onaka ga itai desu.* _______________________________

2. *Hanako-san wa me ga kirei desu.* _______________________________

3. *Kirin wa kubi ga nagai desu ka.* _______________________________

4. *Nihon-jin wa hana ga hikui desu ne.* _______________________________

5. *Makoto-kun wa atama ga yoku nai desu.* _______________________________

6. *Tom-kun no kami wa kuroku nai desu.* _______________________________

Translate into rōmaji:

7. My arms are itchy. _______________________________

8. I have a pain in my leg. _______________________________

9. My father has big hands. _______________________________

10. Elephants have long noses. _______________________________

11. Japanese people are not tall. _______________________________

12. The English teacher doesn't have a loud voice.

____

14.6. 📀 *Say sentences implying that you have pain at the following parts of your body, using the sentence structure _ wa _ ga _ desu. The correct answers are recorded on the track for Exercise 14.6.*

1. head ____

2. leg ____

3. arm ____

4. eye ____

5. stomach ____

WRITING EXERCISE: KATAKANA FOR *A, I, U, E* AND *O*

Practice the five katakana characters ア， イ， ウ， エ and オ.

ア ア

イ イ

ウ ウ ウ

エ エ エ

オ オ オ

What you must remember from this lesson to proceed to the next lesson:

Suki na, kirai na, jōzu na, heta na and **hoshii** use the sentence structure _ **wa** _ **ga** "adjective + **desu.**"

_ **wa** _ **ga** "adjective + **desu**" is used to describe people.

15 Yoko Is More Beautiful Than I Am. But Hanako Is the Most Beautiful of All.

In this lesson you will learn:

Speaking
To describe how something is done
To talk with the words "very" and "not very"
To make comparisons

Grammar
To use adverbs
To convert the adjectives you've learned into adverbs
To understand comparisons of adjectives
To use the comparative degree with the particle **yori**
To use the superlative degree with the adverbs **ichi-ban** and **mottomo**

In the previous two lessons, you have learned to use adjectives:

1. To describe nouns,

2. As complements and

3. To express your emotions (such as liking and disliking), opinions on ability (such as being good or bad at a particular skill), desire or "wanting something" with **hoshii,** and to describe people.

Also, you have finally learned to say "I love you" to someone special. But, if you think that saying "I love you" is the ultimate for your relationship and your language study, you are mistaken. You are more than just a pretty face: you have personality and character, and you want to express them. So, bearing that in mind, you are now going to learn more sentence structures in Japanese.

In this lesson, you will learn to express *comparison of adjectives* in Japanese. Let me refresh your memory of comparison of adjectives in the English language. Each adjective has three degrees of comparison: they are the positive, the comparative and the superlative. The *positive degree* is the ordinary form of an adjective (e.g., *tall* of "I am tall"). The *comparative degree* is used to compare two individuals (e.g., *taller* of "I am taller than Makoto"). The *superlative degree* is used to mark the most outstanding of more than two individuals (e.g., *tallest* of "I am tallest of all"). Some adjectives form their comparative and superlative forms by putting -*er* and -*est* on ordinary form of adjectives (e.g., tall, tall*er*, tall*est*; big, bigg*er*, bigg*est*; and so on). Some adjectives use *more, most, less* and *least* to form comparatives and superlatives (e.g., beautiful, *more* beautiful, *most* beautiful; busy, *less* busy and *least* busy), and some adjectives have totally different forms (e.g., good, *better, best;* bad, *worse, worst;* and so on).

You will also learn adverbs in this lesson. Adverbs describe adjectives, verbs and adverbs. For example, *very* of "a *very* delicious apple" describes the adjective *delicious; fast* of "I drive *fast*" describes the verb *drive;* and *very* of "I drive *very* fast" describes the adverb *fast*. Most adverbs are formed by adding -*ly* to adjectives in English; for example, *quick* of "She walks with *quick* steps" is an adjective while *quickly* of "She eats her dinner *quickly*" is an adverb.

ADVERBS

A Japanese adverb is usually placed immediately before the adjective, verb or adverb that it describes.

Making Adverbs from *I*-Adjectives

The following adjectives will appear in this section.

I-*Adjectives*

hayai quick, rapid, early	*osoi* late, slow

By converting final **i** of **i**-adjectives into **ku,** you may make adverbs.*

Examples: Adjectives	*Adverbs*
hayai quick, rapid, early, fast	*hayaku* quickly, rapidly, early, fast
ōkii big	*ōkiku* big
omoshiroi interesting	*omoshiroku* interestingly
osoi late, slow	*osoku* late, slowly
takai expensive, high	*takaku* expensively, highly
tanoshii enjoyable	*tanoshiku* enjoyably
yasui cheap	*yasuku* cheaply
yoi good	*yoku* well, thoroughly, fully, frequently, often, a lot

You must be careful when you are translating an English adjective or adverb into Japanese. For example, *fast* of "I drive a car fast" is an adverb describing *drive*, while the *fast* of "I drive a fast car" is an adjective describing *car;* they are different words in Japanese. Similarly, when you are

*A Japanese **i**-adjective conjugates (changes its ending) and it has five different forms. One of them is the form ending with **ku** (instead of **i**) and its function is that of describing a verb, just as an English adverb does. Although they are defined as adjectives in Japanese grammar, I have defined them as adverbs in accordance with English grammar.

translating a Japanese word which looks like an adverb ending with **ku,** you must be careful to check that it is not followed by **nai:** a negative **i**-adjective has the form **_ku nai.**

Note that the adverb **yoku,** *well,* has many more meanings than just that of converting **yoi,** *good,* into an adverb.

The adverbs obtained from **i**-adjectives by changing **i** into **ku** describe verbs only.

Examples

Otōsan wa Amerika e yoku ikimasu.	*Father goes to America often.*
Otōto wa gohan o tanoshiku tabemasu.	*The younger brother eats meals enjoyably.*
Watashi wa resutoran ni osoku ikimasu.	*I shall go to the restaurant late.*
Watashi wa kore o anata ni yasuku urimasu.	*I shall sell you this cheaply.*

The Adverbs *Totemo* (or *Taihen*) and *Amari*

The adverb **totemo** (or **taihen**) is used to mean *very* when it describes a positive adjective or adverb; it is used to mean *a lot* or *much* when it describes a verb.

The following examples show **totemo** describing adjectives, adverbs and a verb respectively.

Examples

totemo oishii ringo	*a very delicious apple*
totemo tanoshii eiga	*a very enjoyable movie*
Hiroshi-kun wa totemo omoshiroi hito desu.	*Hiroshi is a very interesting person.*
Ano totemo shizuka na hito wa Kazuko-san desu.	*That very quiet person is Kazuko.*
Watashi wa kore o totemo takaku urimasu.	*I shall sell this very expensively.*
Tom-kun wa Eigo o totemo hayaku hanashimasu.	*Tom speaks English very fast.*
Hiroshi-kun wa gohan o totemo tabemasu.	*Hiroshi eats rice a lot.*

The adverb **amari** is used to mean *(not) very* when it describes a negative adjective or adverb describing a negative verb; it is used to mean *(not) a lot* or *(not) much* when it describes a negative verb.

Examples

amari oishiku nai sakana	*not very delicious fish*
Amari takaku nai sakana o kudasai.	*May I have (some) not very expensive fish please?*
Kono inu wa amari rikō de wa nai desu.	*This dog is not very clever.*
Watashi wa gakkō e amari hayaku ikimasen.	*I don't go to school very early.*
Watashi wa tegami o amari kakimasen.	*I don't write letters much.*
Tom-kun wa gohan o amari tabemasen.	*Tom does not eat rice much.*

Here are the Japanese adverbs meaning very that you have learned.

totemo *very* (with adjectives and adverbs); *a lot, much* (with verbs)

taihen *very* (with adjectives and adverbs); *a lot, much* (with verbs)

amari *(not) very* (with negative adjectives and adverbs describing negative verbs);
(not) a lot, (not) much (with negative verbs)

More Adverbs

Adverbs

dō *how, in what way*	**sō** *so, in that way*
mada *not yet* (used with negative verbs)	**sorosoro** *soon*
mata *again*	**sukoshi** *a little*
mō *already*	**sugu** *immediately*
motto *more*	**takusan** *much, many, a lot, plenty*
naze *why*	**tokidoki** *sometimes*
sakki *a little while ago*	**yagate** *soon, presently, before long*
	yukkuri *slowly*

Examples

Motto tabemasen ka.	*Would you like to eat more?*
Hanako-san wa mada kimasen.	*Hanako has not come yet.*
Motto yukkuri onegai shimasu.	*Could you (speak) more slowly please?*
Otōsan wa (hon o) takusan kaimasu.	*Father buys (books) plenty.*
Watashi wa Eigo o sukoshi hanashimasu.	*I speak English a little.*
Kono nichi-yōbi ni anata wa gakkō e naze ikimasu ka.	*Why do you go to school this Sunday?*

Conversation 1: With Whom Do You Often Speak Japanese?

Makoto asks Tom about his Japanese speaking habits.

Makoto:	*(Anata wa)* **Nihon-go de dare to yoku hanashimasu ka.**	*With whom do you often speak in Japanese?*
Tom:	*(Boku wa Nihongo de)* **Hanako-san to** *(yoku)* **hanashimasu.**	*I speak with Hanako.*
Makoto:	*(Anata wa Nihon-go de)* **Hiroshi-kun to mo yoku hanashimasu ka.**	*Do you often speak with Hiroshi too?*
Tom:	*(Iie boku wa Hiroshi-kun to)* **amari hanashimasen.**	*No, I don't speak much with him.*
Makoto:	*(Anata wa Hiroshi-kun to)* **naze** *(hanashimasen ka).*	*Why?*
Tom:	**Hiroshi-kun wa** *(Nihongo o)* **totemo hayaku hanashimasu.**	*Hiroshi speaks very fast.*
	Hanako-san wa *(Nihongo o)* **totemo yukkuri hanashimasu.**	*Hanako speaks very slowly.*

15.1. Convert the following adjectives into adverbs.

Adjectives   **Adverbs**

1. *hayai* quick, rapid, early   _hayaku_________________________   quickly, rapidly, early

2. *nagai* long   ___________________________   long

3. *usui* thin   ___________________________   thinly

4. *yasashii* gentle   ___________________________   gently

5. *tanoshii* enjoyable   ___________________________   enjoyably

*15.2. Write either **totemo** or **amari** in the blanks.*

1. ___________________________   *oishii ringo* a very delicious apple

2. ___________________________   *oishiku nai ringo* not a very delicious apple

3. ___________________________   *hayai kisha* a very fast train

4. ___________________________   *hayakunai kisha* not a very fast train

15.3. Write adverbs in the blanks.

1. ___________________________   *watashi wa soko e ikimasu.* I shall go there *immediately.*

2. ___________________________   *anata wa benkyō o shimasu ka.* *Why* do you study?

3. ___________________________   *Hanako-san-tachi wa kimasu.* Hanako and the girls will come *soon.*

4. ___________________________   *mizu o kudasai.* May I have *more* water please?

15.4. Translate into English:

1. *totemo kirei na doresu*____

2. *totemo ōkii hito* ____

3. *amari muzukashiku nai hon* _______________________________________

4. *Watashi wa soko e sugu ikimasu.*

____

5. *Anata wa Hanako-san ga naze suki desu ka.*

____

6. *Hanako-san wa totemo shinsetsu desu.*

____

7. *Ano hito wa amari yūmei de wa arimasen.*

____

8. *Kono eiga wa totemo omoshiroi desu yo.*

____

9. *Boku-tachi wa tenisu o tanoshiku shimasu.*

____

10. *Otōto wa gohan o totemo yukkuri tabemasu.*

____

11. *Pātī ni sukoshi hayaku ikimasen ka.*

____

Translate into rōmaji:

12. very fast train ____

13. not very cute cat ____

14. Hanako is very beautiful. ____

15. Is a big house very expensive? ____

16. This room is not very large. ____

17. My younger brother speaks English very slowly. _________________________

18. My father will come soon. ____

19. May I have more water please? ____

20. I shall eat fast. ____

21. Why do you go to temples? ____

22. May I have a lot of that please? ____

15.5. 💿 *I shall ask some questions about Conversation 1. Reply to each question aloud in Japanese. Correct answers are recorded at the end of this exercise.*

1. ____

2. ____

3. ____

LET'S COMPARE! COMPARISON OF ADJECTIVES

Japanese adjectives do not have comparative (e.g., *larger*) and superlative (e.g., *largest*) forms.

Comparative Degree

The comparative idea is expressed with the following particle.

Particle

___ *yori (more) than* ___

By inserting **C yori,** *(more) than* C, in the sentence structure **A wa** "adjective + **desu,**" you may express the comparative idea: **A wa C yori** "adjective + **desu**" implies *A is adjective-er than C.*

Let's consider **Tom-kun wa ōkii desu,** *Tom is big.* By inserting **Makoto-kun yori,** *(more) than Makoto,* in the sentence, we get **Tom-kun wa Makoto-kun yori ōkii desu,** *Tom is bigger than Makoto.*

Examples

Tom-kun wa ōkii desu.	*Tom is big.*
Tom-kun wa Makoto-kun yori ōkii desu.	*Tom is bigger than Makoto.*
Hanako-san wa kirei desu.	*Hanako is pretty.*
Hanako-san wa Yōko-san yori kirei desu.	*Hanako is prettier than Yoko.*

To reinforce the comparison more, the adverb **motto,** *more,* may be put before adjectives.

Examples

Tom-kun wa Makoto-kun yori motto ōkii desu   Tom is much bigger than Makoto.
Hanako-san wa Yōko-san yori motto kirei desu.   *Hanako is much prettier than Yoko.*

You may also express comparative ideas, by inserting **C yori** into

A wa **B** ga "adjective + desu" as follows:

A wa **C** yori **B** ga "adjective + desu," meaning

A is adjective-er than C;

A wa **B** ga **C** yori "adjective + desu," meaning

B is adjective-er than C.

A is the indirect subject and B is the grammatical subject.

Examples

Otōsan wa Eigo ga jōzu desu.   (My) father is good at English.
Otōsan wa watashi yori Eigo ga jōzu desu.   (My) father is better than I am at English.

This is the case of "A is adjective-er (better) than C."

Otōsan wa Eigo ga jōzu desu.   (My) father is good at English.
Otōsan wa Eigo ga Nihon-go yori jōzu desu.   (My) father is better at English than Japanese.

This is the case of "B is adjective-er (better) than C."

You may note that the above sentence **Otōsan wa Eigo ga Nihon-go yori jōzu desu** may be written as **Otōsan wa Nihon-go yori Eigo ga jōzu desu.** You must guess from **Nihon-go yori** whether it is compared with **otōsan** or **Eigo.**

Superlative Degree

Superlatives are made by putting the following adverbs in front of adjectives.

Adverbs

ichi-ban most, best, number one   *mottomo* most, best

Examples

Ringo wa yasui kudamono desu.   *Apples are cheap fruits.*
Ringo wa ichi-ban/mottomo yasui kudamono desu.   *Apples are the cheapest fruits.*

Watashi wa ichigo ga suki desu.   *I like strawberries.*
Watashi wa ichigo ga ichi-ban/mottomo suki desu.   *I like strawberries most.*

Hiroshi-kun wa se ga takai desu. — *Hiroshi is tall.*

Makoto-kun wa se ga ichi-ban/mottomo takai desu. — *Makoto is tallest.*

Conversation 2: Nozomi Is Fastest

Makoto suggests that Tom go to Kyoto by Nozomi.

There are three types of Shinkansen trains (bullet trains) running from Tokyo to Hakata: in order of speed and elegance, they are called Kodama, Hikari and Nozomi. The Kodama is essentially a second-class Shinkansen, relatively slow with many stops, and gives an overall inferior ride compared to the other two types. The Hikari is a first-class train, relatively fast with few stops, and gives a very comfortable ride. The Nozomi is essentially "super-first-class," very fast with fewer stops, and gives a luxurious ride. Announcements on the trains (for stops, snack service, etc.) are made in both Japanese and English, but the Nozomi is much more English-speaker-friendly than the Kodama.

Makoto:	*(Anata wa Tōkyō kara Kyōto made)* **dono kisha de ikimasu ka.**	*By which train do you go (from Tokyo to Kyoto)?*
Tom:	*(Boku wa)* **Kodama de ikimasu.**	*I'm going by Kodama.*
Makoto:	**Hikari wa Kodama yori hayai desu yo.**	*Hikari is faster than Kodama!*
Tom:	**Boku wa Hikari de ikimasu.**	*I will go by Hikari.*
Makoto:	**Nozomi wa mottomo hayai desu yo.**	*Nozomi is fastest!*
Tom:	**Boku wa Nozomi de ikimasu.**	*I'll go by Nozomi.*

 ## Conversation 3: Which Ice Cream Do You Like Best?

Tom and Hanako discuss ice cream using the following vocabulary.

Nouns

aisukurīmu *ice cream*	**banira** *vanilla*	**chokorēto** *chocolate*

Tom:	*Tōkyō wa totemo atsui desu ne.*	*Tokyo is very hot, isn't it?*
Hanako:	*(Hai) sō desu ne.*	*Yes, it is, isn't it?*
	Aisukurīmu o tabemasen ka.	*Would you like to eat ice cream?*
Tom:	*(Boku wa) aisukurīmu ga suki desu.*	*I like ice cream.*
Hanako:	*(Anata wa) dono aisukurīmu ga ichi-ban suki desu ka.*	*Which ice cream do you like best (most)?*
Tom:	*(Boku wa) chokorēto ga ichi-ban suki desu.*	*I like chocolate best.*
Hanako:	*Watashi wa banira ga chokorēto yori suki desu.*	*I like vanilla more than chocolate.*
Tom:	*Are wa kirai na sensei desu.*	*Look, that's the teacher I dislike (dislikable teacher).*
Hanako:	*(Anata wa ano sensei ga) naze kirai desu ka.*	*Why do you dislike him?*
Tom:	*Ano sensei wa Nihon-go no sensei desu.*	*He is the teacher of the Japanese language.*
	Nihon-go wa totemo muzukashii desu.	*Japanese is very difficult.*
Hanako:	*Anata wa Nihon-go ga jōzu desu yo.*	*You're good at Japanese!*

*15.6 Convert ordinary statements into comparative statements by inserting _ **yori**, more than _.*

1. ***Kore wa yasui desu.*** *This is cheap.*

Insert ***are yori,*** *more than that,* to get:

Kore wa are yori yasui desu.

This is cheaper than that.

2. ***Makoto-kun wa hansamu desu.*** *Makoto is handsome.*

Insert ***Hiroshi-kun yori,*** *more than Hiroshi,* to get:

Makoto is more handsome than Hiroshi.

3. ***Ken-kun wa Chūgoku-go ga jōzu desu.*** *Ken is good at Chinese.*

Insert ***Nihon-go yori,*** *more than Japanese,* to get:

Ken is better at Chinese than Japanese.

4. ***Watashi wa yakyū ga suki desu.*** *I like baseball.*

Insert ***tenisu yori,*** *more than tennis,* to get:

I like baseball more than tennis.

15.7. 🔘 *Say the following sentences in Japanese. You may consult Conversation 2. Correct answers are recorded on the track for Exercise 15.7.*

1. Hikari is faster than Kodama.

2. Nozomi is faster than Hikari.

3. Kodama is the slowest.

4. Nozomi is the fastest.

15.8. 🔘 *I shall ask some questions about Conversation 3. Reply to each question aloud in Japanese. Correct answers are recorded at the end of this exercise.*

1. ______________

2. ____

3. ____

15.9. Translate into English:

1. *Nihon no ie wa Kanada no ie yori semai desu.*

____

2. *Amerika-jin wa Nihon-jin yori hana ga takai desu.*

____

3. *Watashi wa chiri ga rekishi yori motto suki desu.*

____

4. *Watashi wa Nihon-go ga ichiban kirai desu.*

____

5. *Tom-kun wa mottomo hansamu desu.*

____

Translate into rōmaji:

6. The mathematics teacher is kinder than the geography teacher.

____

7. This dog is bigger than my younger brother.

____

8. American grapes are much cheaper than Japanese grapes.

____

9. London is the most expensive capital.

____

10. This temple is the biggest temple in Japan.

____

Practice the five katakana characters カ， キ， ク， ケ and コ.

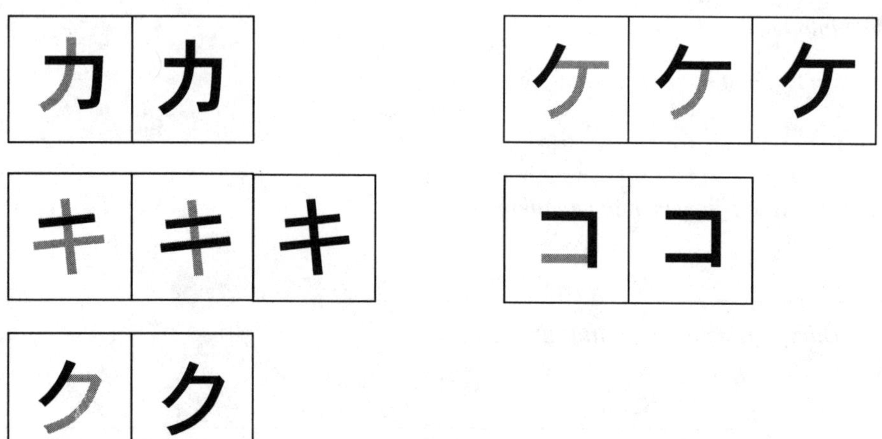

What you must remember from this lesson to proceed to the next lesson:

Adverbs describe adjectives, verbs and adverbs; they precede them.

_ **yori,** *(more) than* _, expresses comparative ideas.

mottomo, *most,* and **ichi-ban,** *most,* express superlative ideas.

16 — That Darned Cat Is in My Garden!

In this lesson you will learn:

Speaking
To talk about positions or locations of things, people and shops
To express "to have"

Grammar
To use the verbs **arimasu** and **imasu**
To understand the difference between the particles **ni** and **de**

In the previous three lessons, you have learned about adjectives:

1. To describe nouns,

2. As complements,

3. To express your emotions (such as liking and disliking),

4. To express your opinions on ability (such as good or bad at a particular skill),

5. To express your desires (such as wanting something),

6. To describe people,

7. To make adverbs and

8. To make comparisons.

In other words, you have learned everything you need to know about adjectives.

In this lesson, you are going to study sentences which express positions or locations of things, people, buildings, etc. You will learn sentences such as "Here is a book," "The cat is in the garden," "Where is the station?," and "There isn't any salt." This sentence structure forms the basis for asking directions, which will be studied in the next lesson.

You will also learn the verb *to have* so that you may be able to say sentences such as "I have a class," "I have a test," "I have a meeting," and so on.

THE VERB *TO BE*

In English, the single verb *to be* can express several different ideas. You can use it to mean:

1. "equals,"

2. "has characteristics of,"

3. "is located" and

4. "is engaged in the activity of."

Typical examples are:

1. This *is* a book. ("this" equals "a book")

2. The book *is* red. ("the book" has the characteristic of "red")

3. Here *is* a book. ("a book" is located at "here")

4. The train *is* running. ("the train" is engaged in the activity of "running")

There are four different categories of words and expressions for *to be* in Japanese.

1. To predicate something with something else, Japanese uses **desu** (lesson 4). That is, **desu** is used to equate one thing with another (*this* with *a book* in sentence 1 above).

2. To indicate condition, or quality, or characteristics, Japanese uses "adjective + **desu**" (lesson 13).

3. The independent verbs **arimasu** and **imasu** may indicate locations/positions.

4. The progressive present tense is expressed by the verb form called **te**-form followed by **imasu** (e.g., **tabete imasu,** *to be eating;* **hanashite imasu,** *to be talking,* **yonde imasu,** *to be reading,* etc.).

In this lesson, you will learn category 3 above of *to be.*

POSITION/LOCATION

Here Is the Book

The following verbs are used to denote position/location.

Verbs (Intransitive)

arimasu to be located/to exist is used to indicate a position/location of a non-living subject.

imasu to be located/to exist is used to indicate a position/location of a living subject.

Arimasu and **imasu** have the sentence structure

place **ni** subject **ga arimasu/imasu.**

The particle **ni** follows the location of the subject and is translated as *at/in;* the particle **ga** follows a grammatical subject (a subject in Japanese, but not necessarily a subject in the English translation).

Examples

Koko ni inu ga imasu.	*Here is a dog. (At this place, a dog is located.)*
Soko ni neko ga imasu.	*There is a cat. (At that place, a cat is located.)*
Niwa ni okāsan ga imasu.	*The mother is in the garden. (In the garden, the mother is located.)*
Koko ni hon ga arimasu.	*Here is a book. (At this place, a book is located.)*
Niwa ni isu ga arimasu.	*A chair is in the garden. (In the garden, a chair is located.)*
Asoko ni basu-sutoppu ga arimasu.	*That (over there) is the bus stop. (Over there, the bus stop is located.)*

    Lesson 16: That Darned Cat Is in My Garden!

Here is a list of shops that you are likely to be interested in visiting. Notice that the suffix **-ya** is put after nouns to make them into shops.

Nouns		*Suffix*
mise shops		*-ya* - *shop*
hana-ya flower shop	*omocha-ya toy shop*	
hon-ya bookstore	*pan-ya bread shop*	
kēki-ya cake shop	*sakana-ya fish shop*	
kudamono-ya fruit shop	*sakaya liquor store*	
niku-ya butcher shop	*sūpāmāketto supermarket*	
(o)kashi-ya confectionery shop	*yaoya vegetable shop*	

And here are some common utensils, spices, and teas.

Nouns		
chawan rice bowl	*koshō pepper*	*kōcha (Indian) tea*
koppu cup	*satō sugar*	*(o)cha green tea*
sara plate	*shio salt*	
	shōyu soy sauce	

The negative tenses for **arimasu** and **imasu** are **arimasen** (or **nai desu**) and **imasen** (or **inai desu**) respectively. We shall be using **arimasen** and **imasen**.

Examples	
Daidokoro ni shio ga arimasen.	*There isn't salt (there is no salt) in the kitchen.*
Niwa ni neko ga imasen.	*There isn't a cat in the garden.*

The particle **mo**, corresponding to *also/too*, replaces **ga** or follows **ni**.

Examples	
Koko ni shio ga arimasu.	*Here is the salt.*
Koko ni koshō mo arimasu.	*Here is the pepper also (as well as salt).*
Koko ni neko ga imasu.	*Here is a cat.*
Asoko ni mo neko ga imasu.	*There too is a cat.*
Koko ni shio mo koshō mo arimasen.	*There is neither salt nor pepper here.*

Interrogatives **dare**, *who*, **doko**, *where*, and **nani**, *what*, are used in the same way as in lesson 5.

Examples	
Koko ni ringo ga arimasu.	*Here is an apple.*
Doko ni ringo ga arimasu ka.	*Where is an apple?*
Koko ni ringo ga arimasu.	*Here is an apple.*
Koko ni nani ga arimasu ka.	*What is here?*
Niwa ni otōsan ga imasu.	*Father is in the garden.*
Niwa ni dare ga imasu ka.	*Who is in the garden?*

A reply to the question _ **ni** _ **ga arimasu/imasu ka** uses the sentence structure **hai arimasu/ imasu** or **iie arimasen/imasen**.

A question is asked

Heya ni terebi ga arimasu ka.	*Is there a TV in the room?*

Possible replies are

Hai arimasu.	*Yes, there is.*
Iie arimasen.	*No, there isn't.*

 ## Conversation 1: Is Your Father or Mother at Home Now?

A stranger visits Tom's parents while they are out shopping.

Woman:	*Ima (o)uchi ni otōsan ka okāsan ga imasu ka.*	*Is (your) father or mother at home now?*
Tom:	*(Ima uchi ni) otōsan mo okāsan mo imasen.*	*Neither (my) father nor (my) mother is at home.*
	San-ji made ni otōsan to okāsan wa depāto kara kaerimasu.	*They will be back from the department store by 3 o'clock.*
Woman:	*Yo-ji ni (watashi wa) mata kimasu.*	*I'll come again at 4 o'clock.*

Japanese garden.

EXERCISES

16.1.

1. *Circle the words that make sense in the blank for the sentence Daidokoro ni _ ga arimasu.*

shio   koshō   satō   otōsan   shōyu   onīsan   watashi   neko   koppu

2. *Circle the words that make sense in the blank for the sentence Daidokoro ni _ ga imasu.*

kōcha   (o)cha   satō   neko   okāsan   sara

        Lesson 16: That Darned Cat Is in My Garden!

16.2. *I shall describe my mother's grocery shopping habits. Answer the questions in rōmaji.*

1. **Okāsan wa doko de kaimono o shimasu ka.**

____

2. **Sūpāmāketto ni hito ga ōzei imasu ka.**

____

3. **Sūpāmāketto wa benri desu ka. (Sūpāmāketto wa) fuben desu ka.**

____

4. **Sūpāmāketto ni oishii pan ga arimasu ka.**

____

5. **Doko ni oishii pan ga arimasu ka.**

____

6. **Okāsan wa niku-ya to sakana-ya e mo ikimasu ka.**

____

16.3. *I shall ask some questions about Conversation 1. Listen to the questions, and reply to each question aloud in Japanese. Correct answers are recorded at the end of this exercise.*

1. ____

2. ____

3. ____

4. ____

16.4. *Translate into English:*

1. *Asoko ni depāto ga arimasu.* ____

2. *Soko ni Makoto-kun ga imasu.* ______________________________________

3. *Niwa ni otōsan to okāsan ga imasu.* __________________________________

4. *Koko ni shio mo koshō mo arimasu.* __________________________________

5. *Daidokoro ni neko ga imasu. Niwa ni mo neko ga imasu.*

____

6. *Koko ni nani ga arimasu ka.* _______________________________

7. *Doko ni anata no pan-ya ga arimasu ka.*

____

Translate into rōmaji:

8. Over there, (there) are father's eyeglasses.

____

9. At that fruit shop, (there) are very delicious apples and oranges.

____

10. In the hospital, (there) are medical doctors and nurses.

____

11. Betty is not in the garden. (In the garden, there is not Betty.)

____

12. Where is the bank? ____

13. What is over there? _______________________________________

14. Who is in the house? ______________________________________

I DON'T HAVE MONEY BUT I HAVE (SPARE) TIME

Arimasu is also used to express *to have* where the item in possession is not an animate (living) object. It has the sentence structure

> **indirect subject** wa **grammatical subject** ga arimasu.

Wa follows an *animate* indirect subject (a subject, in English translation).

Ga follows a grammatical subject (an object, in English translation).

        Lesson 16: That Darned Cat Is in My Garden!

Let us consider the sentence **watashi wa tesuto ga arimasu. Watashi wa** is translated as *as for me*, and **tesuto ga arimasu** is translated as *a test exists*. So the literal translation is *as for me, a test exists*. But it is more appropriate to translate the sentence as *I have a test*. Here are some words which may come in handy with this sentence structure.

Nouns

jikan (spare) time	*kane* money	*pūru* pool	*tesuto* test

Examples

Anata wa jikan ga arimasu ka.	*Do you have (spare) time?*
Hai arimasu.	*Yes, I do.*
Watashi wa (o)kane ga arimasen.	*I don't have money.*
Kono neko wa namae ga mada arimasen.	*This cat does not have a name yet.*

In the sentence structure **_ ni _ ga arimasu, arimasu** may be translated as *to have* as well as *to be located* or *to exist*, as shown in the following examples.

Examples

Depāto ni toire ga arimasu.	*Department stores have toilets. (At department stores, there are toilets.)*
Gakkō ni pūru ga arimasen.	*The school has no swimming pool. (At the school, there is not a swimming pool.)*

Since both **ni** and **de** can mean *at/in* in English, you must be careful about which one you use. **De** is used when *an action/event takes place "at/in* the place" while **ni** is used to *locate "at/in* the place."

Examples

Consider *Watashi-tachi wa pātī ga arimasu, We have a party.*

Insert *gakkō de* to get:

Watashi-tachi wa gakkō de pātī ga arimasu.	*We have a party at the school.*
Watashi-tachi wa gakkō de tesuto ga arimasu.	*We have a test at the school.*
Watashi-tachi wa gakkō ni pūru ga arimasu.	*We have a pool at the school.*

Notice that while "a pool" is a thing *located* at the school, "a party" and "a test" are *events that take place* at the school.

 You may talk of having "living things" by using **imasu.**

Examples

Hanako-san wa otōto ga imasu.	*Hanako has a younger brother.*
Obasan wa kodomo ga imasen.	*(My) aunt does not have a child.*

It is interesting to note that you ask for a fish in a shop by saying (mise ni) **sakana ga arimasu ka,** *do you have fish?*, while you say (ike ni) **sakana ga imasu ka,** *is there a fish (in the pond)?* The fish sold at a shop, whether it is dead or alive, is regarded as an object of food and is treated as dead.

Conversation 2: Indian Curry Is Hot! Do You Have Water?

Tom runs into difficulties when he is served a dish of Indian curry at Makoto's house.

I-Adjectives

amai sweet (taste)	*karai* hot (spicy)	*nigai* bitter (taste)	*shio-karai* salty

Makoto:	*(Anata wa)* **ranchi o boku no uchi de tabe-masen ka.**	*Would you like to eat lunch at my house?*
Tom:	**Hai tabemasu.**	*Yes, I would.*
	Makoto's mother serves them lunch.	
Makoto:	*(Kore wa)* **karēraisu desu.**	*This is Indian curry.*
Tom:	*(Anata wa karēraisu o)* **supūn de tabemasu ka.**	*Do you eat it with a spoon?*
Makoto:	**Hai supūn de tabemasu.**	*Yes, I eat it with a spoon.*
Tom:	*(Anata wa)* **naifu to hōku ga arimasu ka.**	*Do you have a knife and a fork?*
Makoto:	**Hai arimasu.**	*Yes, I do.*
Tom:	**Naifu to hōku o kudasai.**	*May I have a knife and a fork please?*
	(Anata wa) **shio ga arimasu ka.**	*Do you have salt?*
Makoto:	**Hai arimasu.**	*Yes, I have.*
	Karēraisu wa karai desu yo.	*Indian curry is hot!*
Tom:	*(Anata wa)* **mizu ga arimasu ka.**	*Do you have water?*
Makoto:	**Hai arimasu.**	*Yes, I have.*
Tom:	**Mizu o kudasai.**	*May I have water please?*
	Karēraisu wa totemo karai desu ne.	*Indian curry is very hot, isn't it?*

Conversation 3: What Should We Buy for Hanako?

Makoto and Tom buy a birthday present for Hanako at a department store.

Noun   Na-Adjective

aidea idea	*suteki na* lovely

Expression

Kore wa dō desu ka	*How about this?, How do you like this?*

Makoto:	*(Boku-tachi wa)* **nani o Hanako-san ni kaimasu ka.**	*What should we buy for Hanako?*
Tom:	**Hon wa dō desu ka.**	*How about a book?*
Makoto:	**Hanako-san wa hon o amari yomimasen.**	*Hanako doesn't read books much.*
Tom:	**Sētā wa dō desu ka.**	*How about a sweater?*

Makoto:	*Sore wa ii aidea desu.*	*That's a good idea.*
	(Boku-tachi wa sētā wa) ikura no sētā ni shimasu ka.	*How much do we want to spend (what price of the sweater do we decide on)?*
Tom:	*Go-sen-en wa dō desu ka.*	*How about ¥5,000?*
Makoto:	*Kore wa boku no ni-sen go-hyaku-en desu.*	*This is my ¥2,500.*

***

Tom:	*Ano sētā wa ikura desu ka.*	*How much is that sweater?*
Clerk:	*(Are wa) nana-sen-en desu.*	*It's ¥7,000.*
Tom:	*(Depāto ni are yori) motto yasui sētā ga arimasu ka.*	*Do you (the department store) have a much cheaper sweater (than that)?*
Clerk:	*Kore wa dō desu ka.*	*How about this?*
Tom:	*(Kore wa) suteki desu. (Kore wa) ikura desu ka.*	*It's lovely. How much?*
Clerk:	*(Kore wa) go-sen-en desu.*	*It's ¥5,000.*
Tom:	*(Kore wa) totemo yasui desu. (Depāto ni) akai sētā ga arimasu ka.*	*It's very cheap. Do you (the department store) have a red sweater?*
Clerk:	*Hai arimasu.*	*Yes, we do.*
Tom:	*(Boku-tachi wa) kore ni shimasu.*	*We'll take this one (we shall decide on this).*

EXAMPLES

16.5. *I shall tell you Hanako's family's plan for tomorrow. Answer the questions in complete sentences in rōmaji.*

1. *Ashita Hanako-san wa nani ga arimasu ka.*

____

2. *Ashita onēsan wa daigaku de jugyō ga arimasu ka.*

____

3. *Ashita onēsan wa nani ga arimasu ka.*

____

4. *Imōto wa gakkō ga arimasu ka.*___________________

5. *Otōsan wa kaisha de nani ga arimasu ka.*

____

6. *Okāsan wa nani ga arimasu ka.* _______________________

16.6. Translate into English:

1. *Ashita no asa watashi-tachi wa Eigo no tesuto ga arimasu.*

____

2. *Ashita watashi wa Hanako-san no bāsudē pātī ga arimasu.*

____

3. *Anata wa kodomo-san ga imasu ka.*

____

4. *Ima watashi wa jikan ga arimasen.*

____

Translate into rōmaji:

5. I have money. ____

6. (My) father has a meeting in Tokyo. _______________________________

7. Do you have a TV in (your) room?_______________________________

8. Do you have an older brother? _______________________________

16.7. I shall ask some questions about Conversation 2. Listen to the questions and reply to each question aloud in Japanese. Correct answers are recorded at the end of this exercise.

1. ____

2. ____

3. ____

4. ____

5. ____

16.8. I shall ask some questions about Conversation 3. Listen to the questions and reply to each question aloud in Japanese. Correct answers are recorded at the end of this exercise.

1. ____

 Lesson 16: That Darned Cat Is in My Garden!

2. ____

3. ____

4. ____

WRITING EXERCISE: KATAKANA FOR *SA, SHI, SU, SE* AND *SO*

Practice the five katakana characters サ， シ， ス， セ and ソ.

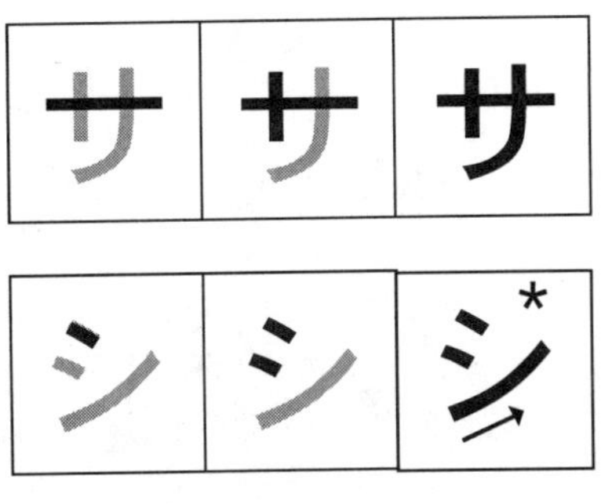

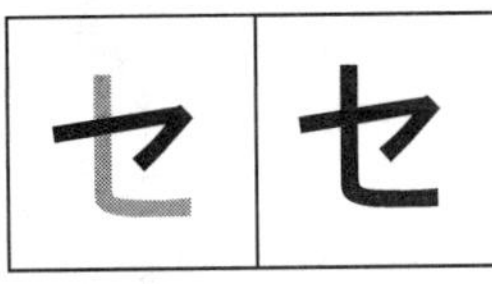

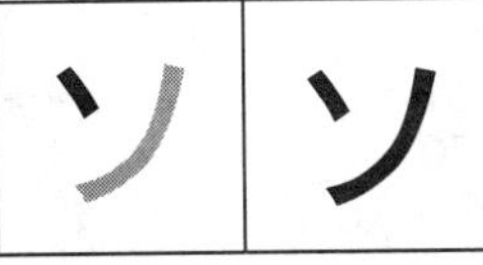

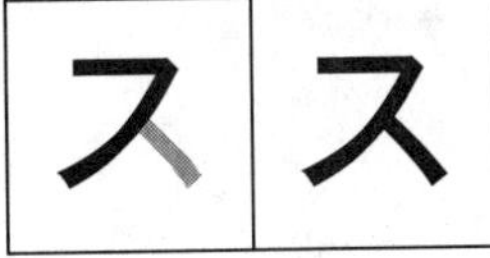

> **What you must remember from this lesson to proceed
> to the next lesson:**
>
> _ **ni** _ **ga arimasu** is used to express the location of a non-living subject.
>
> _ **ni** _ **ga imasu** is used to express the location of an animate (living)
> subject.
>
> _ **wa** _ **ga arimasu/imasu** expresses the idea of "to have."

*Note: This stroke is drawn from the lower end to the higher end.

Lesson 16: That Darned Cat Is in My Garden!   185

17

I'm Lost! Where Is the Station?

In this lesson you will learn:

Speaking

To use words such as "on," "beside," "above" and "below" to describe the location of things

To use words such as "before" and "after" to talk about when you do something

To ask for directions, and understand directions that are given to you

Grammar

To use the particle **no** to connect two nouns

To use the particles **mae** and **ato**

To understand the expressions associated with directions

In the previous lesson, you learned to express locations of things, people, buildings, and so on; you can now say sentences such as "Where is a station?," "The station is over there" and "My sister is in the garden." So when you get lost in Japan, you know how to ask for directions, and don't you ever think that you won't need to. With so many meandering twists and turns, you cannot help but get lost in Japan, and it is just a matter of time before you have to ask for directions to get back to familiar surroundings. Although you know how to ask for directions, you do not yet understand the directions that people will give you.

In this lesson, I shall expand the sentences you have learned in the previous lesson so that you will be able to understand sentences such as "The station is *in front of* the department store" and "The book store is *beside* the post office." You will also learn to understand sentences such as "Turn right at the T-junction" and "Go straight through the traffic light." After all, not every place you want to get to will be visible and easy to find. After this lesson, you can go gallivanting anywhere you fancy without ever worrying about getting lost: you will be able to get back to where you started by asking directions.

NOUN `NO` NOUN

You have learned in lesson 6 that **A no B** indicates that A is a possessor of B (translated as *A's B*), A is the origin of B, or A describes B (translated as *B of/for/in/on A*).

Examples

otōsan no hon	*father's book*	(A is the possessor of B)
Furansu no uta	*French song*	(A is the origin of B)

getsu-yōbi no asa	*Monday morning (morning of Monday)*	(A describes B)
asa no hachi-ji	*eight o'clock in the morning*	(A describes B)
Nihon-go no hon	*a book in the Japanese language*	(A describes B)

Prepositions of Position

No is also used to connect two nouns in cases where, in English, a preposition of position is used. Wow! "Preposition of position" sounds mighty complicated. But don't let it worry you because a *preposition of position* is just a little word placed before a word denoting a position. For example, "at" of "the train *at* the platform" and "in" of "the chair *in* the garden" are prepositions of position. They are placed before "the platform" and "the garden" which describe positions of "the train" and "the chair." So, **A no B** is translated as *B in/at A*. Note that the particle **ni,** *in/at,* or any other particle denoting position (such as **de,** *in/on/at*) may not be used to connect two nouns.

Examples

niwa no isu	*the chair in the garden*
ike no mizu	*pond water (water in the pond)*
sora no tori	*the bird in the sky*
Tōkyō no tatemono	*the building in Tokyo*

Nouns

| *ike* pond | *sora* sky | *tatemono* building |

Is It on the Desk? Beside the Desk? Under the Desk?

Let us look at the following list of "nouns of position."

Nouns of Position

mae front part, position in front	*ue* upper part, space over (something)
ushiro back part, position behind	*shita* lower part, space under (something)
yoko side part, position beside	

| *tonari* next door, position next to | *naka* middle, inside |
| *chikaku* nearby | *soto* outside |

A "noun + **no** + noun of position" produces an adverbial phrase such as "in front of the house," "on the table," "under the desk," etc. For example, **no mae** implies *the position in front of,* **no ue** implies *the upper part of,* **no naka** implies *the inside of,* and so on. Hence, **ie no mae** is literally translated as *the position in front of the house,* which is more appropriately translated as *in front of the house.* In the examples below, the appropriate translations are given, while the literal translations are given in parentheses.

Examples

ie no soto	*outside the house (outside of the house)*
tēburu no ue	*on the table (upper part of the table)*
heya no naka	*in the room (inside of the room)*
ie no mae	*in front of the house (front part of the house)*
tsukue no shita	*under the desk (space under the desk)*

| *okāsan no yoko* | *beside the mother (position beside the mother)* |
| *anata no ushiro* | *behind you (position behind you)* |

Betty-san to Robert-kun wa karate o ie no soto de shimasu.	*Betty and Robert practice karate outside the house.*
Okāsan no ushiro ni otōto ga imasu.	*There is (my) younger brother behind (my) mother.*
Tsukue no ue ni hon ga arimasu.	*There is a book on the desk.*
Niwa no tēburu no shita ni neko ga imasu.	*There is a cat under the table in the garden.*

Do You Wash Your Hands before Dinner? Or after Dinner?

Let us look at the following words:

Nouns

ato (time) after
mae (time) before

"Noun" **no mae/ato** is used to express time *before/after* "noun." They may be followed by **ni**.

Examples

| *Gohan no mae ni watashi wa te o araimasu.* | *I wash (my) hands before meals.* |
| *Ban-gohan no ato ni watashi wa terebi o mimasu.* | *I watch TV after dinner.* |

EXERCISES

17.1. *Say the following phrases using the structure _ **no** _. The correct answers are recorded on the track for Exercise 17.1.*

1. in the house

2. outside the house

3. near the house

4. beside the house

5. in front of the house

6. behind the house

7. on the desk

8. under the desk

17.2. *Write either **no** or **de** in the blanks.*

1. *Cute wa kawa* _____________ *mizu o nomimasu. Cute drinks water in the river.*

2. *Cute wa niwa* _____________ *gohan o tabemasu. Cute eats his meals in the garden.*

3. *Kisha* _____________ *naka de tabemasen ka. Would you like to eat on the train?*

17.3. *Look at the picture and write rōmaji in the blanks.*

1. *Tsukue no* _________________________ *ni hon ga arimasu.*

2. *Tsukue no* _________________________ *ni neko ga imasu.*

3. *Tsukue no* _________________________ *ni isu ga arimasu.*

4. *Tsukue no* _________________________ *ni enpitsu ga arimasu.*

17.4. *Look at the illustration on page 193 and listen to the statements. If the statement is correct, write O; if the statement is wrong, write X.*

1. _______ 2. _______ 3. _______ 4. _______ 5. _______ 6. _______

17.5. *Translate into English:*

1. *Kono inu wa toire no mizu o nomimasu.*

____

2. *Tsukue no ue ni anata no hon ga arimasu yo.*

____

3. *Ie no naka ni otōsan to okāsan ga imasu.*

____

4. *Depāto no chikaku ni hon-ya ga arimasu ka.*

____

5. *Watashi no otōto wa manga o basu no naka de yomimasu.*

____

6. *Gakkō no mae ni byōin ga arimasu.*

____

7. *Ranchi no ato ni anata wa nani o shimasu ka.*

____

8. *Tesuto no mae ni watashi wa benkyō o shimasen.*

____

Translate into rōmaji:

9. Buildings in New York City *(Nyūyōku)* are very tall.

____

10. On the desk, there is a pencil.

____

11. In the sea, there are large fishes.

____

12. In front of the hospital, there is a flower shop.

____

13. The post office is beside that big department store.

____

14. What is on the table in the kitchen?

____

15. After dinner, I take a bath.

____

16. Before the movie, would you like to go to a restaurant?

____

Arimasu is used to ask a direction. Here is a list of words which are associated with directions.

Nouns

hō *direction (of travel/motion)*	**dōro** *road, way, highway*	**hantai** *opposite*
hōkō *direction(s)*	**michi** *road, path, way*	**hidari** *left*
kōsaten *intersection*	**shingō** *traffic light*	**migi** *right*
tsukiatari *T-junction*		

Verbs (Intransitive)

magarimasu turn
norimasu ride (on)

Adverb

massugu straight through

Suffix

-gawa - side

When you want to mention the point (an intersection, a T-junction) at which the turn is to be made (e.g., "turn right *at the intersection*," "go left *at the T-junction*") or proceed further ("go straight *through the intersection*"), the point (an intersection, a T-junction) is followed by **o** as shown below.

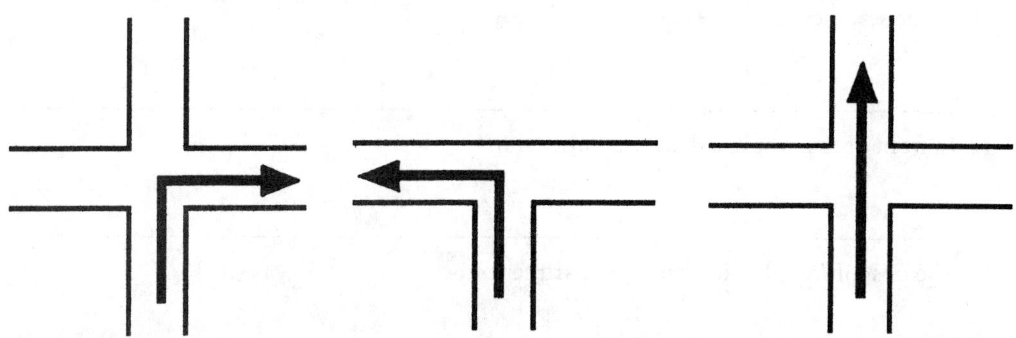

Kōsaten o migi e ikimasu/ magarimasu.

Go/turn (to) right at the intersection.

Tsukiatari o hidari e magarimasu/ikimasu.

Turn/go (to) left at the T-junction.

Kōsaten o massugu ikimasu.

Go straight through (at) the intersection.

 ## Conversation 1: Where Is a Bookstore?

Tom asks Hanako for directions to a bookstore.

Tom:	*Hanako-san. Doko ni hon-ya ga arima-su ka.*	*Where is a bookstore, Hanako?*

Hanako:	*(Anata wa) daigaku no mae de* basu ni norimasu**.*	You get (ride) on a bus in front of the college.

Hanako:	*(Anata wa) daigaku no mae de* basu ni norimasu**.*	You get (ride) on a bus in front of the college.
	(Anata wa) dōbutsuen no mae de basu kara orimasu.*	You get off (from) the bus in front of the zoo.
	Soko kara (anata wa) depāto no hō e massugu ikimasu.	From there, you go straight toward the direction of the department store.
	Hidari-gawa ni yūbinkyoku ga arimasu.	There is a post office on (your) left side.
	(Anata wa) yūbinkyoku no mae no shin-gō o hidari e magarimasu.	You turn to (your) left at the traffic light in front of the post office.
	Migi-gawa ni hon-ya ga arimasu.	On (your) right side, there is the book-store.

Conversation 2: Where Is a Bus Stop?

Tom is ready to return and can't find a bus stop; he asks a man for help.

Tom:	*Sumimasen. Koko wa doko desu ka.*	Excuse me. Where is this place?
Man:	*(Koko wa) Higashi-kōen no yoko desu yo.*	This (place) is beside Higashi Park!
Tom:	*Doko ni basu-sutoppu ga arimasu ka.*	Where is a bus stop?
Man:	*(Anata wa) doko e ikimasu ka.*	Where are you going?
Tom:	*(Boku wa) eki e ikimasu.*	I'm going to the station.
Man:	*(Anata wa) ano shingō o migi e magarimasu.*	Turn right at that traffic light.
	(Anata wa) depāto no hō e massugu ikimasu.	Go straight in the direction of the department store.
	Depāto no hantai-gawa ni basu-sutoppu ga arimasu.	At the opposite side of the depart-ment store, there's a bus stop.
	Basu-sutoppu wa ginkō no mae desu.	The bus stop is in front of the bank.

*It should be understood that **de** denotes an action taking place *on/at/in* a location while **ni** denotes *on/at/in* the location.

"A vehicle" + **ni norimasu means *ride on* "a vehicle."

Buses

Japanese metro (inner city) buses are one-man buses equipped with prerecorded messages and signs to tell you the next stops. The fare may be fixed or based on the distance of your ride. A bus has usually two doors, one near the driver and one halfway along the bus (the locations of the doors are the same as in most metro buses in the U.S.). You get on a bus at the center door, and you get off from the door near the driver. In the case where the fare depends on the distance you travel, you must take a control ticket with a number from a dispensing machine as you board the bus. At the front of the bus inside, there is a table of numbers with fares below which change accordingly. The numbers represent stops where one got on the bus, and the prices below show the fares at the next bus stop. When you get off the bus from the door near the driver, you put the control ticket and the exact fare in the box provided just beside the driver. There is a change machine beside the driver for coins as well as for bills. In many cities, you can buy a pre-paid bus pass which you can scan through as you get on and off the bus.

For an intercity bus (a bus between cities), you get on and off the bus from the front door near the driver, and you put the exact fare in the box provided just beside the driver when you get off the bus.

Vehicles are driven on the lefthand side of the road in Japan.

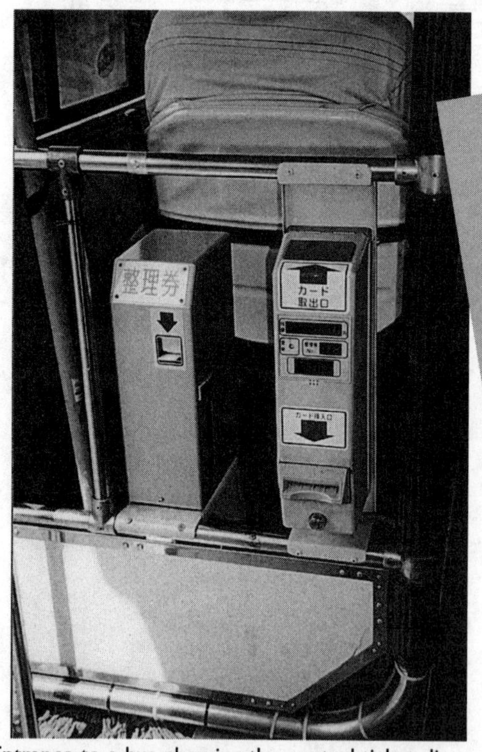

Entrance to a bus, showing the control ticket dispenser. You must take a token or insert and retrieve your pre-paid bus card.

Pre-paid bus cards.

EXERCISES

17.6. Look at the map. You are driving a car, going from southwest to northeast. Say aloud what you can see at each exit, using the sentence structure _ **ni** _ **ga arimasu.** *Correct answers are recorded on the track for Exercise 17.6.*

1. ______________________________

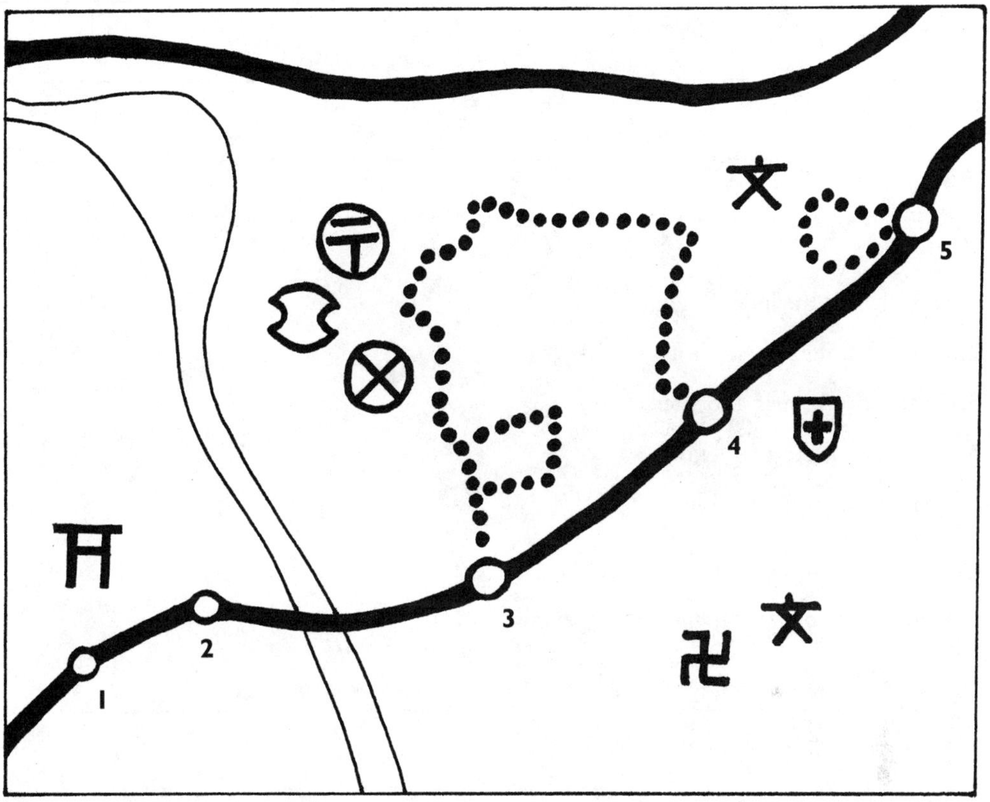

*This symbol for "temple" is one you may see frequently in Japan.

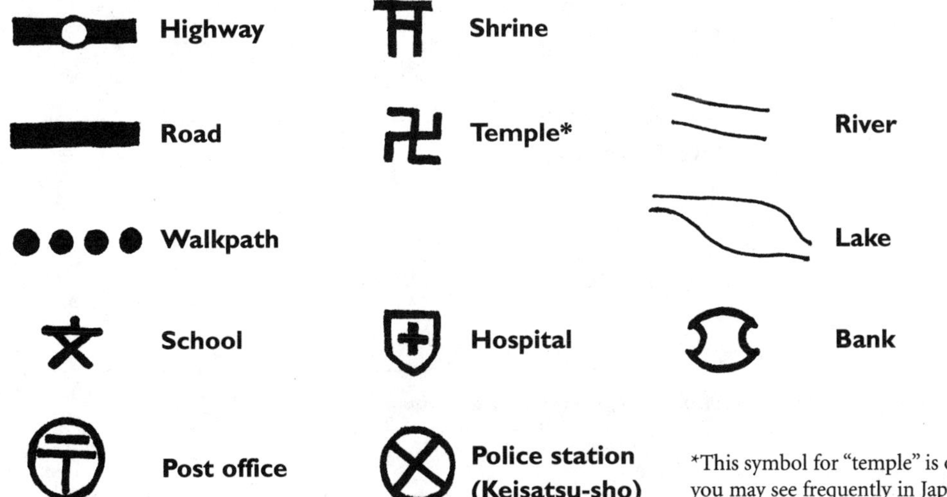

2. ____

3. *Hidari-gawa ni* _______________________________________

   Migi-gawa ni ____

   Ushiro ni ____

4. ____

5. ____

17.7. *Say the following sentences in Japanese. Correct answers are recorded on the track for Exercise 17.7.*

1. Turn right at the intersection

2. Turn left at the intersection

3. Go straight through the intersection

4. Turn right at the T-junction

5. Turn left at the T-junction

17.8. *Translate into English:*

1. *Watashi wa kono michi o massugu ikimasu.*

   ____

2. *Basu wa shingō o migi e magarimasu.*

   ____

3. *(Anata wa) ano tsukiatari o hidari e magarimasu.*

   ____

4. *San-ban no basu wa Higashi-kōen e ikimasu.*

   ____

5. *Watashi wa (o)tera no hantai-gawa de kuruma o tomemasu.*

   ____

6. *(Anata wa) hana-ya no mae no kōsaten o migi e magarimasu.*

   ____

7. (You) go straight through that traffic light.

____

8. (You) turn right at the T-junction.

____

9. This bus will go in the direction of Mt. Atago.

____

10. There is a bread shop at the opposite side of the station.

____

11. (You) turn left before that hotel.

____

12. On (your) left side, there is a post office.

____

WRITING EXERCISE: KATAKANA FOR *TA, CHI, TSU, TE* AND *TO*

Practice the five katakana characters タ, チ, ツ, テ and ト.

 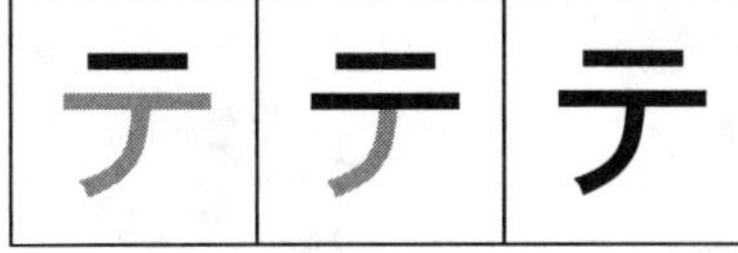

 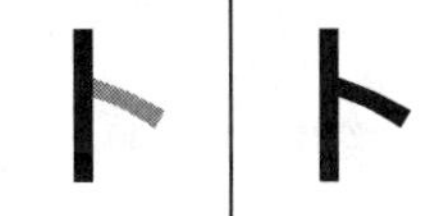

What you must remember from this lesson to proceed to the next lesson:
> **No** is used to join two nouns using the structure **A no B,** and it is translated as *B at/in/of A.*

It Will Rain Tomorrow!

In this lesson you will learn:

Speaking
To talk about things that happen naturally
To talk about people causing things to happen
To talk about things that are being done
To talk about the weather
To talk about what people can do and understand

Grammar
To understand the differences between Japanese and English intransitive verbs
To understand when to use the particles **ga** and **wa** after a subject
To use the verbs **dekimasu** and **wakarimasu**

So far you have learned the following intransitive verbs: **desu,** the verbs of motion, and **arimasu** and **imasu.**

In this lesson, you will learn the difference between Japanese and English intransitive verbs so that you can use Japanese intransitive verbs correctly. You will also learn when to use **wa** and when to use **ga** after subjects for intransitive verbs. You will learn the intransitive verbs **dekimasu** and **wakarimasu** to express abilities, so that you'll be able to say sentences such as "I can speak Japanese," "I understand Japanese," etc. In addition, you will learn how to talk about weather: you will be able to say sentences such as "It will rain tomorrow," "The snow will melt," and so on.

INTRANSITIVE VERBS

Intransitive **V•masu**-verbs (**V•masu**-verbs which may not have direct objects) have the sentence structure

subject **wa/ga V•masu.**

Wa follows a subject responsible for the action.

Ga follows a subject where action is presented as natural occurrence.

You have learned so far that the subjects for the verbs of motion are followed by **wa** (lesson 11) while the subject for **arimasu/imasu** is followed by **ga** (lesson 16). This is not quite true. Because the subtlety of whether to use **wa** or **ga** was a little too much for you to handle at the time, I simplified the rule. Well, you are finally ready for the subtlety of **wa** and **ga,** and I shall now explain it.

Let's consider **watashi wa yama e ikimasu,** *I go to the mountain.* In this sentence, "going to the mountain" is an *action performed* by I. Because **watashi,** *I,* is responsible for the action, it is followed by **wa.**

Let's consider **basu ga kimasu,** *the bus is coming* or *the bus comes.* "The bus coming" is a natural occurrence and hence the subject **basu,** *bus,* is followed by **ga.**

Let's consider **niwa ni otōsan ga imasu,** *father is (located) in the garden.* Because **imasu** means *to be located* or *to exist,* there is no action performed by father: "father" is merely *located* or *exists* in the garden. Hence **otōsan,** *father,* is followed by **ga.** But, the subject may be followed by **wa** if the subject is responsible for being there. For instance, **koko ni watashi wa imasu,** *I shall be here,* implies a decision or determination of the speaker, that is, **watashi** is responsible for being here and therefore it is followed by **wa.**

TWO REASONS FOR WHY THE TRANSLATION OF VERBS IS TRICKY

The translation of an English verb into a Japanese verb (Reason 1) or vice versa (Reason 2) may sometimes be confusing.

Transitive and Intransitive Verbs

REASON 1: In English, in some cases the same verb acts as either a transitive or an intransitive verb.

Example

I stop a car. ("stop" is a transitive verb in this case)

A car stops. ("stop" is an intransitive verb in this case)

In English, the verb "stop" may be both transitive and intransitive. For the sentence with the transitive verb, the direct object for the verb *(a car)* is stated; for the sentence with the intransitive verb, the sentence is complete without a direct object. The sentence with a transitive verb always states the person responsible for the action, while the action is stated as a natural occurrence in the sentence with an intransitive verb.

In Japanese, transitive and intransitive verbs are almost always different. The only exception is **owarimasu** which is both transitive, meaning *finish/end (something),* and intransitive, meaning *be finished;* the intransitive verb **owarimasu** also has a transitive counterpart **oemasu,** *finish (something).*

So when you are translating an English verb that may be either transitive and intransitive, you must make sure of which it is.

     Lesson 18: It Will Rain Tomorrow!

The following example shows that **tomemasu,** *stop (something),* is a transitive verb while **tomari-masu,** *stop,* is an intransitive verb; but both would be translated as *stop* in English.

Example

Watashi wa kuruma o **tomemasu.**	*I stop a car.*
Kuruma ga **tomarimasu.**	*A car stops.*

Here are some intransitive verbs and their transitive counterparts in Japanese, although in English they are same word.

Verbs (Intransitive)

Verbs (Transitive)

Verbs (Intransitive)	Verbs (Transitive)
hajimarimasu begin	*hajimemasu* begin (something)
kowaremasu break	*kowashimasu* break (something)
tomarimasu stop	*tomemasu* stop (something)
ugokimasu move	*ugokashimasu* move (something)

Examples

Benkyō ga hajimarimasu.	*The lesson (study) will start.*
Watashi wa benkyō o hajimemasu.	*I shall start (my) study.*
Koppu ga kowaremasu.	*The cup breaks.*
Watashi wa koppu o kowashimasu.	*I break a cup.*
Basu ga ugokimasu.	*The bus will move.*
Watashi wa tsukue o ugokashimasu.	*I shall move a desk.*

Here are more intransitive verbs in Japanese. You use **arukimasu** for "I *walk,*" but not for "I *walk* my dog" since **arukimasu** is an intransitive verb and cannot be used with direct object "my dog."

Verbs (Intransitive)

aimasu meet	*nemasu* sleep	*furimasu* fall (rain, snow)
arukimasu walk	*okimasu* wake up	*tokemasu* melt
hatarakimasu work	*oyogimasu* swim	*yamimasu* stop (rain, snow)
nakimasu cry	*tomarimasu* stay (overnight)	

It should be pointed out that *meet* is usually transitive in English, but the Japanese equivalent **aimasu** is intransitive and follows **ni.**

Examples

Watashi wa Robert-kun ni hon-ya de aimasu.	*I meet Robert at the bookstore.*
Akachan wa arukimasu.	*The baby walks.*
Watashi wa kisha no naka de nemasu.	*I sleep in the train.*

Below is some vocabulary associated with natural phenomena.

Nouns

Conjunction

Nouns		Conjunction
ame rain	*tenki* weather	*matawa* or
kumo cloud	*kumori* cloudy weather	

niji rainbow	*hare* fine weather
yuki snow	

Examples

Haru yama no yuki ga tokemasu.	*In spring, mountain snow melts.*
Gogo ame ga yamimasu.	*(The) rain will stop in the afternoon.*
Ashita yuki ga furimasu.	*It will snow tomorrow.*

Active and Passive Verbs

Before going to the second reason that the translation of some Japanese verbs into English is sometimes confusing, let me explain English *verbs of doing* (action verbs) in some detail. You may remember that there are two types of verbs of doing (page 310): transitive verbs, which have direct objects, and intransitive verbs, which do not have direct objects but make a complete thought. Let us consider the sentence with a transitive verb: "I eat the apple." The verb "eat" is called an active verb because the subject, "I," *performs an action* of "eating." The sentence "I eat the apple" may be put in a different way without altering its meaning: "the apple is eaten by me." The verb "is eaten" is called a *passive verb* because the subject "the apple" is described as *experiencing rather than performing the action*. Notice that the direct object of the active verb is now the subject of the passive verb. Any sentence with an active transitive verb (the sentence with a direct object) may be made into a sentence with a passive verb in English; the passive verb is obtained by putting the verb "to be" (*is, am, are*) in front of the verb past particle (past particles of *eat* and *make* are *eaten* and *made*). Sentences with intransitive verbs may not be made into passive forms since they do not have direct objects. In Japanese, passive verbs may not be obtained from active verbs as in English.

Now let me state the second reason that the translation of some Japanese verbs into English verbs is tricky.

REASON 2: In some cases, Japanese intransitive verbs are translated as passive verbs in English. Here are some of them.

Verbs (Intransitive)

dekimasu be made, be produced, be possible	*kikoemasu* be heard
kimarimasu be decided	*miemasu* be visible
okuremasu be late	*umaremasu* be born
tsukimasu be accompanied, be included	*wakarimasu* be understandable

Examples

Pan ga dekimasu.	*The bread is made.*
Ongaku ga niwa de kikoemasu.	*The music is heard in the garden.*
Watashi wa deito ni okuremasu.	*I shall be late for a date.*
Resutoran ga kimarimasu.	*The restaurant is decided (upon).*

When you are translating a Japanese verb into English, care must be taken to determine whether it is an active verb or a passive verb in the English translation.

 **Conversation I: Do You Have a Room?**

Tom visits a youth hostel. The following vocabulary appears in the conversation.

*chekkuauto** check out	*kagi* key
*ik-kai*** *first floor*	*yūsuhosuteru* youth hostel

Tom:	*Konnichiwa. (Yūsuhosuteru ni) heya ga ari-masu ka.*	*Good afternoon. Do you (the youth hostel) have a room?*
Clerk:	*Hai arimasu.*	*Yes, we do.*
Tom:	*(Heya wa) ikura desu ka.*	*How much is it?*
Clerk:	*(Heya wa) go-sen-en desu. Asa-gohan to ban-gohan ga tsukimasu.*	*It's ¥5,000. Breakfasts and dinners are included.*
Tom:	*(Yūsuhosuteru ni) furo ga arimasu ka.*	*Do you (the youth hostel) have a bath?*
Clerk:	*Hai arimasu. (Furoba wa) ik-kai desu.*	*Yes, we do. It's on the first floor.*
Tom:	*Kyō boku wa (yūsuhosuteru ni) tomarima-su.*	*I'll stay tonight (today).*
	Ashita ame ga furimasu ka.	*Will it rain tomorrow?*
Clerk:	*Hai furimasu.*	*Yes, it will.*

*18.1. Write **wa** or **ga** in the blanks and then translate the sentences into English.*

1. *Isu _ga_ kowaremasu yo.*   <u>The chair will break!</u>

2. *Sorosoro basu _____________ kimasu yo.* _______________________________________

3. *Sugu eiga _____________ hajimarimasu.* _______________________________________

4. *Kono natsu watashi _____________ Eigo no benkyō o hajimemasu.*

____

5. *Kisha _____________ ugokimasu yo.* _______________________________________

6. *Ōkii yama _____________ miemasu.* _______________________________________

Che of **chekkuauto** is introduced as a new Japanese syllable to describe the sound of an English word, which has now become a Japanese word.
Ichi + kai, *one + floor,* has undergone a phonetic change and become **ik-kai,** *first floor.*

7. *Watashi-tachi* _______________ *jugyō ni okuremasu yo.*

____

8. *Tori no koe* _______________ *niwa de kikoemasu.*

____

18.2. *I shall say a sentence such as "I break a cup," "I stop a car," etc. Change it into a sentence using the format "A cup breaks," "A car stops," etc. and say it aloud. Correct answers are recorded at the end of this exercise.*

1. ____

2. ____

3. ____

4. ____

18.3. *Listen to the track for Exercise 18.3. I shall tell you about my father's work days. Answer the questions in rōmaji.*

1. *Otōsan wa nan-ji ni okimasu ka.* ____

2. *Otōsan wa kaisha e basu de ikimasu ka.* _______________________________________

3. *Otōsan wa doko de hatarakimasu ka.* ____

4. *Otōsan wa nan-ji ni uchi e kaerimasu ka.* ____________________________________

18.4. *Look at the weather forecast. Say the weather forecast for each day of the week aloud. The correct answers are recorded at the end of this exercise.*

1. ____

SUN	MON	TUE	WED	THU	FRI	SAT
日	月	火	水	木	金	土

                Lesson 18: It Will Rain Tomorrow!

2. ____

3. ____

4. ____

5. *Kinyōbi wa kumori matawa hare desu.* ________________________

6. ____

7. ____

18.5. Translate into English:

1. *Ashita yuki ga furimasu.* ________________________

2. *Roku-gatsu ni onīsan no ie ga dekimasu.*

____

3. *Otōto wa tomodachi to pūru de oyogimasu.*

____

4. *Kuruma ga ie no mae de tomarimasu.*

____

5. *Otōsan wa kuruma no kōjō de hatarakimasu.*

____

6. *Akachan wa okāsan no ude no naka de nakimasen.*

____

7. *Nan-ji ni Nihon no eiga ga hajimarimasu ka.*

____

Translate into rōmaji:

1. The rain will stop soon. ________________________

2. When does that mountain snow (snow on the mountain) melt?

____

3. The mother's voice is heard from the house next door.

____

4. In summer, I'll swim in the sea. _______________________________________

5. The mountain is visible. _______________________________________

6. In the spring, I'll meet my uncle in Canada.

____

7. In March, the older brother moves to America.

____

WHAT FOLLOWS A SUBJECT? *WA* OR *GA*?

In this section, I am going to sum up what you have learned so far about **wa** and **ga**.

Desu is an intransitive verb and is used in the sentence structure _ **wa** _ **desu**. As you can see, the subject is always followed by **wa**. Most of the "adjective + **desu**" constructs have the sentence structure _ **wa** "adjective + **desu**"; the subject is also always followed by **wa**. Some of the adjectives (**suki na, kirai na, jōzu na, heta na, itai, kayui** and **hoshii**) have the sentence structure _ **wa** _ **ga** "adjective + **desu**". **Wa** follows what is the subject in the English translation (it's the topic or indirect subject in Japanese) and **ga** follows the object or something else in the English translation (the grammatical subject in Japanese).

Intransitive verbs **wakarimasu** and **dekimasu** (to be discussed in the following section) have the sentence structure _ **wa** _ **ga** wakarimasu/dekimasu. **Wa** follows what is the subject in the English translation (the topic or indirect subject in Japanese) and **ga** follows what is the object in the English translation (the grammatical subject in Japanese).

The verbs of motion (lesson 11), **arimasu** and **imasu,** and some of those listed in the vocabulary in this lesson, are intransitive verbs (they may not have direct objects). They use the sentence structure _ **ga/wa** V•**masu**. **Wa** follows the subject when the subject is responsible for the action, while **ga** follows the subject when the action occurs naturally.

Noh play.

     Lesson 18: It Will Rain Tomorrow!

Examples

Ojisan wa *Amerika kara kimasu.*	*(My) uncle comes from America.*
Kisha ga *kimasu.*	*The train comes.*

The transitive verbs have the sentence structure _ **wa** _ **o V•masu**. All the transitive verbs are action verbs with their subjects being responsible for the actions; therefore, the subjects are followed by **wa**.

I UNDERSTAND JAPANESE! I CAN SPEAK JAPANESE!

Dekimasu, *be made/produced/possible*, and **wakarimasu**, *be understandable*, may be translated as follows.

Examples

Pan ga dekimasu.	*The bread is made.*
Wain ga dekimasu.	*The wine is produced.*
Tenisu ga dekimasu.	*Tennis is possible.*
Eigo ga wakarimasu.	*The English language is understandable.*

Dekimasu/wakarimasu may be used to express abilities with the sentence structure

> indirect subject **wa** grammatical subject **ga dekimasu/wakarimasu.**

Wa follows the indirect subject (subject in the English translation) and **ga** follows the grammatical subject (object in the English translation).

Let us consider **watashi wa Nihon-go ga dekimasu**. It may be translated as *as for me, Japanese is possible*. Of course, *I can speak (do) Japanese* is a more appropriate translation in English. Hence **dekimasu** may be thought of as *can do* in English and should be translated according to context.

Examples

Watashi wa Nihon-go ga dekimasu.	*I can speak Japanese (I can do Japanese).*
Watashi wa ryōri ga dekimasu.	*I can cook (I can do cooking).*

Note that **dekimasu**, *can do,* expresses the "ability" of the verb **shimasu**, *do,* and is translated according to context.

Examples

Watashi wa tenisu o shimasu.	*I play tennis.*
Watashi wa tenisu ga dekimasu.	*I can play tennis.*
Watashi wa suiei o shimasu.	*I swim.*
Watashi wa suiei ga dekimasu.	*I can swim.*

You may use the following adverbs, and those learned before, to express abilities in detail.

māmā so and so   *zenzen not at all, entirely* (used with negative verbs)

Examples

Watashi wa Nihon-go ga sukoshi dekimasu.	*I can speak Japanese a little.*
Okāsan wa suiei ga zenzen dekimasen.	*Mother cannot swim at all.*
Anata wa Nihon-go ga yoku wakarimasu ne.	*You understand Japanese well, don't you?*

A direct answer to a question **_ wa _ ga dekimasu/wakarimasu ka** has the form **hai dekimasu/ wakarimasu** or **iie dekimasen/wakarimasen,** just as does **suki/kirai desu.**

 **Conversation 2: Hanako Meets Tom's Grandpa**

Hanako meets Tom and his grandfather on a street and decides to go to town with them. The following vocabulary appears in the conversation.

Noun

machi town

Tom:	*Hanako-san Ohayōgozaimasu.*	*Good morning Hanako.*
Hanako:	*Ohayōgozaimasu.*	*Good morning.*
Tom:	*(Kore wa) boku no ojīsan desu.*	*This is my grandfather.*
Hanako:	*Hajimemashite. (Watashi wa) Hanako desu. Dōzo yoroshiku.*	*How do you do. I am Hanako. Pleased to meet you.*
	Hanako and Grandpa bow to each other.	
Hanako:	*(Anata no) ojīsan wa Nihon-go ga wakarimasu ka.*	*Does your grandfather understand Japanese?*
Tom:	*Iie zenzen wakarimasen.*	*No, he doesn't understand at all.*
	Ojīsan wa Eigo to Furansu-go ga wakarimasu.	*(My) grandfather understands English and French.*
	(Ojīsan wa) Doitsu-go mo sukoshi dekimasu.	*He can speak German a little too.*
Hanako:	*Watashi wa Eigo ga sukoshi dekimasu.*	*I can speak English a little.*
Tom:	*Boku-tachi wa machi e ikimasu.*	*We are going to town.*
	Anata mo (machi e) ikimasen ka.	*Would you like to go too?*
Hanako:	*Hai ikimasu.*	*Yes, I would.*
	(Watashi-tachi wa machi e) nan de ikimasu ka.	*How (With what) do we go?*
Tom:	*(Boku-tachi wa machi e) takushī de ikimasu.*	*By taxi.*
	Ojīsan wa amari arukimasen.	*(My) grandfather does not walk much.*

 A Japanese taxi driver wears a navy-blue uniform with white gloves. He is not as friendly as one in the West. He will not come out and open the door for you; instead he will use a lever at his seat to open and close the back door (on the left side only) for you. So, stand out of the way and don't touch the door. He will not help you with your luggage either. Tipping is rarely done in Japan.

18.6. 🔘 *Listen as Tom talks about his family's ability with the Japanese language. Write rōmaji in the blanks.*

1. _________________________________ wa Nihon-go ga mottomo dekimasen.

2. _________________________________ wa Nihon-go ga sukoshi dekimasu.

3. _________________________________ wa onīsan yori Nihon-go ga dekimasu.

4. _________________________________ wa Nihon-go ga ichiban dekimasu.

18.7. Translate into English:

1. *Anata wa kono e ga wakarimasu ka.*

____

2. *Watashi wa Nihon-go ga sukoshi wakarimasu.*

____

3. *Anata wa nan no supōtsu ga dekimasu ka.*

____

4. *Otōto wa kuruma no unten ga dekimasen.*

____

5. *Ano hito wa Nihon-go ga zenzen dekimasen yo.*

____

Translate into rōmaji:

6. I don't understand Hanako at all. _________________________________

7. My younger brother can do judo. _________________________________

8. I cannot study at home. _________________________________

9. Mother cannot speak English at all. _________________________________

10. Do you understand Hanako's English? _________________________________

Practice the five katakana characters ナ, ニ, ヌ, ネ and ノ.

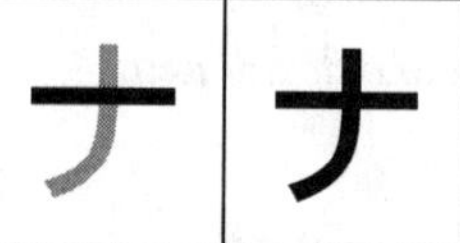 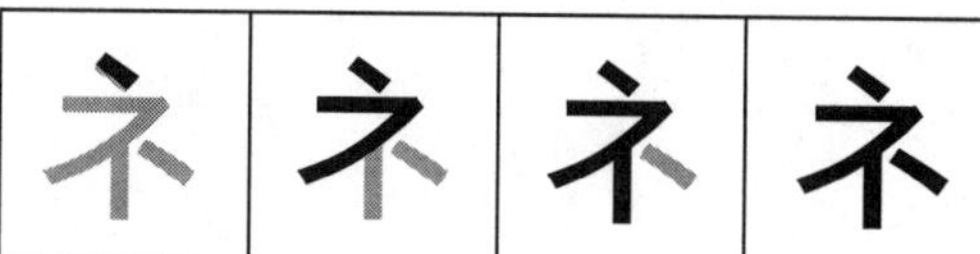

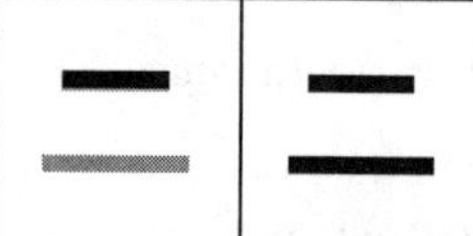 

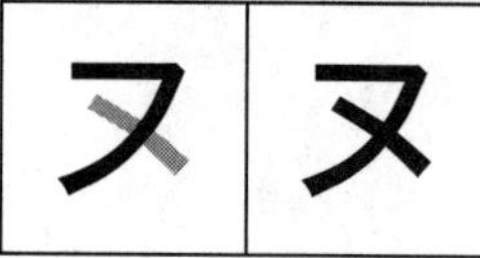

What you must remember from this lesson to proceed to the next lesson:

Intransitive **V•masu**-verbs have the sentence structure _ **wa/ga V•masu** where

wa follows the subject responsible for the action and

ga follows the subject where action is presented as natural occurrence.

We express abilities with the sentence structure _ **wa** _ **ga dekimasu/wakarimasu** where

wa follows the indirect subject (subject in the English translation) and

ga follows the grammatical subject (object in the English translation).

 Lesson 18: It Will Rain Tomorrow!

19 It All Happened Yesterday

So far, you have studied the present tense in detail and you can say almost anything you may want to say in the present tense. You also know that the present tense and the future tense for **V•masu-** verbs are the same.

In this lesson, you will study the past tense so that you may talk about what you did yesterday, last year and so on.

PAST, PRESENT AND FUTURE TENSE IN JAPANESE

In the English language, verbs have three basic tenses: they are the present tense, past tense and future tense. Let us look at the following three sentences.

1. I eat an apple.
2. I ate an apple.
3. I shall eat an apple.

In sentence 1, the verb expresses an action going on at the present time, and it is said to be in the present tense. In sentence 2, the verb expresses an action that happened in the past, and it is said to be in the past tense. In sentence 3, the verb expresses an action which will happen in the future, and it is said to be in the future tense.

In the English language, each tense may be classified into 3 more specific categories. Let us look at the following three sentences in the present tense.

1. I eat an apple.
2. I am eating an apple.
3. I have eaten an apple.

In sentence 1, the action is stated most simply in present, and it is said to be in the present simple tense. In sentence 2, the action is continuing at present; it is in the present continuous tense.

In sentence 3, the action is complete (has been made perfect) now; it is in the present perfect tense. In a similar way, you have the past simple, past continuous, past perfect, future simple, future continuous and future perfect tenses in English.

Tenses for Japanese verbs are much simpler than tenses in English. There are two basic tenses: the present tense and the past tense. Japanese uses the same **V•masu**-verb for the present and future tenses, but there is no confusion between the present and future tenses because the rest of the sentence makes the tense clear with a word or phrase such as *tomorrow, now,* or *next year.* Each tense has simple and continuous forms. Hence Japanese has the present simple, present continuous, past simple and past continuous tenses. In this book, we shall study only the present simple and past simple tenses.

Here are words, both nouns and adverbs, which clarify the tenses of sentences.

Nouns and Adverbs*

kinō yesterday	*kyonen* last year	*sen-shū* last week
kyō today	*kotoshi* this year	*kon-shū* this week
ashita tomorrow	*rainen* next year	*rai-shū* next week
itsuka someday		
	sen-getsu last month	*kesa* this morning
mai-asa every morning	*kon-getsu* this month	*konban* this evening
mai-ban every evening	*rai-getsu* next month	
mai-nen every year		
mai-nichi every day	*ototoi* the day before yesterday	
mai-shū every week	*asatte* the day after tomorrow	

You may have noticed the following prefixes from the vocabulary above.

Prefixes

kon- this (-getsu, -shū)

mai- every (-asa, -ban, -nen, -nichi, -shū)

rai- next (-getsu, -nen, -shū)

sen- last (-getsu, -shū)

IT ALL HAPPENED YESTERDAY

You may form the past simple tense by converting

    1. **desu** into **deshita,**

    2. **de wa arimasen** into **de wa arimasen deshita,**

    3. **V•masu** into **V•mashita,**

    4. **V•masen** into **V•masen deshita,**

    5. **_i desu** into **_katta desu** and

    6. **_ku nai desu** into **_ku nakatta desu.**

*In Japanese grammar these words are defined as nouns, except **itsuka** which is defined as a pronoun. Here, I have followed the structure of English grammar and defined them as nouns and adverbs.

1. *Koko wa hon-ya desu.* — *This is a bookstore.*
   Koko wa hon-ya deshita. — *This was a bookstore.*

2. *Ano hito wa Betty-san de wa arimasen.* — *She is not Betty.*
   Ano hito wa Betty-san de wa arimasen deshita. — *She was not Betty.*

3. *Watashi wa pan o tsukurimasu.* — *I make bread.*
   Watashi wa pan o tsukurimashita. — *I made bread.*

   Watashi wa gakkō e ikimasu. — *I go to school.*
   Watashi wa gakkō e ikimashita. — *I went to school.*

   Watashi wa amimono o shimasu. — *I knit.*
   Watashi wa amimono o shimashita. — *I knitted.*

   Koko ni hon ga arimasu. — *Here is a book.*
   Koko ni hon ga arimashita. — *Here was a book.*

   Koko ni neko ga imasu. — *Here is a cat.*
   Koko ni neko ga imashita. — *Here was a cat.*

   Ame ga furimasu. — *It rains. (Rain falls.)*
   Ame ga furimashita. — *It rained. (Rain fell.)*

4. *Kyō otōsan wa shigoto o shimasen.* — *Today, father does not work.*
   Kinō otōsan wa shigoto o shimasen deshita. — *Yesterday, father did not work.*

   Kyō watashi wa gakkō e ikimasen. — *Today, I do not go to school.*
   Kinō watashi wa gakkō e ikimasen deshita. — *Yesterday, I did not go to school.*

For the "**i**-adjective + **desu,**" you may obtain past simple tenses by replacing **_i desu** with **_katta desu**. The negative past simple tense may be obtained by replacing **_ku nai desu** with **_ku nakatta desu**.

5. *Kono ki wa chiisai desu.* — *This tree is small.*
   Kono ki wa chiisakatta desu. — *This tree was small.*

6. *Kono bideo wa omoshiroku nai desu.* — *This video is not interesting.*
   Kono bideo wa omoshiroku nakatta desu. — *This video was not interesting.*

The past simple "**na**-adjective (without **na**) + **desu**" is obtained by replacing **desu** with **deshita**. The negative past simple tense may be obtained by replacing **de wa arimasen** with **de wa arimasen deshita**. In other words, **desu** of the "**na**-adjective (without **na**) + **desu**" conjugates while **na**-adjective (without **na**) remains unchanged.

1. *(O)tera wa shizuka desu.* — *The temple is quiet.*
   (O)tera wa shizuka deshita. — *The temple was quiet.*

2. *Ano hito wa rikō de wa arimasen.* — *He is not clever.*
   Ano hito wa rikō de wa arimasen deshita. — *He was not clever.*

The times listed in the vocabulary on page 212, except those starting with **mai-**, are called "relative times," that is, the time which depends on when "now" is. For example, **sen-getsu**, *last month*, is a relative time because it means April if it is May now, but it means July if it is August now.

 When you refer to a relative time, you do not put **ni** after it.

Examples

Sen-getsu watashi wa Amerika e ikimashita.	*Last month, I went to America.*
Watashi wa sen-getsu Amerika e ikimashita.	*I went to America last month.*

 **Conversation 1: What Did You Do Yesterday?**

Tom and Hanako talk about what they did yesterday.

Adverbs*	Conjunction	Noun
korekara *from now on*	dakara *so, therefore*	ten *mark, score*
sorekara *after that, and then*		

Verb (Intransitive)	Verb (Transitive)	Suffix
asobimasu *play, amuse, enjoy*	torimasu *score*	-ten *mark*

Hanako:	*Kinō anata wa nani o shimashita ka.*	*What did you do yesterday?*
Tom:	*Asa (boku wa) daigaku e ikimashita.*	*In the morning, I went to a class (college).*
	Hiru (boku wa) daigaku kara kaerimashita.	*In the afternoon, I returned (home) from school.*
	Sorekara (boku wa) yakyū o Hiroshi-kun-tachi to shimashita.	*After that, I played baseball with Hiroshi and the guys.*
	Sorekara (boku wa) ban-gohan o tabe-mashita.	*After that, I ate an evening meal.*
	Yoru (boku wa) terebi o mimashita.	*At night, I watched television.*
Hanako:	*Itsu (anata wa) benkyō o shimashita ka.*	*When did you study?*
Tom:	*Kinō (boku wa) benkyō o shimasen deshita.*	*Yesterday, I did not study.*
	Ototoi (boku-tachi wa) sūgaku no tesuto ga arimashita ne.	*The day before yesterday, we had the mathematics test, didn't we?*
	Boku wa hyaku-ten o torimashita.	*I scored 100.*
	Dakara kinō (boku wa) asobimashita.	*So, yesterday, I played.*
Hanako:	*Watashi wa totemo warui ten o tori-mashita.*	*I scored a very bad mark.*
	Dakara kinō (watashi wa) sūgaku no benkyō o shimashita.	*So, I studied mathematics yesterday.*
	Korekara (watashi wa) mata benkyō o shi-masu.	*Now, I'll study again.*

*****Korekara** is defined as a noun and **sorekara** is defined as a conjunction in Japanese grammar. I have defined both as adverbs in accordance with English grammar.

 ## Conversation 2: I Forgot My Briefcase in a Bus

Tom visits the office in a bus terminal to retrieve a briefcase which he left on a bus this morning.

Tom: *Sumimasen.* — Excuse me.

Kyō (no) asa (boku wa) basu no naka ni kaban o wasuremashita. — This morning, I forgot (my) briefcase in a bus.

Clerk: *(Basu wa) nan-ji no basu deshita ka.* — What time was the bus?

Tom: *(Basu wa) asa no hachi-ji deshita.* — It was 8 o'clock in the morning.

Clerk: *(Basu wa) nan-ban (no basu) deshita ka.* — What number was it?

Tom: *(Basu wa) san-ban (no basu) deshita.* — It was number 3.

(Basu wa) Handa-yama kara eki e iki-mashita. — It went from Mt. Handa to the station.

Clerk: *Kaban no naka ni nani ga arimashita ka.* — What was in the briefcase?

Tom: *(Kaban no naka ni) hon to enpitsu to tenisu no bōru ga arimashita.* — There were books, pencils and a tennis ball.

Clerk: *Kore (wa anata no kaban) desu ka.* — Is this it?

Tom: *Hai sō desu. Dōmo arigatō gozaimasu.* — Yes, it is. Thank you very much.

EXERCISES

19.1. Convert the rōmaji sentences in the present tense into the past tense by filling in the blanks, and then translate them into English.

1. *Kyō wa yoi (o)tenki desu ne.*

Kinō wa yoi (o)tenki <u>*deshita ne*</u>.

<u>*The weather was good yesterday, wasn't it?*</u>

2. *Kyō no tesuto wa yasashii desu yo.*

Kinō no tesuto wa ______________________.

____

3. *Watashi wa Hanako-san ga suki desu.*

Kyonen watashi wa Hanako-san ga ______________________.

____

4. *Kyō wa sui-yōbi de wa arimasen yo.*

Kinō wa ______________________.

____

5. *Kyō wa samuku nai desu ne.*

Kinō wa _________________________________.

____

6. *Kono (o)kashi wa amari oishiku nai desu ne.*

Kono (o)kashi wa ______________________________.

____

7. *Kyō otōsan wa ryokō kara kaerimasu.*

Kinō _____________________________.

____

8. *Kono haru onēsan wa kekkon shimasu.*

Kyonen no haru _______________________________.

____

9. *Kyō watashi-tachi wa uchi de pātī ga arimasu.*

Kinō ________________________________.

____

10. *Konshū watashi-tachi wa mai-nichi bangohan ni karēraisu o tabemasu.*

Senshū ________________________________.

____

19.2. 💿 *I shall read Tom's essay about his summer vacation. Answer the following questions in rōmaji.*

1. *Kyonen no natsu Tom-kun wa doko e ikimashita ka.*

____

2. *Tom-kun wa doko ni tomarimashita ka.*

____

3. *Tom-kun wa Amerika o ryokō shimashita ka.*

____

     Lesson 19: It All Happened Yesterday

4. *Tom-kun wa doko ga ichiban suki deshita ka.*

____

5. *Mai-nichi Tom-kun wa nani o shimashita ka.*

____

6. *Tom-kun wa nani-go o Amerika de hanashimashita ka.*

____

7. *Amerika wa suzushikatta desu ka.*

____

8. *Tom-kun no natsu-yasumi wa tanoshii natsu-yasumi deshita ka, (Tom-kun no natsu-yasumi wa) tsumaranai natsu-yasumi deshita ka.*

____

19.3. Complete the table below.

Meaning	Present Tense	Negative Present	Past Tense	Negative Past
to eat	tabemasu	tabemasen	tabemashita	tabemasen deshita
	mimasu			
to be	desu			
	asobimasu			
	shimasu			
to be located	imasu			
	yasui desu			
	baka desu			
to be good at	jōzu desu			
	wakarimasu			

19.4. Translate into English:

1. *Ano hito wa Makoto-kun no onīsan deshita.*

____

2. *Kinō Furansu-go no uta ga yūsuhosuteru de kikoemashita.*

____

3. *Kyonen no natsu koko ni ōkii ki ga arimashita.*

____

4. *Sen-getsu watashi-tachi wa kaimono o Amerika de shimashita.*

____

5. *Kinō boku wa isu o otōsan to tsukurimashita.*

____

6. *Kinō boku-tachi wa Nihon no eiga o gakkō de mimashita.*

____

7. *Sen-shū anata wa nan no hon o yomimashita ka.*

____

8. *Kinō anata wa nani o ranchi ni tabemashita ka.*

____

9. *Kyonen kono ki wa chiisakatta desu yo.*

____

10. *Asoko wa Hanako-san no ie de wa arimasen deshita ne.*

____

11. *Kinō boku wa ban-gohan o tabemasen deshita.*

____

12. *Sen-shū otōto wa gakkō e ikimasen deshita.*

____

13. *Kono hon wa omoshiroku nakatta desu yo.*

____

14. *Watashi wa Betty-san ga suki de wa arimasen deshita.*

____

15. *Kinō watashi wa kore ga dekimasen deshita.*

____

Translate into rōmaji:

16. That was a temple._______________________________________

17. Last year, I went to America by airplane.

____

18. Yesterday night, I studied Japanese with Hanako.

____

19. Did you read the book yesterday?

____

20. Yesterday, there was a newspaper on the desk.

____

21. The long travelling has finished. _______________________

22. Yesterday, I had a headache._______________________________

23. Kyoto was a very interesting city. _______________________

24. That wasn't my briefcase. _______________________________

25. Last evening, I did not eat dinner._______________________

26. I did not play tennis with Makoto yesterday.

____

27. I did not read this book. ____

28. I did not understand the movie at all._____________________________________

29. The film was not interesting.____

30. Betty was not good with Japanese. ____

19.5. 🔘 *I shall ask some questions on Conversation 2. Reply to each question aloud in Japanese. Correct answers are recorded at the end of this exercise.*

1. ____

2. ____

3. ____

4. ____

5. ____

WRITING EXERCISE: KATAKANA FOR *HA, HI, FU, HE* AND *HO*

Practice the five katakana characters ハ， ヒ， フ， ヘ *and* ホ.

   Lesson 19: It All Happened Yesterday

**What you must remember from this lesson to proceed
to the next lesson:**

The past simple tense of verbs is formed by converting the present simple tense of

desu	into	**deshita,**
de wa arimasen	into	**de wa arimasen deshita,**
V•masu	into	**V•mashita,**
V•masen	into	**V•masen deshita,**
_i desu	into	**_katta desu** and
_ku nai desu	into	**_ku nakatta desu.**

20 Tomorrow Is Another Day!

So far, you have studied the present simple tense and the past simple tense. You also know that the future simple tense has the same form as the present simple tense for **V•masu**-verbs.

In this lesson, you will practice the future tense thoroughly so that you will have no doubt as to whether a **V•masu**-verb is used in the present tense or the future tense. You will also learn the future tense of the verb **desu**.

I WILL DO EVERYTHING TOMORROW

You have learned (in lesson 7, page 57) that the present and future tenses for **V•masu**-verbs have the same form in Japanese, but there is rarely any confusion because the context usually removes any ambiguity as may be seen below.

Examples

Rainen watashi-tachi wa Amerika e ikimasu.	*Next year, we will go to America.*
Ashita watashi wa Eigo no benkyō o shimasu.	*Tomorrow, I will study English.*
Korekara watashi wa ongaku o kikimasu.	*From now (on), I will listen to music.*
Korekara okāsan wa gohan o tsukurimasu.	*From now (on), (my) mother will make a meal.*
Ashita watashi wa e o kakimasen.	*Tomorrow, I will not draw a picture.*
Ashita ame ga furimasu.	*It will rain tomorrow. (Tomorrow, rain will fall.)*
Rai-shū gakkō ga hajimarimasu.	*Schools will start next week.*

In the above examples, you may have noticed that words specifying the future (such as *tomorrow, next year,* etc.) are included in each sentence. In a conversation, once a speaker establishes the time frame, it is not necessary to mention it again, as we can see in the following conversation.

Conversation 1: What Are You Doing Tomorrow?

Tom asks Makoto what he is going to do tomorrow.

Tom:	*Ashita (anata wa) nani o shimasu ka.*	*What are you doing tomorrow?*
Makoto:	*(Boku wa)* **otōto to machi e ikimasu.**	*I'll go to town with my younger brother.*
Tom:	*(Anata wa)* **nani o machi de shimasu ka.**	*What will you do in town?*
Makoto:	*(Boku-tachi wa)* **hon-ya e ikimasu.**	*We're going to bookstores.*
	(Boku-tachi wa) **hon o kaimasu.**	*We are going to buy books.*
	(Boku-tachi wa) **depāto e mo ikimasu.**	*We'll go to department stores too.*
	Anata mo (machi e boku-tachi to) iki-masen ka.	*Would you like to go too?*

20.1

1. Circle the words associated with future tense.

ashita   rainen   senshū   raishū   sengetsu   ototoi   asatte   korekara   kinō   kyonen   raigetsu

2. Circle the words associated with past tense.

ashita   rainen   senshū   raishū   sengetsu   ototoi   asatte   korekara   kinō   kyonen   raigetsu

20.2.   *I shall ask some questions on Conversation 1. Reply to each question aloud in Japanese, and write your answers. Correct answers are recorded at the end of this exercise.*

1. ____

2. ____

3. ____

4. ____

20.3. Translate into English:

1. Asatte wa getsu-yōbi desu. _______________________

2. Ashita otōsan to okāsan wa Igirisu kara kaerimasu.

____

3. Rai-shū onīsan no ie ga dekimasu.

____

4. *Assatte watashi wa ban-gohan o Betty-san no ie de tabemasu.*

____

5. *Ashita no eiga wa omoshiroku nai desu yo.*

____

6. *Ashita watashi wa anata o eki de machimasu ne.*

____

7. *Rai-shū kono hon o anata ni kaeshimasu.*

____

8. *Ashita watashi wa tenisu o shimasen.*

____

9. *Rai-shū no sui-yōbi ni gakkō ga hajimarimasu.*

____

10. *Rai-shū kaimono ni ikimasen ka.*

____

Translate into rōmaji:

11. Tomorrow will be Sunday._______________________________

12. Someday, I will study French. _______________________________

13. Tomorrow, (my) younger brother and I will go to the temple.

____

14. What will you do tomorrow?

____

15. Tomorrow morning, I'll draw a picture of the mountain.

____

16. Next year, will your grandfather come to Japan?

____

17. Tomorrow, I will not watch television.

____

18. Next year, I will buy an expensive blue coat.

____

19. Next month, a baby will be born to (my) aunt.

____

20. Tomorrow, I'll put on this dress.

____

I WILL BE A TEACHER SOMEDAY

Unlike **V•masu**-verbs, the verb **desu** does not express the future tense unless the subjects indicate the future as shown in the examples below.

Verb (Intransitive)
narimasu become

Examples
Ashita *wa atatakai desu yo.*   *Tomorrow will be warm!*
Ashita *no tesuto wa muzukashiku arimasen.*   *Tomorrow's test will not be difficult.*

The idea of the future tense for **desu** is expressed by using **narimasu,** *to become,* in the future tense. The future tense for _ **wa** _**desu** is

> **subject** **wa** **complement** **ni narimasu**

where **wa** follows a subject and **ni** follows a complement.

Example
Watashi *wa sensei* **desu.**   *I am a teacher.*
Raigetsu watashi wa sensei ni narimasu.   *Next month, I will be a teacher.*

The future tense for _ **wa** "**i**-adjective + **desu**" is

> **subject** **wa** **_ku narimasu.**

The future tense for _ **wa** "**na**-adjective (without **na**) + **desu**" is

> **subject** **wa** "na-adjective (without **na**)" **ni narimasu.**

> The future tense for _ **wa** _ **ga** "**na**-adjective (without **na**) + **desu**" is
>
> **indirect subject** **wa** **grammatical subject** **ga** "**na**-adjective (without **na**)" **ni narimasu.**

Examples

Kono inu wa ōkii desu.	*This dog is big.*
Kono inu wa sugu ōkiku narimasu.	*This dog will be big soon.*
Yoru gakkō wa shizuka desu.	*At night, school is quiet.*
Yoru gakkō wa shizuka ni narimasu.	*At night, school will be quiet.*
Anata wa tenisu ga jōzu desu.	*You are good at tennis.*
Itsuka anata wa tenisu ga jōzu ni narimasu.	*Someday, you will be good at tennis.*

The negative future tense may be obtained by changing **narimasu** into **narimasen**.

Examples

Hanako-san wa sensei ni narimasen.	*Hanako will not be a teacher.*
Ashita wa atsuku narimasen.	*It will not be hot tomorrow.*
Koko wa benri ni narimasen yo.	*This place will not be convenient!*
Ano hito wa taisō ga jōzu ni narimasen.	*He will not be good with gymnastics.*

 **Conversation 2: It's Cold Today!**

Tom and Hanako talk about the temperature.

Tom:	*Kyō wa samui desu ne.*	*It is cold today, isn't it?*
Hanako:	*Gogo (wa) atatakaku narimasu yo.*	*It will be warm in the afternoon!*
	Hachi-gatsu wa totemo atsuku narimasu yo.	*It will be very hot in August!*
Tom:	*Ku-gatsu wa (hachi-gatsu yori) suzushiku narimasu ka.*	*Will it be cooler in September?*
Hanako:	*Hai (ku-gatsu wa) hachi-gatsu yori suzushiku narimasu.*	*Yes, it will be cooler than in August.*

EXERCISES

20.4. *I shall tell you what everyone thinks of becoming when he/she grows up. Join the person with what he/she thinks of becoming.*

Tom	a judo instructor
Mari	a nurse
Makoto	a white collar worker
Hanako	a school teacher
Ken	a medical doctor

20.5. Complete the table below.

Adjective	Meaning	"Adjective + *desu*"	Meaning	Future Tense
nagai	long	*nagai desu*	to be long	*nagaku narimasu*
hoshii	desirous			
muzukashii				
benri na				
rippa na				

20.6. I shall ask some questions on Conversation 2. Reply to each question aloud in Japanese, and write your answers. Correct answers are recorded at the end of this exercise.

1. ____

2. ____

3. ____

4. ____

20.7. Translate into English:

1. *Raigetsu Akiko-obasan wa okāsan ni narimasu.*

____

2. *Nihon-go no benkyō wa muzukashiku narimasu ka.*

____

3. *Itsuka ano hito wa yūmei ni narimasu yo.*

____

4. *Pātī no ato daidokoro wa kitanaku narimasu.*

____

5. *Anata wa Nihon no rekishi ga suki ni narimasu yo.*

____

6. Someday, you will be good at tennis. _______________________________

7. Will you become a medical doctor someday? _______________________________

8. Next year, skirts will be short! _______________________________

9. This tree will not be big. _______________________________

10. You will like Japanese food. _______________________________

JAPANESE CUSTOMS AND CULTURE

Christmas and New Year's Day

Most Japanese people do not celebrate Christmas: to them, Christmas is just another day. For those who acknowledge it, a parent buys a Christmas cake at a bakery, and the family eats it at Christmas. Small children hang up stockings on Christmas Eve somewhere in the houses, although Japanese houses have no fireplaces. Some close friends may exchange gifts at Christmas.

Little shrine for the author's grandparents.

Japanese people celebrate New Year's Day, and preparations for the New Year's Day celebration are considerable. The whole nation goes through cleaning rituals as the end of the year approaches: everywhere and everything are cleaned, especially the areas that have been ignored until then. By New Year's Eve, Japanese housewives have prepared most of the food that the family and the guests will eat during the New Year's Day holiday. On New Year's Eve, people eat soba (Japanese thin buckwheat noodles) either with a dipping sauce or in a hot broth. You are expected to slurp it down your throat loudly. It signifies that the coming year will go smoothly, just as

Students write their wishes to pass university entrance examinations on wooden blocks and hang them in the shrine which honors a famous scholar. Those wooden blocks, sold at shrines, are not cheap by any means!

Inside of a Japanese temple.

the noodles go through the throat. Celebration of New Year's Day may last from three to seven days, and, during that period, every house is an open house, except those in mourning. People visit their immediate superiors, and those with whom they will be associating in the New Year, as well as their families, relatives and friends. Japanese people also send special New Year greeting postcards, to be delivered in the New Year, just like Christmas cards are sent in the West; some cards are printed and some are handwritten. On New Year's Day, people visit shrines to pray to various gods for a prosperous new year. New Year's Day holiday is a great time for children, who get some money from every relative they meet during the holiday.

Japanese Religious Beliefs

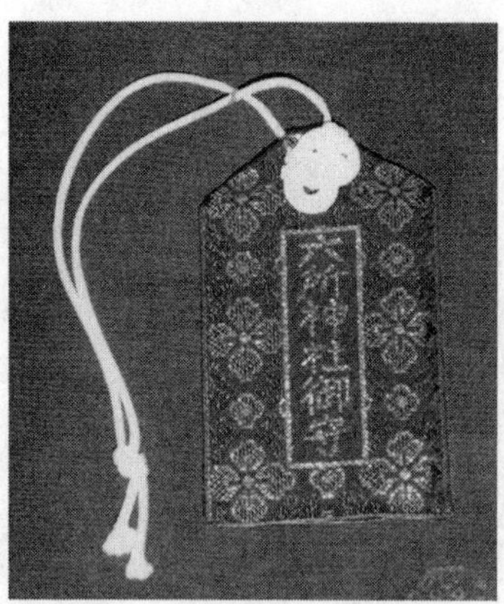

(O)mamori is a little pouch that almost every Japanese person carries around. It is a talisman to protect against disaster or ward off evil; one buys it from a shrine.

Concepts of religion among Japanese people are very different from those of Westerners. In the Shinto religion, which is an ancient native Japanese religion well established before the introduction of Buddhism in the sixth century, people believe that when one dies, his spirit leaves the body and becomes a god who stays somewhere near his descendants in a sacred place such as a shrine, a mountain, etc. So, people worship ancestors, and every household has a miniature shrine on a small shelf near the ceiling for worshipping the dead. Every day, people give boiled rice first to the dead, before they eat any. The sun, mountains, wind, rain, trees, rocks and other natural phenomena are believed to be inhabited by individual gods. If worshipped, a god would be benevolent towards people, but, if neglected, a god would be provoked to wrath and might cause a calamity, so people

Lesson 20: Tomorrow Is Another Day!

choose to worship gods. For example, it is customary to hold a ceremony for purifying a building site before any construction may even start. The ceremony is led by a Shinto priest, and is meant to appease the god living there for the massive changes that will be made to the land. Shinto has many rituals like these which have become second nature to all Japanese people, irrespective of their religion. These are often performed for form's sake, rather than because of a strong religious feeling of piety. Shinto offers no philosophical teaching or moral code, but places great emphasis on fertility and ritual purity. For example, to purify people (after they return from funerals) or earth (before a sumo wrestling match), they throw salt on them. People generally go to

The Great Buddha, a seated bronze image of 11.4 meters, was built in the middle of the thirteenth century in Kamakura.

shrines whenever they want something in return—for example, when they want to pass a university entrance examination, or they want to have a successful year, or they want to have a baby. They are also supposed to revisit the shrines to thank the gods if their wishes come true.

On the other hand, Buddhism, which is the major religion in Japan, has no god. Buddhism has moral codes and a complex philosophical system of thought centering on the principles of mercy and humanity. It condemns killing and emphasizes the links among all things. According to Buddhism, any life on earth is that of suffering, and therefore this earth is seen as the equivalent

A shrine.

of hell. Reincarnation is a part of Buddhist belief, and the ultimate goal of life is to reach the end of the cycles of reincarnation. Shaka, the founder of Buddhism, teaches that this is done by achieving enlightenment. Enlightenment may be obtained through faith and behavior. When one finally reaches the state of enlightenment, one is called a buddha. But on the other hand, if one behaves badly, one may be reborn as a lower-ranking creature such as a cat, an insect, or worse, depending on one's entire past behavior. This may go on forever, and one may become many different creatures until one obtains enlightenment. You may hear quite often in Japan that when a complete stranger is kind to you, he may have been associated with you in a previous life. Or, if an insect or a bird seems to linger around your house, someone may tell you that it may be a deceased relative or acquaintance of yours. Buddhism, originating in India, came to Japan through China and Korea, where it was transformed by the local religions, and then was also influenced by Shintoism. There are many sects in Japanese Buddhism, and some of them have even adopted the Shinto belief that the dead become buddhas instantly, just as the dead become gods in Shinto.

Buddhist altar in a home, to commemorate the dead.

Christianity was introduced to Japan in 1549, but less than 1 percent of the population is currently Christian.

Daily life in Japan has little connection with religion, except for funeral ceremonies, which are usually Buddhist with deep religious significance. A interesting characteristic of Japanese religions is that they are not mutually exclusive: almost all Japanese families consider themselves as belonging to one of many Buddhist sects, yet you will find some homes with Shinto shrines as well as Buddhist altars. Many Shinto and Buddhist beliefs and practices have merged over the years. In Japan, a person might be a Buddhist, but practice Shinto rituals; he/she might be married at a Shinto or Christian ceremony, which is becoming popular with young couples, and he/she might have a Buddhist funeral.

In Buddhism, people believe that a judgement is handed down on each person's spirit forty-nine days after death. Then the spirit is reborn in one of the six realms or four states of heaven, listed here in order from the worst to the best: the hell; the realms of Hungry Ghost; Beasts; Asuras; Titans; human; sravaka; the Prateya-Buddha; the Bodhisatva; and the complete enlighted Nirvana (Buddha). The spirit's individual "case" is reviewed after 100 days, one year and three years, just in case a mistake was made. During the Tokugawa Period (also known as the Edo Period), the three years was extended to 33 years.

Harakiri, cutting of the belly to die, was performed by a samurai ceremonially to prevent the humiliation of capture by an enemy, to protest with his life against the conduct of his lord, as a death sentence imposed by the authority, as a suicide on the death of his lord, or to "wipe the slate clean" when he failed. From the time he was a small boy, a samurai was trained to be completely indifferent to death and suffering. On top of that, a samurai accepted contradicting Buddhism and Shinto tenets which affected his attitude towards death, and caused him to be very willing to die: he believed that thirty-three years after a death, the spirit moved from the Buddhist temple, where the body was buried, to a shrine to become a Shinto god which was a reincarnation of a Buddha or Bodhisatva. In other words, the spirit of the dead attains enlightenment after wandering around for thirty-three years.

When a person dies in Japan, the body is cremated, and the ashes are kept in an urn in the house for forty-nine days. During this period, rites are held at the household altar every seven days. Relatives and friends come together for memorial services held 100 days after the death, and then on the first, second, twelfth and sixteenth anniversaries.

WRITING EXERCISE: KATAKANA FOR *MA, MI, MU, ME AND MO*

Practice the five katakana characters マ, ミ, ム, メ and モ.

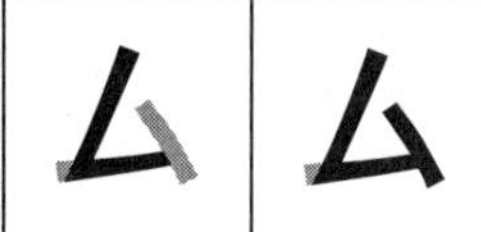

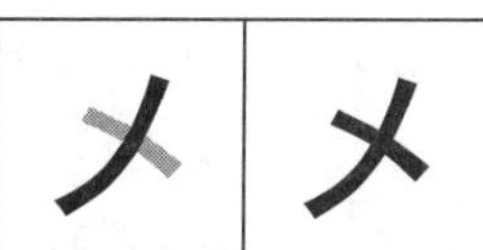

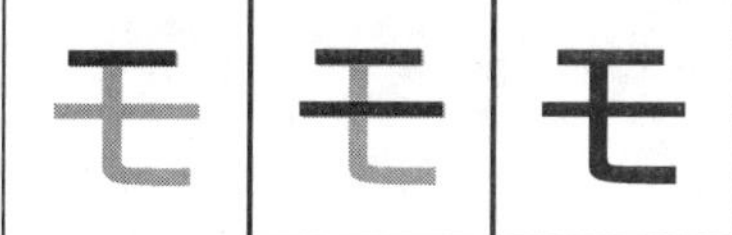

**What you must remember from this lesson to proceed
to the next lesson:**

For **V•masu**-verbs, the present tense and the future tense have the same
form.

The future tense for _ **wa** _ **desu** is _ **wa** _ **ni narimasu.**

The future tense for _ **wa** "**i**-adjective + **desu**" is _ **wa** _**ku narimasu.**

The future tense for _ **wa** (_ **ga**) "**na**-adjective (without **na**) + **desu**" is _
wa (_ **ga**) "**na**-adjective (without **na**) **ni narimasu.**"

   Lesson 20: Tomorrow Is Another Day!

Shall I Suggest?
Or Shall I Demand?

In this lesson you will learn:

Speaking
To suggest that someone do things with you: *"Let's _"*
To order someone to do something
To visit a doctor and describe how you feel physically

Grammar
To use **V•mashō** to make a polite request
To use **V•nasai** to make an imperative sentence

You have learned the present simple, past simple and future simple tenses so far. You may have realized that Japanese verbs are fairly regular and easy compared with English verbs. The past simple tense is obtained by changing **V•masu** into **V•mashita** and **desu** into **deshita** without any exception, while in English, on the other hand, the past simple and perfect tenses must usually be learned individually (e.g., *eat, ate, eaten; cut, cut, cut; walk, walked, walked; take, took, taken* are the present simple, past simple and past perfect tenses respectively). That is in addition to the fact that the future simple tense for a **V•masu**-verb has the same form as that of the present simple tense, and the future simple tense for **desu** is expressed with another verb, **narimasu.** You cannot ask verbs to be much easier than that!

Although tenses are relatively few and simple compared to English, Japanese expresses many ideas by changing the **masu** of **V•masu**-verbs. These changes are fairly regular and easy, and you are going to learn some of them in this lesson. For example, by changing **masu,** you may express an imperative (giving an order or instruction), such as "Eat the dinner!" or "Study mathematics!," and a polite imperative such as "Let's eat dinner" or "Let's study mathematics."

LET'S DO THINGS TOGETHER!

By dropping the subject, and converting **V•masu** into **V•mashō,** you can produce a polite imperative sentence that may be translated as *Let's _* .

Examples

Watashi wa hon o yomimasu.	*I read a book.*
Hon o yomimashō.	*Let's read a book.*

Yama e ikimashō.	Let's go to the mountain.
Nihon-go no benkyō o shimashō.	Let's study Japanese.
Nemashō.	Let's sleep.
Pūru de oyogimashō.	Let's swim in the pool.

 Conversation 1: Would You Like to Go to Kyoto Tomorrow?

Tom and Hanako plan to go to Kyoto.

Nouns		**Verb (Intransitive)**
jikanhyō timetable	*tokkyū* super express	*tsukimasu* arrive

Hanako:	*Ashita Kyōto e ikimasen ka.*	Would you like to go to Kyoto tomorrow?
Tom:	*Hai (Boku wa Kyōto e) ikimasu.*	Yes, I would.
Hanako:	*Kyōto ni (o)tera to jinja ga takusan ari-masu yo.*	There are a lot of temples and shrines in Kyoto!
Tom:	*(Boku-tachi wa Kyōto e) nan de ikimasu ka.*	How (With what) are we going to Kyoto?
Hanako:	*Shinkansen de ikimashō.*	Let's go by Shinkansen.
Tom:	*Nan-ji ni (boku-tachi wa Kyōto e) iki-masu ka.*	What time do we leave (go)?
Hanako:	*Jikanhyō o mimashō.*	Let's look the timetable.
Tom:	*Shichi-ji sanjūgo-fun no Kodama de ikimashō.*	Let's go by a Kodama at 7:35.
	(Boku-tachi wa Kyōto ni) jūichi-ji nijūgo-fun ni tsukimasu.	We'll arrive at 11:25.
Hanako:	*Shichi-ji gojūrop-pun no Nozomi wa jū-ji jūip-pun ni (Kyōto ni*) tsukimasu.*	The Nozomi at 7:56 will arrive (at Kyoto) at 10:11.
	(Kyōto e) Nozomi de ikimashō.	Let's go by Nozomi.
Tom:	*Nozomi wa totemo hayai desu ne.*	The Nozomi is very fast, isn't it?
Hanako:	*Nozomi wa tokkyū desu.*	The Nozomi is a super express.

Torii at The Heian Shrine, Kyoto.

Kinkakuji (Golden Pavilion), Kyoto.

*__ ni tsukimasu** means *arrive at _.*

<table>
<tr><td colspan="8" align="center">TOKYO – NAGOYA – KYOTO – HIROSHIMA – HAKATA
(TŌKAIDŌ & SANYŌ SHINKANSEN)</td></tr>
<tr><td>Stations</td><td></td><td></td><td>H</td><td>K</td><td>H</td><td>N</td></tr>
<tr><td>Tokyo</td><td>東京</td><td>Lv.</td><td>7:30</td><td>7:35</td><td>7:33</td><td>7:56</td></tr>
<tr><td>Shin-Yokohama</td><td>新横浜</td><td>Lv.</td><td>|</td><td>7:52</td><td>7:50</td><td>|</td></tr>
<tr><td>Odawara</td><td>小田原</td><td>Lv.</td><td>|</td><td>8:13</td><td>8:07</td><td>|</td></tr>
<tr><td>Atami</td><td>熱海</td><td>Lv.</td><td>|</td><td>8:22</td><td>|</td><td>|</td></tr>
<tr><td>Mishima</td><td>三島</td><td>Lv.</td><td>|</td><td>8:36</td><td>|</td><td>|</td></tr>
<tr><td>Shin-Fuji</td><td>新富士</td><td>Lv.</td><td>|</td><td>8:49</td><td>|</td><td>|</td></tr>
<tr><td>Shizuoka</td><td>静岡</td><td>Lv.</td><td>|</td><td>9:02</td><td>|</td><td>|</td></tr>
<tr><td>Kakegawa</td><td>掛川</td><td>Lv.</td><td>|</td><td>9:24</td><td>|</td><td>|</td></tr>
<tr><td>Hamamatsu</td><td>浜松</td><td>Lv.</td><td>|</td><td>9:36</td><td>|</td><td>|</td></tr>
<tr><td>Toyohashi</td><td>豊橋</td><td>Lv.</td><td>|</td><td>9:56</td><td>|</td><td>|</td></tr>
<tr><td>Mikawa-Anjo</td><td>三河安城</td><td>Lv.</td><td>|</td><td>10:13</td><td>|</td><td>|</td></tr>
<tr><td>Nagoya</td><td>名古屋</td><td>Lv.</td><td>9:24</td><td>10:29</td><td>9:30</td><td>9:34</td></tr>
<tr><td>Gifu-Hashima</td><td>岐阜羽島</td><td>Lv.</td><td>|</td><td>10:43</td><td>9:47</td><td>|</td></tr>
<tr><td>Maibara</td><td>米原</td><td>Lv.</td><td>|</td><td>11:01</td><td>10:02</td><td>|</td></tr>
<tr><td>Kyoto</td><td>京都</td><td>Lv.</td><td>10:07</td><td>11:25</td><td>10:24</td><td>10:11</td></tr>
<tr><td>Shin-Osaka</td><td>新大阪</td><td>Lv.</td><td>10:23</td><td>11:41</td><td>10:40</td><td>10:26</td></tr>
</table>

N: Nozomi   H: Hikari   K: Kodama

Shinkansen train timetable.

Conversation 2: It's Tokyo Station

Tom and Hanako arrive at Tokyo station.

Nouns

jidō-kippu-uriba *automatic ticket dispensing area*
midori-no-madoguchi *train reservation office*
shiteiseki *reserved seats*

Adverbs

ōzei *many people*   ***zenbu*** *all, everything, completely*

Hanako:	*(Koko wa) Tōkyō eki desu.*	This is Tokyo station.
Tom:	*(Koko ni) hito ga ōzei imasu ne.*	There are many people (here), aren't there?
	Asoko ni jidō-kippu-uriba ga arimasu.	There is an automatic ticket dispensing area over there.
	Kippu o asoko de kaimashō.	Let's buy tickets over there.

Hanako:	*Nozomi wa zenbu shiteiseki desu.*	*The Nozomi is all reserved seats.*
	(Watashi-tachi wa shiteiseki no kippu o) **midori-no-madoguchi de kaimasu.**	*We buy (tickets for reserved seats) at the reservation office.*
Tom:	**Midori-no-madoguchi e ikimashō.**	*Let's go to the reservation office.*

***

Hanako:	**Nozomi wa Tōkyō kara Kyōto made ikura desu ka.**	*How much is the Nozomi from Tokyo to Kyoto?*
Clerk:	**(Kippu wa) roku-sen go-hyaku-en desu.**	*It's ¥6,500.*
Hanako:	**(Kippu o) ni-mai kudasai.**	*May I have two tickets please?*

JAPANESE CUSTOMS AND CULTURE

Trains

Japanese bullet trains, known as **Shinkansen,** are world-famous for their speed, safety and comfort. They are used for long-distance travel. There are six Shinkansen lines. Each Shinkansen line has two or three different types of trains (faster ones making fewer stops) and they have a special names for each line. For instance, for the line between Tokyo and Hakata, there are three types of Shinkansen: they are called Nozomi, Hikari and Kodama, in decreasing order of their speeds. Each Shinkansen has three types of cars (except Nozomi which does not have jiyūseki): **gurinsha** (first class with reserved seats), **shiteiseki** (reserved seats) and **jiyūseki** (non-reserved seats). Gurinsha and shiteiseki cost extra. You need two tickets to board a Shinkansen, one for the basic fare (the charge for the distance; it may be used for any other types of trains) and another one for the supplementary fare (the charge for the speed of a particular type of Shinkansen train, and a seat for a particular car). Shinkansen are equipped with dining cars, toilets, powder rooms and public telephones. As the train passes through different regions, vendors come around selling specialty food

Shinkansen train.

Shinkansen train tickets.

Shinkansen-guchi.

Lost and Found.

Shinkansen (jidō)-kippu-uriba.

Otearai.

Otearai.

Annaisho.

Seisansho.

Kippu-uriba.

gift items from the region as well as drinks, snacks, boxed meals and magazines. Shinkansen are equipped with recorded messages to announce the next stops, and screens to tell the most updated news and the current speed of the train. Some of the long-distance trains have sleeping cars.

There are other types of trains for traveling shorter distances. There are as many as four types of trains for each line. They are **tokkyū** (super express), **kyūkō** (express), **kaisoku** (limited express or rapid) and **futsū** (ordinary) in decreasing order of their speeds. Faster trains make fewer stops than slower ones. Whether one uses a **tokkyū, kyūkō, kaisoku** or **futsū,** the fare is usually the same (the basic fare), and some of them have reserved seats, for which there is an additional charge.

When Japanese main line trains pull up to the platforms, they always stop so that the doors are aligned at the same spots on the platform. These points are marked and the passengers line up at them.

Except for the reserved seats, all the tickets may be bought from **jidō-hanbaiki** (ticket vending machines) as well as at **kippu uriba** (ticket selling counters).

Conversation 3: Makoto Is in a Hospital

Hanako tells Tom of Makoto's hospitalization due to a ski accident.

Nouns

hone bone	*mimai* a visit (to inquire about the health)
kēki cake	*nyūin* admission into a hospital
minna everyone	*taiin* discharge from a hospital
shukudai homework	*hana* flower
sukī ski, skiing	

Verb (Transitive)

orimasu break (bone, stick)

Verbs (Intransitive)

nyūin shimasu be admitted into a hospital

taiin shimasu be discharged from a hospital

Hanako:	*Kinō Makoto-kun wa byōin ni nyūin shimashita*.*	Yesterday, Makoto was admitted to a hospital.
Tom:	*(Sore wa) naze desu ka.*	Why?
Hanako:	*(Makoto-kun wa) ashi no hone o sukī de orimashita.*	He broke (his) leg bone while skiing.
Tom:	*Jugyō no ato (Makoto-kun no) (o)mimai ni ikimashō.*	After the lecture, let's go for a visit.
Hanako:	*Sō shimashō. Byōin no mae ni hana-ya e ikimasen ka.*	Let's do that. Would you like to go to a flower shop before the hospital?
	(O)hana o Makoto-kun ni kaimashō.	Let's buy flowers for Makoto.
Tom:	*Makoto-kun wa hana ga suki de wa arimasen.*	Makoto doesn't like flowers.
	(Makoto-kun wa) tabemono ga suki desu yo. Ōkii kēki o kaimashō.	He likes food! Let's buy a big cake.
Hanako:	*Kēki o byōin no mae no kēki-ya de kaimashō.*	Let's buy a cake at the cake shop in front of the hospital.
Tom:	*Sore wa ii desu ne.*	That's good, isn't it?

***

Tom:	*Makoto-kun Konnichiwa. Kore wa kēki desu.*	Hi (good afternoon), Makoto. This is a cake.
	(Kore wa) Hanako-san to boku kara desu.	It's from Hanako and me.
Makoto:	*Arigatō. (Kore wa) ōkii kēki desu ne. Minna de tabemashō.*	Thank you. It's a big cake, isn't it? Let's all eat!
Tom:	*(Anata no) ashi wa dō desu ka.*	How's your leg?
Makoto:	*Kinō (boku wa ashi ga) totemo itakatta desu.*	Yesterday, it was very painful.
	Kyō (boku wa ashi ga) amari itaku arimasen.	Today, it's not very painful.
Tom:	*Itsu (anata wa byōin kara) taiin shimasu* ka.*	When will you be discharged from the hospital?

*The intransitive verb **nyūin shimasu** follows **ni** while the intransitive verb **taiin shimasu** follows **kara**.

Makoto: *Asatte (boku wa) taiin shimasu.*

        (Boku-tachi wa) shukudai ga takusan ari-masu ka.

Tom: *Hai arimasu.*

The day after tomorrow (I'll be discharged from the hospital).

Do we have a lot of homework?

Yes, we do.

EXERCISES

Exercise 21.1. 🔘 *I shall suggest that we do things together. Write what they are in English.*

1. *Let's listen to Japanese music.* ____________________

2. ____________________

3. ____________________

4. ____________________

5. ____________________

6. ____________________

7. ____________________

21.2. Translate into English:

1. *Ashita no hachi-ji ni depāto no mae de aimashō.*

____

2. *Kono ringo o ojīsan ni agemashō.*

____

3. *Ashita tomodachi o hiru-gohan ni manekimashō.*

____

4. *Kore o kaimashō.*

____

5. *Natsu umi de oyogimashō.* ____

6. *Korekara benkyō o shimashō.* ____

7. *Ashita yama e ikimashō.* ____

Translate into rōmaji:

8. Let's watch TV tonight. ____

9. Let's study Japanese next year. ____

10. Let's put on warm sweaters. ____

11. Let's eat (our) dinner. ____

12. Tomorrow morning, let's go to the department store by bus.

____

13. Let's get good grades tomorrow. ____

14. Let's play. ____

21.3. 🔘 *I shall ask some questions about Conversation 1. Reply to each question aloud in Japanese, and write down your answers. Correct answers are recorded at the end of this exercise.*

1. ____

2. ____

3. ____

4. ____

5. ____

6. ____

7. ____

     Lesson 21: Shall I Suggest? Or Shall I Demand?

21.4.  *I shall ask some questions about Conversation 3. Reply to each question aloud in Japanese, and write down your answers. Correct answers are recorded at the end of this exercise.*

1. ____

2. ____

3. ____

4. ____

5. ____

DO AS I SAY, OR ELSE!

You may form an imperative (that is, give an order or instruction) by converting **V•masu** into **V•nasai**.

subject **wa** object **o V•nasai**

subject **wa V•nasai**

This form of a sentence is most commonly used by a mother to a child or by a teacher to a student. Since the order or instruction is made by an older person to a younger person, **-san** and **-kun** are often dropped. The subject is usually followed by **wa**.

Examples

Robert wa hon o yominasai.	*Read the book, Robert!*
Betty wa benkyō o shinasai.	*Study, Betty!*
Tom wa nenasai.	*Go to bed (Sleep), Tom!*
Anata wa koko ni inasai.	*Stay here (Be here)!*
Koko e kinasai.	*Come here!*

Conversation 4: I Don't Feel Well

Tom visits a hospital and uses the following medically-related vocabulary and expressions.

Nouns	Na-Adjective	Suffix
hokenshō health insurance card	*dame na* not good	*-do* degree
iro color		
kaze a cold		
kibun feeling		
kusuri medicine		
netsu body temperature, fever		
taionkei clinical thermometer		

hakarimasu measure, weigh   *hajimete* for the first time
nomimasu take (medicine)
yasumimasu be absent from, rest from, take time off from

Expressions

(Anata wa) dō shimasu ka.	*What will you do (about it)?*
(Anata wa) dō shimashita ka.	*What's wrong/happened/the-matter (with you)?*

Tom:	*Sumimasen. (Boku wa) atama ga itai desu.*	*Excuse me. I have a headache.*
Nurse:	*Kono byōin wa hajimete desu ka.*	*Is this (your) first time in this hospital?*
Tom:	*Hai.*	*Yes.*
Nurse:	*(Anata wa) hokenshō ga arimasu ka.*	*Do you have a health insurance card?*
Tom:	*Hai. Kore (wa boku no hokenshō) desu.*	*Yes. This is it.*
Nurse:	*(Anata wa) kao (no) iro ga yoku nai desu ne. Netsu o hakarimashō.*	*You don't look well, do you? Let's take (measure) (your) temperature.*

***

Doctor:	*(Anata wa) dō shimashita ka.*	*What's wrong?*
Tom:	*(Boku wa) atama ga itai desu.*	*I have a headache.*
	(Boku wa) netsu ga arimasu.	*I have a fever.*
	(Boku wa) kibun ga warui desu.	*I feel bad (I have bad feeling).*
Doctor:	*Taionkei o kudasai. (Anata wa) netsu ga san-jū hachi-do arimasu.*	*May I have the thermometer please? You have a fever of 38 degrees Celsius.*
	Kore wa kaze desu. Kyō daigaku o yasuminasai.	*This is a cold. Stay home (be absent) from college today!*
	Ie de nenasai. Mizu o takusan nominasai. Furo wa dame desu.	*Sleep at home! Drink plenty of water! Don't take a bath (a bath is not good).*
	Kyō to ashita kono kusuri o nominasai.	*Take this medicine today and tomorrow!*
Tom:	*Dōmo arigatō gozaimashita. Sayōnara.*	*Thank you very much. Good-bye.*

EXERCISES

21.5. 🔘 *I shall "order" you to do things. Write what they are in English.*

1. *Get well fast!* _______________________________________

2. _______________________________________

3. _______________________________________

4. _______________________________________

5. _______________________________________

6. _______________________________________

21.6. 🔘 *I shall ask some questions about Conversation 4. Reply to each question aloud in Japanese, and write down your answers. Correct answers are recorded at the end of this exercise.*

1. ____

2. ____

3. ____

4. ____

21.7. Translate into English:

1. *Amy wa tegami o heya de kakinasai.*

____

2. *Robert wa miruku o neko ni agenasai.*

____

3. *Ashita Kimi to Betty wa gakkō e basu de ikinasai.*

____

4. *Tom wa soto de asobinasai.*

____

5. *Betty wa Furansu-go no benkyō o shinasai.*

____

6. *Jūni-ji ni ranchi o tabenasai.*

____

7. *Ashita Ken wa kono hon o yominasai.*

____

Translate into rōmaji:

8. Betty, clean your room! ____

9. Go to school, Makoto! ____

10. Eat the tomato, Robert! ____

11. Kimi, come here! ____

12. Before a meal, wash your hands, Tom!

____

13. Becky, come into the house!

____

14. It is 11 o'clock already! Go to bed (sleep)!

____

Practice the three katakana characters ヤ, ユ and ヨ.

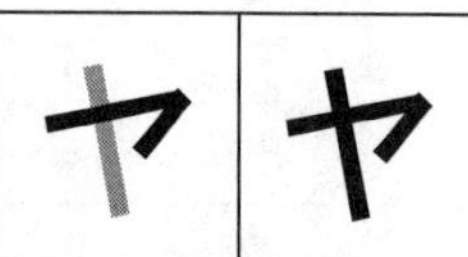

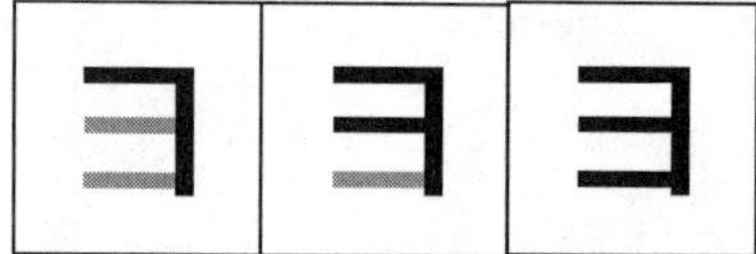

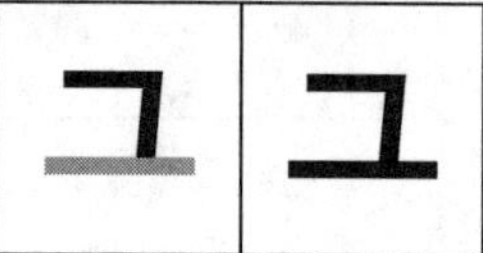

What you must remember from this lesson to proceed to the next lesson:

An imperative sentence is formed by changing **V•masu** into **V•nasai.**

A polite imperative sentence is formed by dropping the subject and changing **V•masu** into **V•mashō**; it is translated as *Let's _.*

22 *Some and Any*

Speaking
To express quantities with the words "some" and "any"

Grammar
To understand the use of **ka, demo** and **mo** after interrogatives

In the previous lesson, you learned to express the imperative (ordering a listener to do something) and the polite imperative (suggesting that a listener do something with you) by changing **masu** of **V•masu**-verbs.

In this lesson, you will learn expressions using *some* and *any*, such as *someday, something, somebody, somewhere, anytime, anything, anyone, anywhere*, etc. Those words are constructed by putting **ka/demo/mo** after interrogatives (question words) in Japanese.

THE PARTICLES *KA, DEMO* AND *MO*

Since interrogatives are the starting point of this lesson, let's review the interrogatives you have learned so far. They are:

dare who	*dore* which one	*itsu* when
doko where	*dono* "noun" which "noun"	*nan/nani* what

Remember that **nan** is used before a word starting with **n/t/d**; **nani** is used in all other cases. Except for **dono,** which is an adjective, all the interrogatives above are pronouns.

Some: Interrogative + KA + Positive Verb

"Interrogatives + **ka** + positive verbs" give the following expressions:

dareka somebody	*doreka* something	*itsuka* someday
dokoka somewhere	*dono* "noun" *ka* some "noun"	*nanika* something

Any: Interrogative + DEMO + Positive Verb

"Interrogatives + **demo** + positive verbs" give the following expressions:

dare demo anyone, everyone	*dore demo* anything	*itsu demo* anytime
doko demo anywhere, everywhere	*dono* "noun" *demo* any "noun"	*nan demo* anything, everything

(Not) Any: Interrogative + MO + Negative Verb

"Interrogatives + **mo** + negative verbs" give the following expressions:

dare mo *(not) anyone*	***dore mo*** *(not) any of them*	***itsu mo*** *(not) anytime*
doko mo *(not) anywhere*	***dono "noun" mo*** *(not) any "noun"*	***nani mo*** *(not) anything*

HOW DO WE USE *SOME* AND *ANY* IN SENTENCES?

We can make a sentence with one of the above expressions like this: we start with a "basic statement" and find the word which may be replaced by the expression; then check the particle which follows the word we are replacing with the expression, and follow the rules below.

Rules:

1. If the word you are replacing is followed by the particle **wa/ga/o,** the particle must be dropped.

2. If the word you are replacing is followed by the particle **ni/e** and if the expression you are replacing it with ends with **demo/mo,** the particle **ni/e** must be put in between the interrogative word and **demo/mo** of the expression.

3. If the word you are replacing is followed by the particle **ni/e** and if the expression ends with **ka, ni/e** follows the **ka** of the expression.

The above rules sound complicated. Well, it is much easier to see what they mean by going through the following examples. Let us start with "basic statements" and see how the basic statements change with the expressions.

Let us consider a basic statement **Watashi wa <u>ringo o</u> tabemasu,** *I shall eat an apple.*

We want to change "I shall eat an apple" into "I shall eat something," "I shall eat anything" and "I shall not eat anything." **Ringo** is the word to be replaced with the expressions (something, anything and (not) anything). Because **ringo** is a "thing," **nani/nan** is the interrogative word to be considered (**dore** and **dono ringo** may be considered also). Hence, to replace **ringo** we have expressions **nanika,** *something,* **na***n* **demo,** *anything,* and **nani mo,** *(not) anything.* (You may recall that **nan** is used if it is followed by a word starting with **n/t/d; nani** is used in all other cases.) Since **ringo** is followed by **o, o** must be omitted from the new sentences with the expressions (rule 1). Putting it all together, we get:

Watashi wa ringo o *tabemasu.*	*I shall eat an apple.*
Watashi wa nanika *tabemasu.*	*I shall eat something.*
Watashi wa nan demo *tabemasu.*	*I shall eat anything.*
Watashi wa nani mo *tabemasen.*	*I shall not eat anything.*

Note that **nani mo** must be followed by a negative verb to mean *(not) anything.*

Let's do the same thing with another sentence, **Watashi wa <u>eki e</u> ikimasu,** *I will go to the station.*

     Lesson 22: Some and Any

We want to change "I will go to the station" into "I will go somewhere," "I will go anywhere" and "I will not go anywhere." **Eki** is the word to be replaced with the expressions. Because **eki** is a "place," **doko** is the interrogative word to be considered. Hence we have expressions **dokoka,** *somewhere,* **doko demo,** *anywhere,* and **doko mo,** *(not) anywhere* to replace **eki**.

Consider the expression **dokoka,** *somewhere,* first. Since **eki** is followed by **e** and the expression ends with **ka, e** must follow **ka** (rule 3). Hence we get: **Watashi wa <u>dokoka e ikimasu</u>,** *I will go somewhere.*

Now consider the expression **doko demo,** *anywhere.* Using rule 2, **e** must be put in between **doko** and **demo** in the new sentence. Hence we get: **Watashi wa <u>doko e demo</u> ikimasu,** *I will go anywhere.*

Now consider the expression **doko mo,** *(not) anywhere.* Using rule 2, **e** must be put in between **doko** and **mo.** Changing the positive verb into the negative verb, we get: **Watashi wa <u>doko e mo</u> ikimasen,** *I will not go anywhere.*

Well, that wasn't too bad, was it?

Conversation: I'm Full

Makoto suggests activities to Hanako and Tom. Hanako is very agreeable while Tom is very unsociable. The following vocabulary lists ippai, *which may be used in many ways.*

	Na-*Adjective*	*Adverb*	*Noun*
ippai	*full*	*plenty*	*one cupful, one drink (alcoholic)*

Makoto:	*Nani ka tabemasen ka.*	*Would you like to eat something?*
Hanako:	*(Watashi wa)* **nan demo** *tabemasu yo.*	*I'll eat anything!*
Tom:	*Boku wa* **nani mo** *tabemasen. (Boku wa) onaka ga ippai desu.*	*I won't eat anything. I'm full.*
	Sakki (boku wa) **hiru-gohan o tabe-mashita.**	*A little while ago, I ate (my) lunch.*
	(Boku wa yakisoba o) **ippai tabe-mashita.**	*I ate plenty.*
Makoto:	*Korekara nani ka minna de shimasen ka.*	*Would you like to do something (from) now, with all of us?*
Hanako:	*(Watashi wa)* **nan demo** *shimasu yo.*	*I'll do anything!*
Tom:	*Boku wa* **nani mo** *shimasen.*	*I won't (do anything).*
	Korekara boku wa uchi e kaerimasu. Dareka boku no uchi e kimasu.	*I'll go back to (my) house (from) now. Somebody's coming to my house.*
Makoto:	*Ashita dokoka e minna de ikimasen ka.*	*Would you like to go somewhere tomorrow, with all of us?*
Hanako:	*(Watashi wa)* **doko e demo** *ikimasu. Atago-yama wa dō desu ka.*	*I'll go anywhere. How about Mt. Atago?*
Tom:	*Boku wa* **doko e mo** *ikimasen. Ashita (boku wa) isogashii desu.*	*I won't go anywhere. I'm busy tomorrow.*

22.1. 🔘 *Say the following words aloud in Japanese. Correct answers are recorded on the track for Exercise 22.1.*

1. somebody

2. somewhere

3. someday

4. anyone

5. anywhere

6. anytime

7. (not) anyone

8. (not) anywhere

9. (not) anytime

22.2. Translate into rōmaji:

1. I will read these books. _*Watashi wa kono hon o yomimasu.*_

I will read some books. ________________________

I will read any book. ________________________

I will not read any book. ________________________

2. I will buy this. _*Watashi wa kore o kaimasu.*_

I will buy something. ________________________

I will buy anything. ________________________

I will not buy anything. ________________________

3. I will give this to you. _*Watashi wa kore o anata ni agemasu.*_

I will give this to somebody. ________________________

I will give this to anybody. ________________________

I will not give this to anybody. ________________________

22.3. Translate into English:

1. *Watashi wa nani mo hoshiku nai desu.*

____

2. *Watashi wa dore mo kaimasen.* _____________________________

3. *Nanika nomimasen ka.* ___________________________________

4. *Watashi wa doreka yomimasu.* _____________________________

5. *Dareka kono video o mimasen ka.* __________________________

6. *Dare mo yama e ikimasen deshita.* __________________________

7. *Kono neko wa dare demo suki desu.* _________________________

8. *Itsu demo watashi wa tenisu o shimasu yo!*

____

9. *Dono basu ga eki e ikimasu ka. Dono basu demo eki e ikimasu.*

____

Translate into rōmaji:

10. This dog eats anything. __________________________________

11. I won't buy any fruit. ____________________________________

12. Would you like to go somewhere? ___________________________

13. Nobody goes to school on Sundays. __________________________

14. I did not see anything. ___________________________________

15. I will not buy any dress. _________________________________

16. My elder brother can do anything. __________________________

17. Makoto does not come to a party ever (any time).

____

18. Would you like to go to a mountain someday?

____

Practice the five katakana characters ラ， リ， ル， レ and ロ.

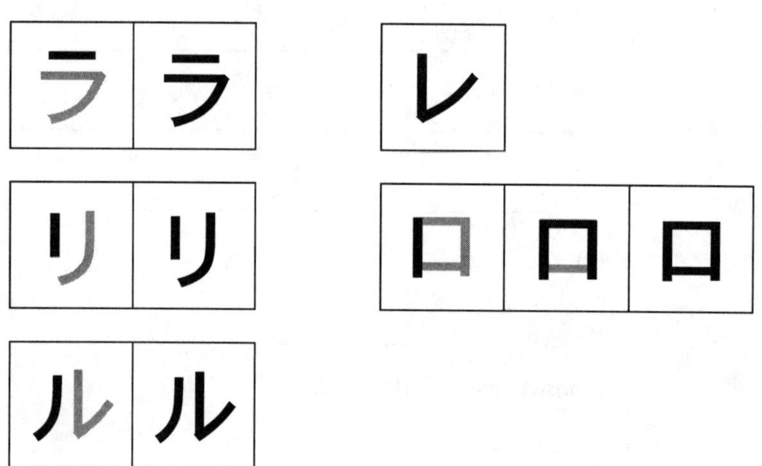

What you must remember from this lesson to proceed to the next lesson:

An interrogative + **ka** + a positive verb produces *some*.

An interrogative + **demo** + a positive verb produces *any*.

An interrogative + **mo** + a negative verb produces *not any*.

Lesson 22: Some and Any

23 Desires

By now, you should be fairly comfortable and confident with carrying on conversations with Japanese people. You may also notice that you are approaching the end of learning the Japanese sentence structures: this is, after all, the last lesson dealing with sentence structures.

It is natural for you to want to be more forceful and assertive of your desires now. Instead of visiting shrines, watching baseball games and eating noodles like your Japanese friends want to do, wouldn't it be nice to do things that you want to do for a change? In this lesson, you will learn to do just that: you will learn to say sentences such as "I don't want to go to the temple," "I don't want to watch Japanese TV," "I want to eat steak," "I want to watch movies in English," and so on. You will also learn adjective clauses.

Let me explain what an adjective clause is. You know that an adjective describes a noun. While an adjective is a single word, an adjective clause is a collection of words (containing a verb) that describes a noun. For example, *big* of "I eat the big apple" is an adjective describing "the apple," while *which is big* of "I eat the apple which is big" is an adjective clause because *which is big* is a collection of words (containing the verb *is*) describing "the apple." It is worth noting that every adjective may be written as an adjective clause in English. An adjective clause may begin with *which, when, where, that,* etc., depending on the word it describes. For example, in the sentence "My brother went to America where he wanted to go for a long time," *where he wanted to go for a long time* is an adjective clause describing America; because the word *America* is a place, the adjective clause describing it starts with *where*.

You may be wondering why I want to teach you complicated sentences such as ones including adjective clauses. After all, I have told you that every complicated sentence should be rewritten in several simpler sentences when you are a beginner in a foreign language. For example, "My brother went to America where he wanted to go for a long time" should be expressed in two sentences: "My brother went to America" and "He wanted to go there for a long time." Well, although the sentences containing adjective clauses are fairly complicated in English, they are very simple in Japanese. Once you have learned to express your desire ("want to do something"), you can make adjective clauses with no extra work, so I just cannot resist the temptation of teaching it to you!

The sentences with transitive verbs, _ **wa** _ **o V•masu,** may be transformed to express desire by changing **o** into **ga** and **V•masu** into **V•tai desu.**

subject **wa** object **ga V•tai desu**

The sentences with intransitive verbs, _ **wa/ga V•masu,** may be transformed to express desire by changing **ga** into **wa** and **V•masu** into **V•tai desu.**

subject **wa V•tai desu**

The Japanese verbs **V•tai desu** may be translated as *want to _.*

Examples

Watashi wa hon o yomimasu.	*I read a book.*
Watashi wa hon ga yomitai desu.	*I want to read a book.*
Okāsan wa ryokō o shimasu.	*Mother travels.*
Okāsan wa ryokō ga shitai desu.	*Mother wants to travel.*
Otōsan wa Doitsu e ikimasu.	*Father goes to Germany.*
Otōsan wa Doitsu e ikitai desu.	*Father wants to go to Germany.*
Watashi wa nemasu.	*I sleep.*
Watashi wa netai desu.	*I want to sleep.*
Koko ni neko ga imasu.	*Here is a cat.*
Koko ni watashi wa itai desu.	*I want to be here.*

You may notice in the above example that *want to be here* expresses "my desire" and therefore the subject is not followed by **ga,** which follows a subject when the action is stated as a natural occurrence.

Anata wa nani ga nomitai desu ka.	*What do you want to drink?*
Anata wa nani ga shitai desu ka.	*What do you want to do?*
Anata wa dono hon ga yomitai desu ka.	*Which book do you want to read?*
Anata wa doko e ikitai desu ka.	*Where do you want to go?*

When an expression "interrogative + **ka/demo/mo** (e.g., **dareka, dokoka, doreka,** etc.)" is used, the rules on page 248 hold.

Examples

Anata wa nanika tabetai desu ka.	*Do you want to eat something?*
Anata wa dokoka e ikitai desu ka.	*Do you want to go somewhere?*
Watashi wa doko e demo ikitai desu.	*I want to go anywhere.*
Dareka nanika tabetai desu ka.	*Does somebody want to eat something?*
Yoru dare demo netai desu.	*At night, everybody wants to sleep.*

(O)bentō—a meal in a box.

 Conversation 1: Would You Like to Go to a Mountain Tomorrow?

Hanako and Tom go on a trip to a mountain.

Verbs (Intransitive)	**Noun**
sukimasu be empty, not to be crowded	*bentō* meal in a box
tsukaremasu to be tired	

Hanako:	*Ashita yama e ikimasen ka.*	*Would you like to go to a mountain tomorrow?*
Tom:	*(Boku wa yama e) ikitai desu.*	*I'd like to.*
	(Boku wa) yama de e ga kakitai desu.	*I want to draw a picture on the mountain.*
Hanako:	*Watashi wa hana ga mitai desu.*	*I want to see flowers.*
	(Watashi wa) tori no koe mo kikitai desu.*	*I want to listen to the cries of birds too.*
	Nan-ji ni (watashi-tachi wa) ikimasu ka.	*What time will (do) we go?*
Tom:	*Asa-gohan no ato wa dō desu ka.*	*How about after breakfast?*
Hanako:	*Nan-ji ni (anata wa) asa-gohan o tabemasu ka.*	*What time do you eat (your) breakfast?*
Tom:	*Shichi-ji ni (boku wa asa-gohan o) tabemasu.*	*I eat at 7 o'clock.*
Hanako:	*Hachi-ji ni ie o demashō.*	*Let's leave (our) houses at 8 o'clock.*
	Watashi wa (watashi-tachi no) (o)bentō o tsukurimasu.	*I shall make our lunch (in boxes).*
Tom:	*(Boku-tachi wa) dono yama e ikimasu ka.*	*To which mountain are we going?*
Hanako:	*Atago-yama wa dō desu ka*	*How about Mt. Atago?*
Tom:	*(Sore wa) ii desu ne.*	*That's good, isn't it?*
Hanako:	*Korekara watashi wa (o)bentō o tsukurima-su.*	*Right now (from now) I will make our lunch (in boxes).*
	Dewa mata ashita.	*See you tomorrow.*
***		
Tom:	*Yama wa kirei desu ne.*	*The mountain is beautiful, isn't it?*
	(Boku-tachi wa) yoku arukimashita ne. *(Anata wa) tsukaremashita ka.*	*We walked a lot, didn't we? Did you get tired?*

*When **mo**, *also/too*, refers to the word followed by **ga**, **ga** is omitted (page 100).

Hanako:	*Iie (Watashi wa tsukaremasen deshita).*	*No, I didn't.*
	(Watashi wa) **onaka ga sukimashita.****	*I am hungry (As for me, the stomach is empty).*
	*(Watashi wa) (o)***bentō ga tabetai desu.**	*I want to eat lunch.*
Tom:	*(O)***bentō o tabemashō.**	*Let's eat.*

I DON'T WANT TO

subject wa **object** ga/o **V•taku nai desu**

You may make negative statements by converting **V•tai desu** into **V•taku ari-masen** or **V•taku nai desu**. We shall use **V•taku nai desu** in this book. The object may be followed by either **ga** or **o**.

Examples

Watashi wa hon ga/o yomitaku nai desu.	*I do not want to read the book.*
Watashi wa Eigo ga/o naraitaku nai desu.	*I do not want to learn English.*
Tarō-kun wa sumō ga/o shitaku nai desu.	*Taro does not want to do sumo.*
Inu wa heya kara detaku nai desu.	*The dog does not want to go out of the room.*
Otōto wa arukitaku nai desu.	*The younger brother does not want to walk.*

A direct answer to a question _ **wa** _ **ga** _**tai desu ka** is either **hai _tai desu** or **iie _taku nai desu**.

EXERCISES

23.1. Complete the table below.

masu	Meaning	"Want to" Form	"Don't Want to" Form
naraimasu	learn	*naraitai desu*	*naraitaku nai desu*
okurimasu			
shimasu			
		hajimetai desu	
aimasu			
aitaku nai desu			
	come	*kitai desu*	

**Same sentence structure as "I have a headache!," page 160.

23.2. *I shall tell you what I want to do. Write what it is in English.*

1. ____

2. ____

3. ____

4. ____

5. ____

23.3. *Listen to the track for Exercise 23.2 again. Convert the sentences into negative statements and say them. You may check your replies against the correct answers recorded on the track for Exercise 23.3.*

1. ____

2. ____

3. ____

4. ____

5. ____

23.4. *Translate into English:*

1. *Anata wa dono zasshi ga yomitai desu ka.*

____

2. *Ima watashi wa nakitai desu.* ________________________________

3. *Onīsan wa kawa de oyogitai desu.*________________________________

4. *Kyō watashi wa ban-gohan ga/o tabetaku nai desu.*

____

5. *Watashi wa benkyō ga/o shitaku nai desu.*

____

6. *Kyō otōto wa gakkō e ikitaku nai desu.*

____

7. *Watashi wa netaku nai desu.*_______________________________

8. *Ashita watashi-tachi wa dokoka e ikitai desu ne.*

____

9. *Anata wa nanika shitai desu ka.* _____________________________

10. *Dareka koko ni itai desu ka.* ______________________________

11. *Dareka mizu ga nomitai desu ka.*

____

12. *Watashi wa nani mo tabetaku nai desu.*

____

13. *Watashi wa doko e mo ikitaku nai desu.*

____

Translate into rōmaji:

14. I want to watch a video tonight. ____________________________

15. I want to eat steak for dinner. _____________________________

16. I want to buy a coat in spring.______________________________

17. I want to walk. ____

18. That cat wants to go out from the room.

____

19. In summer, I want to marry Robert in America.

____

20. Mother wants to buy an Italian handbag.

____

21. I do not want to meet Betty. _______________________________

22. I do not want to swim today. _______________________________

                    Lesson 23: Desires

23. Does anybody want to drink cold water?

____

24. In summer, I want to work at a company somewhere.

____

25. I do not want to meet anyone. ____________________________

26. Nobody wants to clean. _________________________________

23.5. 💿 *I shall ask some questions on Conversation 1. Reply to each question aloud in Japanese. Correct answers are recorded at the end of this exercise.*

1. ____

2. ____

3. ____

4. ____

23.6. 💿 *I shall ask some questions on Conversation 1 on lesson 22. Listen to the questions on the track for Exercise 23.6. Reply to each question aloud in Japanese. Correct answers are recorded at the end of this exercise.*

1. ____

2. ____

3. ____

YESTERDAY, I WANTED TO

You may convert to the past tense by changing **_tai desu** into **_takatta desu.**

Examples

Watashi wa hon ga yomitakatta desu.	*I wanted to read a book.*
Watashi wa Amerika e ikitakatta desu.	*I wanted to go to America.*
Watashi wa ryokō ga shitakatta desu.	*I wanted to travel.*
Amerika ni watashi wa itakatta desu.	*I wanted to be in America.*

Anata wa nani ga nomitakatta desu ka.	*What did you want to drink?*
Anata wa nani ga shitakatta desu ka.	*What did you want to do?*
Anata wa dokoka e ikitakatta desu ka.	*Did you want to go somewhere?*

EXERCISES

23.7. 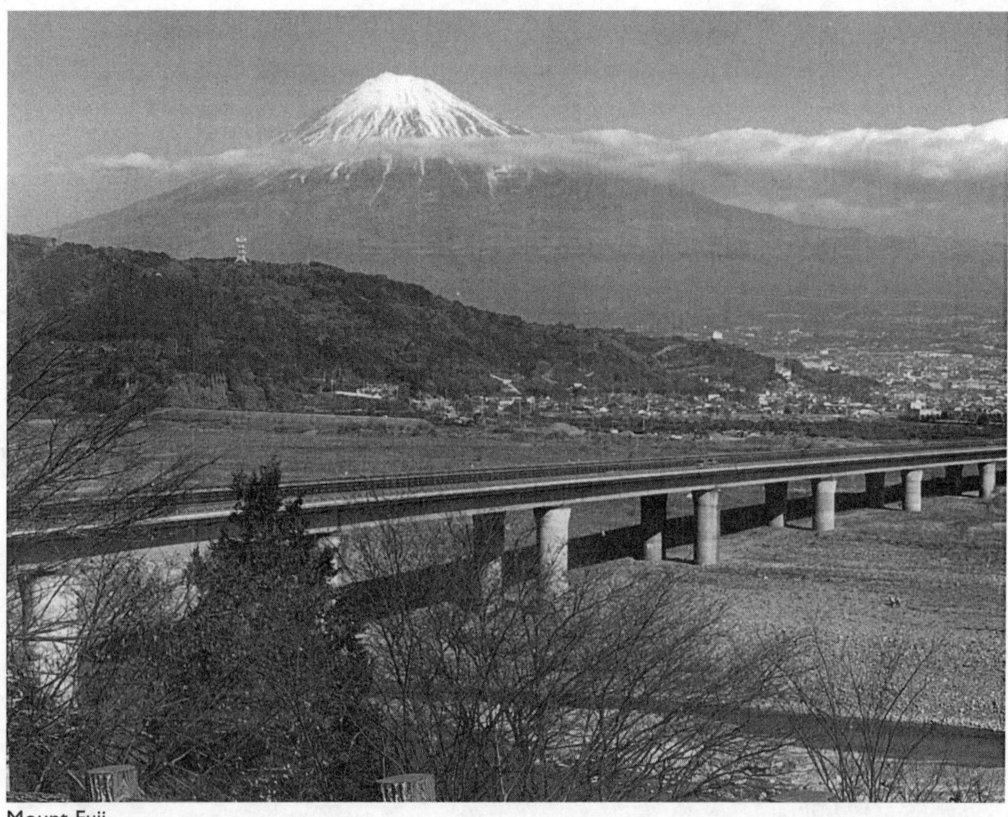 Listen to the track for Exercise 23.2 again. Convert the sentences into past tense and say them aloud. Correct answers are recorded on the track for Exercise 23.7.

1. ____

2. ____

3. ____

4. ____

5. ____

Mount Fuji.

Lesson 23: Desires

23.8. Translate into English:

1. *Watashi wa yama no e ga kakitakatta desu.*

____

2. *Kyonen ojīsan wa Amerika e kaeritakatta desu.*

____

3. *Natsu-yasumi ni onēsan wa hatarakitakatta desu.*

____

4. *Watashi wa machi de kaimono ga shitakatta desu.*

____

5. *Anata wa nan no benkyō ga shitakatta desu ka.*

____

6. *Anata wa dono fuku ga kaitakatta desu ka.*

____

Translate into rōmaji:

7. I wanted to go to England last year.

____

8. My mother wanted to buy a very expensive dress.

____

9. I wanted to drive a car. ____________________________________

10. I wanted to drink coffee. __________________________________

11. Last summer my younger brother wanted to travel.

____

12. I wanted to take photographs of the beautiful mountains.

____

 You may make the negative past tense by changing **_taku nai desu** into **_taku nakatta desu** (or by changing **_taku arimasen** into **_taku arimasen deshita**). The object may be followed by either **ga** or **o**.

Examples

Kinō watashi wa benkyō ga/o shitaku nakatta desu.	*Yesterday, I did not want to study.*
Imōto wa ban-gohan ga/o tabetaku nakatta desu.	*The younger sister did not want to eat an evening meal.*
Watashi wa Amerika kara kaeritaku nakatta desu.	*I did not want to return from America.*
Onīsan wa daigaku e ikitaku nakatta desu.	*The elder brother did not want to go to the university.*
Robert-kun wa kekkon shitaku nakatta desu.	*Robert did not want to get married.*
Watashi wa yama de netaku nakatta desu.	*I did not want to sleep on the mountain.*

EXERCISES

23.9. Listen to the track for Exercise 23.2 again. Convert the sentences into negative past tense and say them aloud. Correct answers are recorded on the track for Exercise 23.9.

1. ____

2. ____

3. ____

4. ____

5. ____

23.10. On a separate piece of paper, complete the conjugations below for each of the V•masu-verbs that follow.

V•masu-verb:	*hanashimasu (to talk)*
"Want to" Form:	*hanashitai desu*
"Don't Want to" Form:	*hanashitaku nai desu*
"Wanted to" Form:	*hanashitakatta desu*
"Did Not Want to" Form:	*hanashitaku nakatta desu*

1. *nomimasu* 2. *machimasu* 3. *ikimasu* 4. *arukimasu*

     Lesson 23: Desires

23.11. Translate into English:

1. Kyonen watashi wa Nihon e kitaku nakatta desu.

____

2. Watashi wa kisha kara oritaku nakatta desu.

____

3. Otōto wa Furansu-go ga/o naraitaku nakatta desu.

____

4. Otōsan wa kono kuruma ga/o kaitaku nakatta desu.

____

Translate into rōmaji:

1. I did not want to go to Germany. _____________________________________

2. I did not want to invite Robert to my birthday party.

____

3. I did not want to meet you._____________________________________

4. Yesterday, my younger sister did not want to study math.

____

ADJECTIVE CLAUSES: _TAI / TAKATTA / TAKU-NAI / TAKU-NAKATTA_

Nouns

koto thing (abstract)	*mukashi* long time ago	*toki* time, moment
keshō make-up	*mono* thing (article)	*tokoro* place

_tai may act as an adjective clause by itself and it precedes the word it describes. It is translated as *which/when/where/that (somebody) wants to _*. The subject of the adjective clause is the same as that of the main clause.

Examples

tabetai okashi	*the candy* which *(somebody) wants to eat*
shitai koto	*the thing* that *(somebody) wants to do*
ikitai toki	*the moment* when *(somebody) wants to go*
ikitai tokoro	*the place* where *(somebody) wants to go*

Tabetai, shitai and **ikitai,** above, describe the nouns **okashi, koto, toki** and **tokoro,** and they may be translated as *which/that/when/where somebody wants to eat/do/go.* Notice that the translation for the adjective clauses starts with *which, that, when* and *where* according to the nouns they describe.

The easiest way to make a sentence with an adjective clause is as follows. First, make a sentence without the adjective clause, and then insert the adjective clause in front of the noun it describes. Let's make the sentence *I buy the fruit that I want to eat.* First, consider *I buy the fruit:* **watashi wa kudamono o kaimasu.** Insert **tabetai,** *that I want to eat* in front of **kudamono** to get **Watashi wa tabetai kudamono o kaimasu,** *I buy the fruit that I want to eat.*

The following examples show adjective clauses in sentences. You may notice that the subjects of the adjective clauses are the same as those of the main clauses. For example, in the last three sentences, **yomitai hon** is translated as *the book that I want to read, the book that you want to read* and *the book that she wants to read,* respectively, because the subjects of the main clauses are **watashi, Miki** (implying you) and **Miki-san** (implying she), respectively.

Examples

Watashi wa tabetai *mono o kaimasu.*	*I buy* what I want to eat. *(I buy the things* that I want to eat.*)*
Watashi wa ikitai *tokoro e ikimasu.*	*I go* where I want. *(I go to the place* where I want to go.*)*
Ikitai *toki ni ikinasai.*	*Go* when you want! *(Go at the moment* when you want to go!*)*
Watashi wa shitai *koto o shimasu.*	*I do* what I want. *(I do the thing* that I want to do.*)*
Kaitai *fuku wa takai desu.*	*The dress* that I want to buy *is expensive.*
Watashi wa yomitai *hon o yomimasu.*	*I read the book* that I want to read.
Miki wa yomitai *hon o yominasai.*	*Miki, read the book* that you want to read!
Miki-san wa yomitai *hon o yomimasu.*	*Miki reads the book* that she wants to read.

_taku nai, _takatta and **_taku nakatta** are adjective clauses for the negative present, past and negative past, respectively.

Examples

yomitai hon	*the book that (somebody) wants to read*
yomitaku nai hon	*the book that (somebody) does not want to read*
yomitakatta hon	*the book that (somebody) wanted to read*
yomitaku nakatta hon	*the book that (somebody) did not want to read*
Kaitai *kutsu wa totemo takai desu.*	*The shoes* that I want to buy *are very expensive.*
Korekara watashi wa shitaku nai *rekishi no benkyō o shimasu.*	*From now on, I shall study history,* which I do not want to do.
Kinō onīsan wa ikitakatta *Amerika e ikimashita.*	*Yesterday, (my) elder brother went to America* where he wanted to go.
Watashi wa kaitaku nakatta *takai kutsu o kaimashita.*	*I bought the expensive shoes* that I did not want to buy.

           Lesson 23: Desires

23.12. 🔘 *Say the following phrases aloud. Correct answers are recorded on the track for Exercise 23.12.*

1. when (I) want to go

2. when (I) do not want to go

3. when (I) wanted to go

4. when (I) did not want to go

5. the person (I) want to meet

6. the person (I) do not want to meet

7. the person (I) wanted to meet

8. the person (I) did not want to meet

23.13. 🔘 *I shall say some adjective clauses in Japanese. Choose the English translation of what I say from the list and write down the correct letter.*

1. ___________   a. the thing that I want to eat

2. ___________   b. the thing that I do not want to eat

3. ___________   c. the thing that I wanted to eat

4. ___________   d. the thing that I did not want to eat

5. ___________   e. the place I want to go

6. ___________   f. the place I do not want to go

7. ___________   g. the place I wanted to go

8. ___________   h. the place I did not want to go

23.14. Translate into English:

1. **Watashi wa shitai koto ga arimasen.** ____

2. **Koko wa kitakatta tokoro desu.** ____

3. **Aitakatta hito wa Amerika e ikimashita.**

____

4. *Kore wa tabetakatta kudamono desu.*

5. *Noritakatta basu ga ikimashita.* _______________________________________

6. *Kyō watashi wa kinō tabetakunakatta kudamono o tabemasu.*

Translate into rōmaji:

7. At this shop, there isn't a thing that I want to buy.

8. I don't do things that I don't want to do.

9. Yesterday, I saw the movie that I wanted to see.

10. This is the book that I wanted to read.

11. My elder brother went to a party to which he did not want to go.

12. Right now (from now), I am going to read the book that I did not want to read yesterday.

JAPANESE ADJECTIVES HAVE TENSES!

You may recall that every adjective may be written as an adjective clause. For example, the adjective *big* of "I eat a big apple" may be replaced by the adjective clause *that is big* of "I eat an apple that is big." Since adjective clauses have a past tense, you may be wondering if adjectives have a past tense also.

For **i**-adjectives, you may obtain past and negative past adjectives by changing **_i** with **_katta** and **_ku nakatta,** respectively.

      Lesson 23: Desires

Examples

omoshiroi hon	*the book that is interesting (the interesting book)*
omoshiroku nai hon	*the book that is not interesting (the uninteresting book)*
omoshirokatta hon	*the book that was interesting*
omoshiroku nakatta hon	*the book that was not interesting*

Ano omoshirokatta hito wa Tarō-kun no ojīsan desu.	*That person who was interesting is Taro's grandfather.*
Watashi wa kono karēraisu o kinō no oishiku nakatta niku de tsukurimashita.	*I made this Indian curry with yesterday's meat, which was not delicious.*

For **na**-adjectives, you may obtain past and negative past adjectives by replacing **na** with **datta** and **de (wa) nakatta** respectively.

Examples

suki na hito	*the person (somebody) likes*
suki de (wa) nai hito	*the person (somebody) does not like*
suki datta hito	*the person (somebody) liked*
suki de (wa) nakatta hito	*the person (somebody) did not like*

Ima boku wa mukashi kirai datta Nihon ga suki desu.	*Now, I like Japan, which I disliked a long time ago.*
Mukashi kirei de nakatta Hanako-san wa ima (o)keshō de kirei ni narimashita.	*Hanako, who was not pretty a long time ago, has become pretty with make-up now.*

 ## Conversation 2: I Like Egg Sandwiches

Tom and Hanako are about to eat the boxed lunches. The following vocabulary appears in their conversation.

Na-Adjectives

dai-kirai na very dislikable	*dai-suki na* very likeable

Noun

tamago egg

Hanako:	*(Anata wa)* **tomato to kyūri no sandoicchi** *ga tabetai desu ka. (Anata wa)* **tamago no sandoicchi** *ga tabetai desu ka.*	*Do you want to eat a tomato and cucumber sandwich, or (do you want to eat) an egg sandwich?*
Tom:	*(Boku wa)* **tamago** *(no sandoicchi)* **ga** *tabetai desu.*	*I want egg.*
Hanako:	*(Anata wa)* **mizu ga nomitai desu ka.** *(Anata wa)* **jūsu ga nomitai desu ka.**	*Do you want to drink water or juice?*
Tom:	*(Boku wa)* **jūsu ga nomitai desu.**	*I want juice.*

***

Tom: *Asoko ni mezurashii tori ga imasu.*   *There is a rare bird over there.*
    Kyonen boku wa Nihon e kitaku nakatta desu.   *Last year, I did not want to come to Japan.*
    Boku wa Nihon ga kirai deshita.   *I disliked Japan.*
    Ima boku wa Nihon ga dai-suki desu.   *Now, I like Japan very much.*

EXERCISES

Verbs (Intransitive)

shinimasu die   _ *ni sumimasu* live at, take up residence at _

23.15. Complete the adjective table below.

Meaning	Present	Negative Present	Past	Negative Past
big	ōkii	ōkiku nai	ōkikatta	ōkiku nakatta
	akai			
	isogashii			
	genki na			
	benri na			
	suki na	suki de (wa) nai	suki datta	suki de (wa) nakatta

23.16. 🔘 *I shall say an adjective clause in Japanese. Choose the English translation of what I say from the list and write down the correct letter.*

1. __________   a. the thing that is amusing/interesting

2. __________   b. the thing that is unpleasant (not interesting)

3. __________   c. the thing that was amusing/interesting

4. __________   d. the thing that was unpleasant (not amusing)

5. __________   e. when he is healthy

6. __________   f. when he is not healthy

      Lesson 23: Desires

7. ____________   g. when he was healthy

8. ____________   h. when he was not healthy

23.17. 🔘 *Say the following phrases aloud. Correct answers are recorded on the track for Exercise 23.17.*

1. the person who is kind

2. the person who is not kind

3. the person who was kind

4. the person who was not kind

5. the dog that is cute

6. the dog that is not cute

7. the dog that was cute

8. the dog that was not cute

23.18. Translate into English:

1. *Otōto wa karai karēraisu ga kirai desu.*

____

2. *Kinō watashi-tachi wa omoshiroku nai eiga o gakkō de mimashita.*

____

3. *Hon-ya ni hoshikatta hon ga arimasen deshita.*

____

4. *Watashi wa tanoshiku nakatta toki no koto o kakimashita.*

____

5. *Watashi wa rippa na isha ni naritai desu.*

____

6. *Benri de nai apāto wa yasui desu.*

____

7. *Shinsetsu datta hito wa Hanako-san no onēsan deshita.*

____

8. *Hanako-san wa mukashi jōzu de nakatta tenisu ga totemo jōzu ni narimashita.*

____

9. The long holiday has finished. ____

10. Let's go to the place that is not dangerous.

____

11. That isn't the dog that was noisy. ________________________________

12. I bought the dress that was not too expensive.

____

13. I did a stupid thing yesterday. ____________________________________

14. We took (our) residence at a not very convenient place.

____

15. The person whom I liked got married.

____

16. The grandfather who was not healthy last year died yesterday.

____

Practice the three katakana characters ワ, ヲ *and* ン.

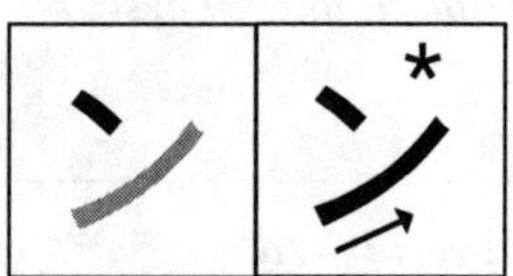

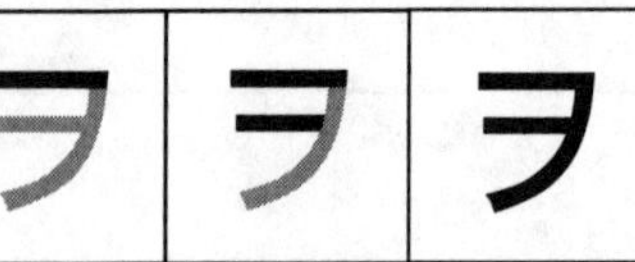

*Note: This stroke is drawn from the lower end to the higher end.

What you must remember from this lesson:

_ **wa** _ **o V•masu** may be converted into the sentence structure _ **wa** _ **ga V•tai desu** to express "want to _."

_**wa/ga V•masu** may be converted into the sentence structure _ **wa V•tai desu** to express "want to _."

The negative present, past and negative past tenses of **V•tai desu** are **V•taku nai desu, V•takatta desu** and **V•taku nakatta desu,** respectively.

V•tai, V•taku nai, V•takatta and **V•taku nakatta,** by themselves, express adjective clauses for present, negative present, past and negative past tenses, respectively.

The present, negative present, past and negative past tenses for **i**-adjectives are **_i, _ku nai, _katta** and **_ku nakatta,** respectively.

The present, negative present, past and negative past tenses for **na**-adjectives are _ **na,** _ **de (wa) nai,** _ **datta** and _ **de (wa) nakatta,** respectively.

24 Let's Read Japanese!

Although you have already learned all the sentence structures there are to learn in this book, you must remember that Japanese is not written in romanized characters, which you have been reading and writing throughout our learning adventures. Romanized characters (called rōmaji) are used to represent the sounds of Japanese in a way that makes it easy for you to read, although Japanese is written in completely different characters.

There are four different types of characters in Japanese. They are hiragana, katakana, kanji and rōmaji (romanized characters). The word **watashi**, *I*, may be written in these four ways as shown below, although you would not write **watashi** in katakana normally.

わたし	ワタシ	私	*watashi*
HIRAGANA	KATAKANA	KANJI	RŌMAJI

Japanese sentences are written in combinations of hiragana, katakana and kanji.

In this lesson, you will learn the differences among hiragana, katakana, kanji and rōmaji so that you will be able to use them correctly. You will also learn to read sentences in hiragana.

DIFFERENCES AMONG HIRAGANA, KATAKANA, KANJI AND RŌMAJI

These are the differences among hiragana, katakana, kanji and rōmaji.

HIRAGANA: Hiragana consists of phonetic symbols representing speech sounds (syllables) and they have no meanings by themselves. There are forty-six different symbols in hiragana. You can write entire sentences with hiragana alone.

KATAKANA: Katakana consists of phonetic symbols representing speech sounds (syllables), just like hiragana. For every hiragana symbol, there is a katakana symbol. The difference between hiragana and katakana is this: Katakana is used mostly for foreign words other than Chinese, for which no Japanese words existed and which became Japanese words after going through some phonetic transformations.

For example, television became テレビ (**terebi**) in Japanese.

Katakana characters are the simplest of all the characters. Each character resembles a combination of a few straight and curved lines in different directions and at different angles.

KANJI: Kanji consists of characters introduced from China many years ago. They were derived from pictographs (pictures) and ideograms (symbols used to represent ideas), and each character represents a complete word or meaning. Kanji characters are the most complicated of all the characters, and they look like pictures for obvious reasons.

Examples
木 *(ki) tree*
人 *(hito) person*

There are more than 50,000 kanji in existence, but only about 1,800 of them are used commonly. Japanese school children spend a great amount of time learning kanji characters at schools. The level of one's education is reflected in the number of kanji characters one uses in one's writing: the more kanji one uses, the more educated one appears to be.

RŌMAJI: Rōmaji characters are combinations of the English alphabet. They represent the Japanese sounds, just as hiragana and katakana do, but in the English alphabet to help English speakers to learn Japanese pronunciation. Although they are taught in schools, they are not customarily used in Japanese writing. Lately, rōmaji has become indispensable when one uses a Japanese word processor: one types sentences in rōmaji, and the word processor converts them into hiragana, katakana or kanji accordingly. This is due to the fact that there are just too many different characters in Japanese and a computer keyboard cannot have that many keys.

When you write a Japanese sentence, you may write it entirely in hiragana. But, if you know kanji for any word, you write it in kanji, and if a word is a "Japanized" imported word, you write it in katakana. Hence, a Japanese sentence is written in a combination of hiragana, katakana and kanji as follows.

A scroll with calligraphy (artistic writing of Japanese characters with brush and ink) of the character 和 decorates a wall.

The sentences below are perceived as being written by an educated person.

Watashi	*wa*	*Tom*	*desu.*	*I am Tom.*
私	は	トム	です。	
↑	↑	↑	↑	
Kanji	Hiragana	Katakana	Hiragana	

Koko	*wa*	*gakkō*	*desu.*	*This is a school.*
ここ	は	学校	です。	
↑	↑	↑	↑	
Hiragana		Kanji	Hiragana	

        Lesson 24: Let's Read Japanese!

The sentences below are perceived as being written by a less educated person.

Watashi   wa   Tom   desu. *I am Tom.*

わたし　は　とむ　です。
　↑　　　↑　　↑　　　　↑

All the characters are in hiragana.

Koko   wa   gakkō   desu. *This is a school.*

ここ　は　がっこう　です。
　↑　　↑　　　↑　　　　↑

All the characters are in hiragana.

HIRAGANA

Syllables in Hiragana

The following table shows the hiragana for each of the rōmaji syllables we've been using.

Vowels

a	あ	i	い	u	う	e	え	o	お

Basic syllables

ka	か	ki	き	ku	く	ke	け	ko	こ
sa	さ	shi	し	su	す	se	せ	so	そ
ta	た	chi	ち	tsu	つ	te	て	to	と
na	な	ni	に	nu	ぬ	ne	ね	no	の
ha	は	hi	ひ	fu	ふ	he	へ	ho	ほ
ma	ま	mi	み	mu	む	me	め	mo	も
ya	や			yu	ゆ			yo	よ
ra	ら	ri	り	ru	る	re	れ	ro	ろ
wa	わ							wo	を
n	ん								

Modified syllables

ga	が	gi	ぎ	gu	ぐ	ge	げ	go	ご
za	ざ	ji	じ	zu	ず	ze	ぜ	zo	ぞ
da	だ	ji	ぢ	zu	づ	de	で	do	ど
ba	ば	bi	び	bu	ぶ	be	べ	bo	ぼ
pa	ぱ	pi	ぴ	pu	ぷ	pe	ぺ	po	ぽ

Ya, Yu, Yo syllables

kya	きゃ	kyu	きゅ	kyo	きょ
sha	しゃ	shu	しゅ	sho	しょ
cha	ちゃ	chu	ちゅ	cho	ちょ
nya	にゃ	nyu	にゅ	nyo	にょ
hya	ひゃ	hyu	ひゅ	hyo	ひょ
mya	みゃ	myu	みゅ	myo	みょ
rya	りゃ	ryu	りゅ	ryo	りょ
gya	ぎゃ	gyu	ぎゅ	gyo	ぎょ
ja	じゃ	ju	じゅ	jo	じょ
bya	びゃ	byu	びゅ	byo	びょ
pya	ぴゃ	pyu	ぴゅ	pyo	ぴょ

It should be stressed that both rōmaji and hiragana are phonetic symbols (romanized spellings in rōmaji and characters in hiragana are associated with speech sounds) and that a syllable in hiragana may be represented by a syllable in rōmaji.

Examples

わ ↔ *wa*

た ↔ *ta*

わたし ↔ *watashi*

Notice that the hiragana in rows 12 to 16, called modified syllables, are obtained by adding "ʹ" to each character in rows 2, 3, 4 and 6, and "°" to row 6, at the upper right corner. In the Japanese language, the sounds of syllables in rows 12 to 15 are considered as harsher versions of the sounds in rows 2, 3, 4 and 6, and they are denoted by two small strokes "ʹ" at the upper right corner of each syllable. In other words, "ʹ" converts a soft sound into a harsher sound. The sounds in row 16 (**pa, pi, pu, pe** and **po**) are regarded as the plosive versions of the sounds in row 6 (**ha, hi, fu, he** and **ho**), and they are written with small circles "°" at the upper righthand corner of **ha, hi, fu, he** and **ho**.

Examples

が *ga* is the harsher sound of か *ka*.

ず *zu* is the harsher sound of す *su*.

ぴ *pi* is the plosive sound of ひ *hi*.

Rows 17 to 27 of the syllable table are called contracted syllables (or Ya, Yu, Yo syllables) because two syllables are contracted to obtain a single syllable. Let's consider the syllable **kya**. When you pronounce **kya**, the syllable starts out as **ki** and ends with **ya**. When the two syllables are pronounced quickly as one syllable, you hear **kya**. When it is written in hiragana, the first letter remains the same but the second letter is written smaller.

Examples

き *ki* + や *ya* → きゃ *kya*

み *mi* + よ *yo* → みよ *myo*

き *ki* + ゆ *yu* → きゅ *kyu*

  Lesson 24: Let's Read Japanese!

Whether a character is of small or usual size, that is, part of a contracted syllable or a whole syllable, makes a great difference to its meaning. For example, いしや means *a stonemason* while いしゃ means *a medical doctor*. You can see that no such confusion arises when they are written in rōmaji (**ishi-ya** and **isha**). The small characters や, ゆ, よ (and つ) are placed at the bottom lefthand corner of the area that a normal-size character would take up, when Japanese is written horizontally; and at the top righthand corner of that area, when Japanese is written vertically.

Example

Isha, medical doctor in hiragana, is written horizontally, and vertically.

いしゃ   い
         し
          ゃ

There are two different hiragana for **ji** and for **zu:** both じ and ぢ are pronounced as **ji,** and both ず and づ are pronounced as **zu.**

EXERCISES

24.1. Consulting the hiragana table, write the following hiragana words in rōmaji, and then translate them into English.

1. こんにちわ______________________________________

2. ただいま______________________________________

3. すみません______________________________________

4. みかん______________________________________

5. りんご______________________________________

6. やさい______________________________________

7. くだもの______________________________________

8. せんせい______________________________________

9. いぬ______________________________________

🔘 *24.2. I shall say a word in Japanese; write it down below in hiragana.*

1. _______________________________ 6. _______________________________

2. _______________________________ 7. _______________________________

3. _______________________________ 8. _______________________________

4. _______________________________ 9. _______________________________

5. _______________________________ 10. ______________________________

HOW TO READ WORDS IN HIRAGANA

Converting rōmaji into hiragana, and vice versa, is fairly straightforward, as we have seen, except when the former have long vowels or double consonants. Here are the rules for converting long vowels and double consonants.

Long Vowels

Let us look at the romanized syllables in the hiragana table.

a appears in the first column in **a, ka, sa, ta, na,** etc. Hence the long vowel **ā** may occur in **ā, kā, sā, tā, nā,** etc. These are pronounced as **a/a, ka/a, sa/a, ta/a, na/a,** etc. They are written as ああ, かあ, さあ, たあ, なあ, etc., in hiragana; e.g., **okāsan** is written as おかあさん.

Similarly, let us look at **i** *in the hiragana table.*

i appears in the second column in **i, ki, shi, chi, ni,** etc. Hence the long vowel **ī** may occur in **ī, kī, shī, chī, nī,** etc. These are pronounced as **i/i, ki/i, shi/i, chi/i, ni/i,** etc. They are written as いい, きい, しい, ちい, にい, etc., in hiragana; e.g., **onīsan** is written as おにいさん.

The long vowel **ū** *may occur in the third column in* **ū, kū, sū, tsū, nū,** *etc.*

These are pronounced as **u/u, ku/u, su/u, tsu/u,** etc. They are written as うう, くう, すう, つう, etc., in hiragana; e.g., **senpūki** is written as せんぷうき.

The long vowel **ē** *may occur in the fourth column in* **ē, kē, sē, tē, nē,** *etc.*

These are pronounced as **e/e, ke/e, se/e, te/e, ne/e,** etc. They are written as えい, けい, せい, てい, ねい, etc., in hiragana. An exception to this rule is **onēsan**, which is written as おね<u>え</u>さん. Most often **ē** occurs in words written in katakana.

The long vowel **ō** *may occur in the fifth column in* **ō, kō, sō, tō, nō,** *etc.*

These are pronounced as **o/o, ko/o, so/o, to/o, no/o,** etc. They are written as おう, こう, そう, とう, のう, etc., in hiragana; e.g., **otōsan** is written as おとうさん. There are some exceptions to this rule.

The most important, and the only one encountered in this book, is that of **ōkii**, which is written as おおきい.

Examples

obāsan おば<u>あ</u>さん	*arigatō* ありが<u>と</u><u>う</u>
ojīsan おじ<u>い</u>さん	*dōzo* ど<u>う</u>ぞ
yūbinkyoku ゆ<u>う</u>びんきょく	*Tōkyō* と<u>う</u>きょ<u>う</u>
otōto おと<u>う</u>と	

In summary, here are our conclusions about the long vowels. い and う each have two different pronunciations.

い is pronounced as **i** except for some long vowels, for which it is pronounced as **e**.

う is pronounced as **u** except for some long vowels, for which it is pronounced as **o**.

When one sees い or う, the only way to correctly pronounce it is to know the pronunciation of the word which contains it.

Double Consonants (kk, pp, tt, ss)

A word with a double consonant in rōmaji is written in hiragana just as it is pronounced, by replacing the "(small pause)" with a small っ.

Examples

Nippon is pronounced as *Ni/(small pause)/po/n,* and written in hiragana as にっぽん.
Similarly, *kitte, kippu* and *zasshi* are written in hiragana as きって, きっぷ and ざっし.

EXERCISES

24.3. Write the pronunciations a, i, u, e or o for the following underlined hiragana.

1. <u>う</u>し   cow   ___*u*___

2. ど<u>う</u>ぞ   Please   ___________

3. おか<u>あ</u>さん   mother   ___________

4. こ<u>う</u>えん   park   ___________

5. よ<u>う</u>ちえん   kindergarten   ___________

6. ありが<u>と</u><u>う</u>   Thank you   ___________

7. おは<u>よう</u>ございます   Good morning   ___________

8. <u>お</u>かえりなさい Welcome home _______________

9. ゆ<u>う</u>びんきょく post office _______________

10. いも<u>う</u>と younger sister _______________

24.4. I shall say a word in Japanese. Write it down below in hiragana.

1. _______________________ 6. _______________________

2. _______________________ 7. _______________________

3. _______________________ 8. _______________________

4. _______________________ 9. _______________________

5. _______________________ 10. _______________________

HOW TO READ JAPANESE SENTENCES

So far we have learned to read words in hiragana. When we read Japanese sentences in hiragana, some rules must be followed.

There are no capital letters in Japanese, and all characters are written the same size, except for the small や, ゆ, よ and っ of double consonants. The small や, ゆ, よ and っ are written about a quarter of the size of the other characters. There is no question mark used in Japanese because the particle **ka,** at the end of a sentence, indicates that it is a question. The end of a sentence is denoted by "。" (period).

The particles **wa, e** and **o** must be written as は, へ and を. In other words, は is pronounced as both **ha** and **wa,** and へ is pronounced as both **he** and **e,** and を is pronounced as both **wo** and **o.**

Examples

<u>Wa</u>tashi <u>wa</u> Hanako desu. The first *wa* is a part of a word, and so it is written as わ. The second *wa* is a particle, and so it is written as は.

Watashi wa <u>e</u>ki <u>e</u> ikimasu. The first *e* is a part of a word, and so it is written as え. The second *e* is a particle, and so it is written as へ.

<u>O</u>tōsan wa ringo <u>o</u> tabemasu. The first *o* is a part of a word, and so it is written as お. The second *o* is a particle, and so it is written as を.

Japanese sentences are written without spaces between words. To make a sentence more readable and to clarify the content, punctuation marks, "、," which are comparable to English commas, are inserted as flexibly as in English. Although there are no spaces between words in written Japanese, to help make your learning easier we shall insert a small space, equivalent to one character, after each particle, each adverb, and each adjective from now on. If there is more than one particle, one after another, a small space will be inserted after the second particle. This is a common practice used to avoid confusion when Japanese children are taught to read and write Japanese.

Japanese sentences are written either horizontally or vertically. Books on mathematics, science, music and foreign languages are usually written horizontally to accommodate Arabic numerals, scientific symbols, musical notes and foreign languages. Novels, and other books that contain only words, are written vertically. It is more common for Japanese people to write Japanese vertically. To do this, you proceed from top to bottom and from right to left. The periods " 。" and punctuation marks " 、" are both placed at the same location as small characters, that is, at the top right half of the square when the sentence is written vertically, and at the bottom left half of the square when the sentence is written horizontally. Usually, Japanese sentences are not written in boxes as they are in the example below; the boxes are provided here only to show you the sizes and positions of various syllables, periods and punctuation marks.

Example

Kore wa nihon no kitte de wa arimasen.

こ	れ	は		に	ほ	ん	の		き	っ	て
で	は		あ	り	ま	せ	ん	。			

When a book is written vertically in Japanese, you open it from what appears to be the back. What is usually the back of an English book is the front of a Japanese book, and vice versa.

EXERCISES

24.5. Convert the following sentences into rōmaji and then translate them into English:

1. ここは　えきです。 ___________________________

____

2. これは　わたしの　いぬです。 ___________________________

____

3. あなたは　すしを　たべますか。 ___________________________

____

4. あした、　わたしたちは　やまへ　いきます。 ___________________________

5. これから、　あなたは　なにを　しますか。_______________________

____

____

6. あそこに　くだものやが　あります。_______________________

____

7. わたしは　はなこです。_______________________

____

🖸 *24.6. I shall say a sentence in Japanese; write it down below in hiragana.*

1. ____

2. ____

3. ____

4. ____

5. ____

JAPANESE CUSTOMS AND CULTURE

Why Is Japanese Written with Kanji, Hiragana and Katakana?

In the beginning, Japanese was a spoken language only. In the fifth century, the Japanese imperial court started to import much advanced culture from Korea and China, and the Chinese method of writing was introduced to Japan. The imperial court employed professional letter writers, who were immigrants from Korea or were descended from immigrants, to write diplomatic correspondence and government documents in Chinese. By the seventh century, a small number of Japanese people had learned Chinese, and they started to write Japanese sentences using Chinese characters. Since the Chinese and Japanese languages are completely different, people devised many systems over the years, but one particular system became prominent, and it is called Manyōgana; the Japanese syllable was written using the Chinese character of the same sound. Although Japanese sentences written in this way were all in Chinese characters, they were incomprehensible to a Chinese person. About 1,000 Chinese characters were used to represent about 100 Japanese syllables, and this became the basis for the future development of hiragana and katakana. During the seventh century, people wrote in either Chinese or Manyōgana. Until the late nineteenth century, Chinese was regarded as the written language for learning, literature and religion, just as Latin was in Europe until the late seventeenth century, and some men continued to write in Chinese.

Meanwhile, katakana had developed by the ninth century to represent Japanese sounds. It was invented by Buddhist monks who had to recite Chinese sutra, which they could not read, and they devised the following scheme. They wrote down the reading of a Chinese character beside it, in Manyōgana. But since there was not enough space to write entire Manyōgana characters, they wrote parts of them, thereby creating katakana. Soon the texts started to appear in Chinese characters mixed with katakana, and this continued through the twelfth century. Also, anthologies of waka (Japanese poetry) came to be written in katakana by the middle of the tenth century.

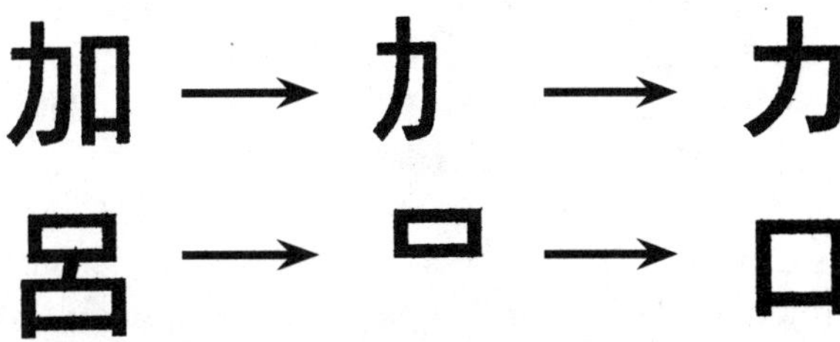

The left half of the Chinese character 加 (pronounced as **ka**) became カ of katakana. The upper half of the Chinese character 呂 (pronounced as **ro**) became ロ of katakana.

In the mid-ninth century, hiragana had developed from Manyōgana (Chinese characters) to represent Japanese sounds. In those days, people used brushes and ink to write Chinese characters, which had (and still have) many strokes. There were three different styles of writing Chinese characters. One was to write characters rigidly (see "a" in the diagram below): the writing brush was lifted off the paper after every stroke. Another was the cursive style in which one rarely lifts the brush off the paper to write a character and a sentence ("c"). It smooths the writing and abbreviates each character. The third style is something in between ("b").

(a)   (b)   (c)

The Chinese script 女, written in three different styles:
(a) **kaisho** (non-cursive style); (b) **gyōsho** (semi-cursive style); (c) **sōsho** (cursive style)

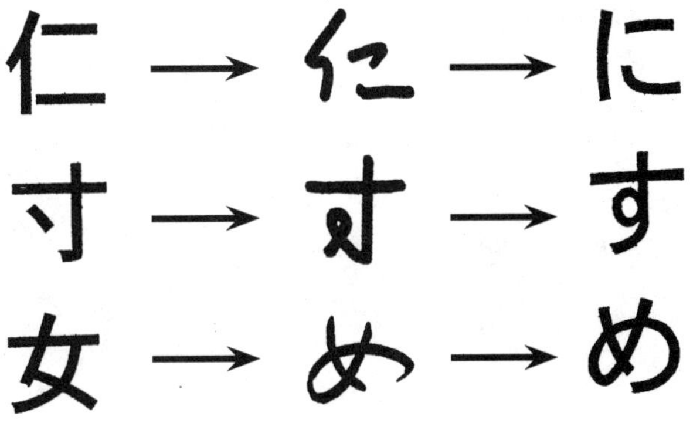

From the cursive style of writing, hiragana was created, after going through abbreviations, and in the beginning it was used only by women.

The Chinese characters 仁 (**ni**), 寸 (**su**) and 女 (**me**) written in **sōsho** (cursive style) were transformed and became hiragana characters に, す and め.

During the Heian period (794–1185), a game of reciting/exchanging waka became an indispensable social entertainment and a way of showing off one's culture and knowledge among the nobles. Waka were studied and recorded in hiragana, with an occasional, rare inclusion of Chinese characters. Similarly, exchanging love letters, in the form of waka written in hiragana, was popular among nobles. Hiragana gained full acceptance when the imperial anthology was written in hiragana in 905, and even educated men started to use hiragana to write narratives around the middle of the tenth century. However, the popularity of hiragana was due to the supreme ascendancy of the Fujiwara family in the imperial court, especially in the late tenth century. The power of the Fujiwara men in the imperial court depended on their women being selected as consorts to emperors. Since emperors and princes (prospective future emperors) had many wives and concubines, competition and intrigues among women were very fierce. The Fujiwara women, especially empresses, were surrounded by extremely well-educated ladies-in-waiting, who taught them what was needed to be desired by prospective future emperors, and it was those ladies-in-waiting for the Fujiwara empresses who produced magnificent novels in hiragana, exalting still further the prestige and the popularity of hiragana. Because men still used Chinese and Manyōgana in the court documents and in their diaries, Chinese characters were often included in hiragana writings. Japanese people continued to write in Chinese, Manyōgana, katakana, katakana with some words in Chinese, hiragana, and hiragana with some words in Chinese. But it was eventually the combination of hiragana, with some words in Chinese, which became the standard way of writing Japanese. Later on, katakana came to be used to write foreign words, other than Chinese, for which no Japanese words existed.

It should be noted that kanji (Japanized ancient Chinese characters), hiragana and katakana all went through simplifications and refinements over the years and resulted in the forms we see today. That is one of the reasons why some kanji are different from those of Chinese characters. The other reason, a somewhat greater factor, is that the Chinese transformed their characters in 1955.

Haiku is an unrhymed poem consisting of 3 lines of 5, 7 and 5 syllables, respectively. Its power and beauty lies in its ability to evoke deep feeling, rather than in what it says. The following haiku by Bashō expresses the loneliness of being quite alone physically and spiritually as the writer approaches the end of his life ("the end of autumn" is a metaphor for the approach of the end of his life).

Kono michi ya
Yuku hito nashi ni
Aki no kure

Along this road
Goes no one
At the end of autumn

     Lesson 24: Let's Read Japanese!

What you must remember from this lesson to proceed to the next lesson:

Japanese sentences may be written entirely in hiragana.

Kanji are used for words originating from China.

Katakana are used to write foreign words, apart from Chinese, which were Japanized.

You must take care when you read a word as to whether a character is small or usual size, as this completely alters the pronunciation and the meaning of the word.

い is pronounced as **i** except for some long vowels for which it is pronounced as **e**.

う is pronounced as **u** except for some long vowels for which it is pronounced as **o**.

は is pronounced as either **ha** or **wa** (for particles).

へ is pronounced as either **he** or **e** (for particles).

を is pronounced as either **wo** or **o** (for particles).

25

Those Darned Imported Words!

In this lesson, you will learn:
To read Japanese characters called katakana

You have learned hiragana in the previous lesson. In this lesson, you will learn another set of characters called katakana.

KATAKANA

Katakana is used in the following situations.

1. Words of foreign origin, other than Chinese, which have become Japanese. Foreign words which did not exist in Japanese and did not have similar sounds in Japanese were modified to fit into the Japanese phonetic system, and are written in katakana.

Examples
Banana became *banana* バナナ.
Radio became *rajio* ラジオ.
Television became *terebi* テレビ.
Baseball became *bēsubōru* ベースボール.

2. Foreign personal names, places and other proper nouns. These are written as closely as possible to the way they are pronounced.

Examples
Smith is pronounced and written as *Sumisu* スミス.
Ann is pronounced and written as *An* アン.
America is pronounced and written as *Amerika* アメリカ.

3. Describing the sounds around us, like the purring of a cat or barking of a dog.

Examples
Wanwan ワンワン for *woof woof*.
Nyā ニャー for *meow*.

Syllables in Katakana

The following is the table of katakana. Unlike hiragana, which is made up of cursive lines, katakana is made up of simpler straight and curved lines.

Vowels

a	ア	i	イ	u	ウ	e	エ	o	オ

Basic syllables

ka	カ	ki	キ	ku	ク	ke	ケ	ko	コ
sa	サ	shi	シ	su	ス	se	セ	so	ソ
ta	タ	chi	チ	tsu	ツ	te	テ	to	ト
na	ナ	ni	ニ	nu	ヌ	ne	ネ	no	ノ
ha	ハ	hi	ヒ	fu	フ	he	ヘ	ho	ホ
ma	マ	mi	ミ	mu	ム	me	メ	mo	モ
ya	ヤ			yu	ユ			yo	ヨ
ra	ラ	ri	リ	ru	ル	re	レ	ro	ロ
wa	ワ							wo	ヲ
n	ン								

Modified syllables

ga	ガ	gi	ギ	gu	グ	ge	ゲ	go	ゴ
za	ザ	ji	ジ	zu	ズ	ze	ゼ	zo	ゾ
da	ダ	ji	ヂ	zu	ヅ	de	デ	do	ド
ba	バ	bi	ビ	bu	ブ	be	ベ	bo	ボ
pa	パ	pi	ピ	pu	プ	pe	ペ	po	ポ

Ya, Yu, Yo syllables

kya	キャ	kyu	キュ	kyo	キョ
sha	シャ	shu	シュ	sho	ショ
cha	チャ	chu	チュ	cho	チョ
nya	ニャ	nyu	ニュ	nyo	ニョ
hya	ヒャ	hyu	ヒュ	hyo	ヒョ
mya	ミャ	myu	ミュ	myo	ミョ
rya	リャ	ryu	リュ	ryo	リョ
gya	ギャ	gyu	ギュ	gyo	ギョ
ja	ジャ	ju	ジュ	jo	ジョ
bya	ビャ	byu	ビュ	byo	ビョ
pya	ピャ	pyu	ピュ	pyo	ピョ

 Lesson 25: Those Darned Imported Words!

The rows 12 to 15 are obtained by adding "゛" to each character in rows 2, 3, 4 and 6. The row 16 is obtained by adding "゜" to each character in row 6. The rows 17 to 27 are obtained by adding small ヤ, ユ and ヨ to the second column of the basic and modified syllables except ヂ. In other words, katakana syllables follow exactly the same rules as those of hiragana syllables.

1. When hiragana has "゛" or "゜," so does katakana.

Examples

ga (が) in hiragana is *ka* (か) + "゛."
ga (ガ) in katakana is *ka* (カ) + "゛."

pa (ぱ) in hiragana is *ha* (は) + "゜."
pa (パ) in katakana is *ha* (ハ) + "゜."

2. When hiragana is followed by a small や, ゆ or よ, so is katakana.

Examples

kya (きゃ) in hiragana is *ki* (き) + *ya* (や).
kya (キャ) in katakana is *ki* (キ) + *ya* (ヤ).

gyu (ぎゅ) in hiragana is *gi* (ぎ) + *yu* (ゆ).
gyu (ギュ) in katakana is *gi* (ギ) + *yu* (ユ).

Since katakana symbols are syllabic, one syllable in katakana may be represented by one syllable in rōmaji, just as in hiragana.

Examples

te ↔ テ
su ↔ ス
tesuto ↔ テスト

Some words are written in a combination of katakana and hiragana.

Example

Amerika-jin literally means *America-person,* hence *Amerika* is written in katakana and *jin* is written in hiragana: アメリカじん.

EXERCISES

25.1. Convert the following katakana into rōmaji and then translate them into English:

1. オレンジ____

2. トイレ____

3. ラジオ____

4. バナナ ____

5. ペン ____

6. プレゼント ____

7. テレビ ____

8. パン ____

9. バス ____

10. トマト ____

11. イギリス ____

12. ナイフ ____

25.2. Listen to the track for Exercise 25.2. I shall say a word in Japanese; write it down below in katakana.

1. _______________________   6. _______________________

2. _______________________   7. _______________________

3. _______________________   8. _______________________

4. _______________________   9. _______________________

5. _______________________   10. _______________________

HOW TO READ WORDS IN KATAKANA

Long Vowels

Converting rōmaji words into katakana is a little easier than converting them into hiragana. All long vowels are indicated by using horizontal lines " ー ," when you write horizontally.

Examples
bōru ボ ー ル
kōhī コ ー ヒ ー
uētā ウ エ ー タ ー

     Lesson 25: Those Darned Imported Words!

When writing katakana vertically, a vertical line " l " is used for long vowels.

Examples

ウ	コ	ボ
エ	l	l
l	ヒ	ル
タ	l	
l		

Double Consonants

For double consonants, the same rule applies as in hiragana: "(short pause)" is replaced by small ッ.

Examples

koppu is pronounced as *ko*/(small pause)/*pu* and written as コップ.

EXERCISES

25.3. Convert the following katakana words into rōmaji.

1. ハンバーガー________________________

2. ジュース________________________

3. カレーライス________________________

4. コーヒー________________________

5. テーブル________________________

6. ラーメン ________________________

7. ステーキ ________________________

8. ホーク ________________________

9. サンドイッチ ________________________

10. セーター ________________________

25.4. Listen to the track for Exercise 25.4. I shall say a word in Japanese; write it down below in katakana.

1. ________________________

2. ________________________

3. ________________________

4. ________________________

5. ________________________

6. ________________________

7. ________________________

8. ________________________

9. ________________________

10. ________________________

25.5. Translate the following sentences into rōmaji and English:

1. わたしの　おかあさんは　アメリカじんです。

____

____

2. おとうさんは　ラジオを　にわで　ききます。

____

____

3. まことくんは　テレビを　みません。

____

____

4. スミスさんは　コーヒーを　のみます。

____

____

5. わたしたちは　ステーキを　たべました。

____

____

6. トイレは　どこですか。

____

____

7. これは　ケリーさんです。

____

____

8. あなたは　フランスじんですか。

____

____

9. イギリスじんは　ごはんを　ナイフと　ホークで　たべます。

____

____

25.6. I shall say a sentence in Japanese; write it down below in hiragana.

1. ____

2. ____

3. ____

4. ____

5. ____

JAPANESE CUSTOMS AND CULTURE

Japanized English Words

The present-day Japanese language contains many Japanized English words, some of which you can recognize easily, such as **aisukurīmu,** *ice cream,* **conpūtā,** *computer,* **banana,** *banana,* **kōhī,** *coffee,* and so on. However, there is a far greater number of Japanized English words that you will, unless you are told, find difficult to recognize that they originated from English. There are patterns of Japanized English words as follows.

1. New words, which may or may not be understandable to native English speakers, from sets of English words: for example, **wan-man-basu,** *one-man-bus,* meaning a bus in which the driver, rather than a conductor, collects the fares.

2. New words from the first two or three syllables of English words: for example, **apāto,** *apartment;* **nega,** *negative* (of a film); **biru,** *building;* **infure,** *inflation.*

3. New words from initials: for example, **ōeru** meaning *office lady.*

4. New words from abbreviating compound words: for example, **wāpuro,** *word processor.*

5. New words from combining Japanese and Japanized English words: for example, Japanese word **ha,** *tooth,* combined with Japanized English word **burasshi,** *brush,* creates **haburashi,** *toothbrush.*

Some Japanese people, thinking that the Japanized English words are English words, are surprised when English-speaking people don't understand them.

What you must remember from this lesson to proceed to the next lesson:

Katakana characters behave like hiragana characters do, except for long vowels.

All long vowels are indicated by using horizontal lines, when writing horizontally, or vertical lines, when writing vertically.

          Lesson 25: Those Damned Imported Words!

26

Pictures Tell It All!

In this lesson, you will learn:
Some kanji

In the previous two lessons, you have learned to read hiragana and katakana. You should be aware of the fact that both hiragana and katakana are symbols representing Japanese speech sounds (syllables) and they usually have no meanings by themselves. A combination of syllables (or a single syllable in some cases) makes a word.

In this lesson, you are going to learn to read some kanji. Unlike characters in hiragana and katakana, each kanji character is a word with a specific meaning.

HOW THE PICTURES BECAME CHARACTERS

At first, Japanese was a spoken language only, and there were no symbols to write Japanese until Chinese characters were introduced from China in the fifth century. Kanji, which originated between 4,000 and 5,000 years ago in China, were originally simple pictures of objects and phenomena in daily life. These illustrations show you some transformations of objects (sun, moon, mountain, river, tree, mouth and eye) into words.

With time, human thinking advanced and pictographic words alone could not express everything people needed to, such as abstract ideas. People started to express abstract ideas using points and lines, and hence developed words from them. These illustrations show you how some abstract ideas (*above*, *below* and *middle*), using points and lines, were transformed into words.

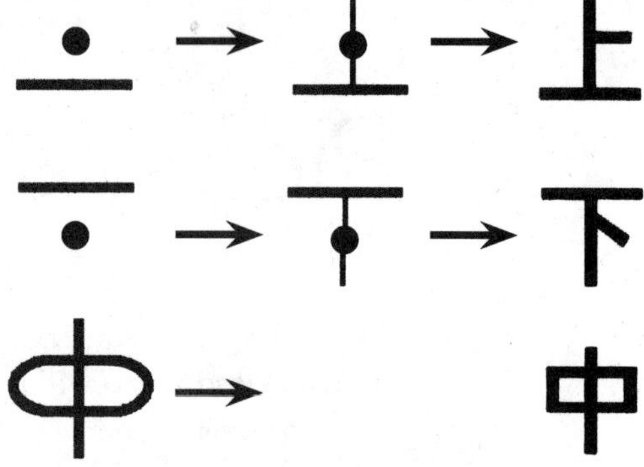

More complicated kanji characters, composed of combinations of simple kanji characters, were developed with time.

木＋木　　→　林　*hayashi wood*　(few trees make a wood)

木＋木＋木　→　森　*mori forest*　　(many trees make a forest)

日＋月　　→　明　*a bright*　　(sun and moon together make things very bright)

As the writing system developed, characters were needed to express even more complicated words, and two or more kanji characters were combined to make one word.

Example

The characters 山 *mountain* and 林 *wood* were combined to make the word related to both *mountain* and *wood*: 山林 **sanrin** *wood in the mountain*

(Note that 山 and 林, pronounced as **yama** and **hayashi** independently, are pronounced as **san** and **rin** when they are combined together.)

Each kanji character may be pronounced in more than one way depending on with what other kanji character(s) it is combined to make another word. So, when you are learning to pronounce kanji, the whole word (a combination of one or more characters) must be remembered, and not just one particular character, as may be seen in the examples below.

Examples

日 and 山 have 4 and 2 different pronunciations, respectively, and they are shown below (the pronunciations of 日 and 山 are underlined).

Since the character 日 was derived from sun and it has the meanings of *sun*, *daytime*, and *day*, it was combined with other kanji characters to make words which are related to either *sun* or *day*.

日　　　*<u>hi</u> sun, daytime, day*
月曜日　*getsuyō<u>bi</u>* Monday*
六日　　*mu<u>ika</u> sixth day of a month, six days*
元日　　*gan<u>jitsu</u> first day of a year*
一日　　*ichi-<u>nichi</u> one day*

***bi** is the phonetic transformation of **hi**.

　　　　　　　　　　　　Lesson 26: Pictures Tell It All!

Since the character 山 was derived from *mountain,* it was used to make words related to *mountain.*

山	*yama*	*mountain*
山林	*sanrin*	*wood in the mountain*
火山	*kazan**	*volcano* (fire and mountain makes volcano)

Although there are more than 50,000 kanji in existence, I have introduced only a few that you should be able to recognize in Japan.

Some kanji characters may have as many as 10 or more different readings for the following two reasons.

REASON 1: When Japanese people started to write Japanese using Chinese characters, a Chinese character was given the pronunciation of the Japanese word of the same meaning. Often, several Japanese words, of similar meanings, were assigned to the same character, resulting in several readings. For example, the Japanese words **hi,** *sun, daytime, day* and **ka,** suffix put after a number to denote the day of a month, were assigned to the character 日. **Hi** and **ka,** the native Japanese words that translate the meaning of the character, are called kun-readings for 日.

REASON 2: The Japanese and Chinese languages were totally different, and the Japanese language had words (combinations of sounds/syllables) which did not exist in the Chinese language. A Chinese character, which had sounds similar to that of a Japanese syllable(s), was used to write that Japanese syllable(s). Also, the Chinese characters, for which there were no Japanese words, were pronounced as closely as possible to that of Japanese syllables. Because Chinese characters were read differently at different times in Chinese history, a Chinese character may have been assigned many different Japanese syllable(s) over time. For example, 日 was read as **nichi** and **jitsu** in Chinese in different times, and both readings were incorporated into Japanese. **Nichi** and **jitsu,** reading kanji in the Chinese way, are called on-readings for 日. Wow! Combining all these factors together, a kanji character ended up with many readings.

Many words were made by combining two kanji characters; these two-character words are usually read character by character, that is, each character is read either on-reading or kun-reading depending on how it was made. Hence, a two-character word may be read as one of on+on, on+kun, kun+kun or kun+on readings. Further, there are many two-character words that cannot be read character by character; that is, the combinations of characters must be read as a whole.

Let us consider 日 which is usually read as **hi/ka/jitsu/nichi.** 今日 is read as **kyō;** 昨日 is read as **kinō;** 明日 is read as **ashita;** 日本 is read as **Nihon/Nippon;** 一日 is read as **tsuitachi,** just to name some examples. The two-character words such as 今日, 昨日, 明日 may also be read as **kon-nichi, saku-jitsu** and **myō-nichi,** and, both **kyō, kinō, ashita** and **kon-nichi, saku-jitsu, myō-nichi** are used commonly, the former being Japanese words assigned to two-character words and the latter being the Chinese reading (on-reading). (The pronunciations of a Japanese word assigned (i) to a two-character word and (ii) to the one-character word, which is used in the two-character word, are totally unrelated.)

*zan is the phonetic transformation of **san.**

It is known that Chinese characters have existed since around 1400 B.C. In the course of time, many different styles of Chinese characters came and went. Kanji, the Japanized Chinese characters, are a somewhat simplified version of Chinese characters used during the period 206 B.C.–8 A.D. in China.

NOW YOU'RE IN JAPAN

The first experience of Japan for anybody going there will probably be a Japanese airport. As you may have hoped, everything is written in both English and Japanese at international airports, and you will have no problem whatsoever in getting to a train station, taxi stand or bus stop.

Departure.

Place to leave coats and luggage while you gallivant at an airport.

Japanese Money

The first Japanese characters you really must understand are those written on Japanese money: after all, you don't want to pay ¥20,000 for your taxi fare, instead of ¥2,000 (although tipping is not customary in Japan, an airport taxi driver is accustomed to foreigners, and he may think that you are being very, very, generous). So, you must study the following Japanese characters carefully. You may notice that ¥ stands for *yen*, just as $ stands for *dollar,* and 円 **-en** at the end of each Japanese currency refers to *yen*.

一万円	*ichi-man-en*	¥ 10,000
五千円	*go-sen-en*	¥ 5,000
千円	*sen-en*	¥ 1,000
五百円	*go-hyaku-en*	¥ 500
百円	*hyaku-en*	¥ 100
五十円	*go-jū-en*	¥ 50
五円	*go-en*	¥ 5
一円	*ichi-en*	¥ 1

Public Transportation

It is quite likely that you will go to a large train station from the airport, to ride on a Shinkansen (long distance super express train) to get closer to your destination. The map on the next page shows you the long distance train lines (Shinkansen lines) and some large cities. The names for Shinkansen lines and some large cities are listed below in Japanese.

Lesson 26: Pictures Tell It All!

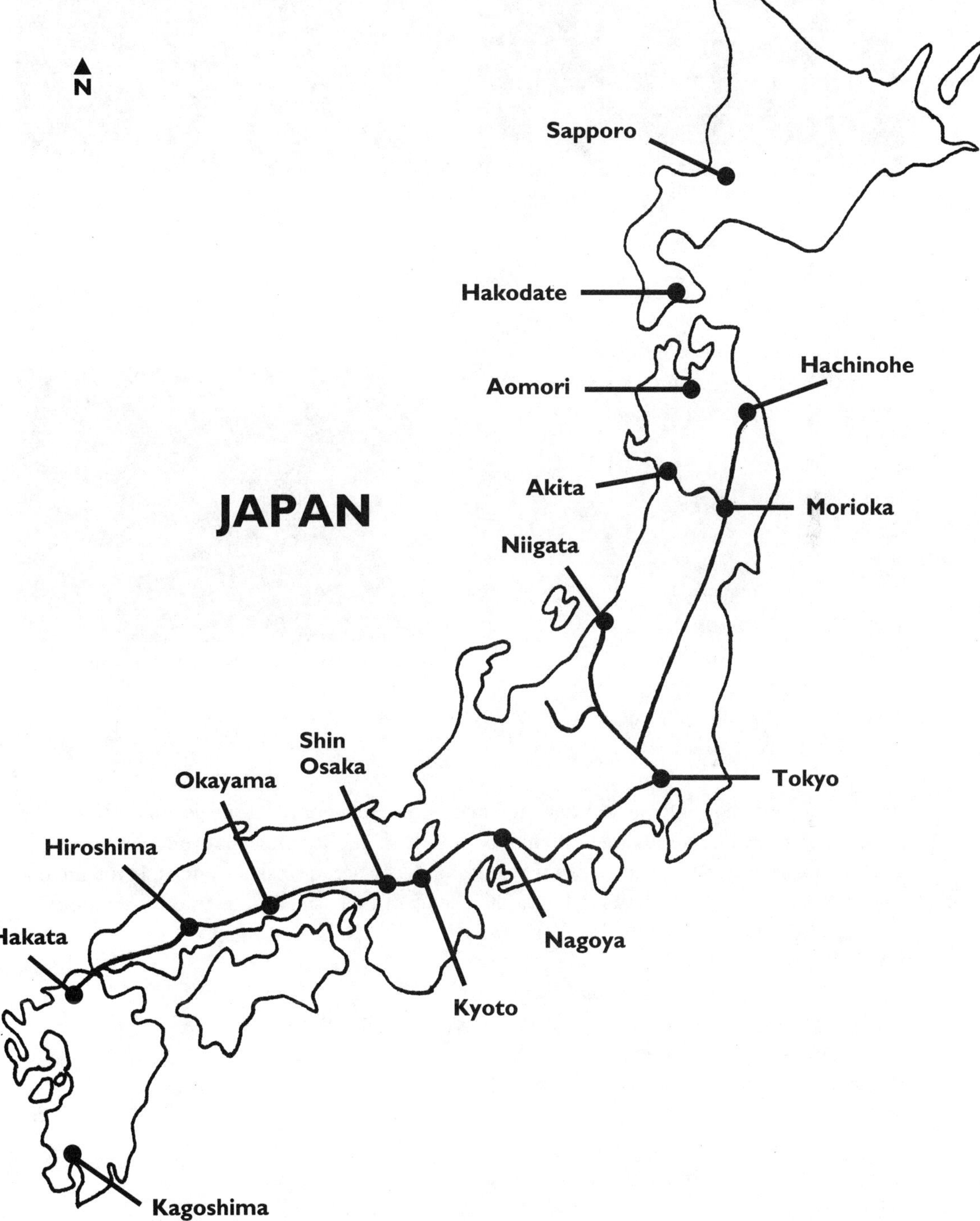

N
JAPAN
Sapporo
Hakodate
Aomori
Hachinohe
Akita
Morioka
Niigata
Shin
Osaka
Okayama
Hiroshima
Hakata
Nagoya
Tokyo
Kyoto
Kagoshima

A sign in a train station with directions to many places.

A sign outside a train station.

東海道新幹線	*Tōkaidō Shinkansen*
山陽新幹線	*Sanyō Shinkansen*
東北新幹線	*Tōhoku Shinkansen*
山形新幹線	*Yamagata Shinkansen*
上越新幹線	*Jōetsu Shinkansen*
札幌	*Sapporo*
盛岡	*Morioka*
新潟	*Niigata*
東京	*Tōkyō*
名古屋	*Nagoya*
京都	*Kyōto*
新大阪	*Shin Ōsaka*
新神戸	*Shin Kōbe*
広島	*Hiroshima*
博多	*Hakata*

Sign for a travel shop which sells Shinkansen tickets.

All you have to do now is to buy a ticket, find the platform for your train, and get on the train. The signs for Shinkansen stations are written in both English and Japanese. But you may as well get used to Japanese characters now since they may be all you see in smaller stations. If you are not alert, you can very easily get on a local train and end up in a very small local station, where you can find only Japanese characters to lead you.

案内所	*annaisho Information*
荷物一時預り所	*nimotsu-ichiji-azukarisho Luggage Check-in*
コインロッカー	*koin-rokkā Coin Lockers*
精算所	*seisansho Fare Adjustment*
バス	*basu Bus*
タクシー	*takushī Taxi*
きっぷうりば	*kippu-uriba Ticket Office*
新幹線のりば	*Shinkansen-noriba Shinkansen Tracks*
JR線のりば	*JR-sen-noriba JR Line Tracks*
電話	*denwa Telephone*
国際電話	*kokusai-denwa International Telephone*
自動きっぷうりば	*jidō-kippu-uriba Automatic Ticket Dispenser (Machines)*

　　　Lesson 26: Pictures Tell It All!

| お手洗 | *otearai Washrooms* |
| みどりの窓口 | *midori-no-madoguchi* Train Reservation Office* |

Now, your Shinkansen trip is over, and you will take a local train, underground, bus or taxi for the rest of the way. So, you need to look for the following characters:

バスの停留所	*basu no teiryūjo bus stop*
地下鉄	*chikatetsu underground, subway*
タクシーのりば	*takushī noriba taxi stand*

If you take a taxi, you could give the taxi driver a piece of paper on which your destination is written in Japanese. But, if you take public transportation, you have to keep your eyes fixed on the display, which tells you the next stop and the fare. Some typical characters you will see on displays are listed below.

病院	*byōin hospital*
動物園	*dōbutsuen zoo*
駅	*eki railway station*
ガソリンスタンド	*gasorin sutando gasoline stand*
飛行場	*hikōjō airport*
ホテル	*hoteru hotel*
銀行	*ginkō bank*
神社	*jinja shrine*
交番	*kōban police station*
公園	*kōen park*
教会	*kyōkai church*
レストラン	*resutoran restaurant*
市役所	*shiyakusho city hall*
旅館	*ryokan Japanese inn*
寺	*tera temple*
郵便局	*yūbinkyoku post office*

幼稚園	*yōchien kindergarten*
小学校	*shōgakkō primary school*
中学校	*chūgakkō secondary school*
高等学校	*kōtōgakkō high school*
大学	*daigaku university, college*

橋	*hashi/bashi bridge*
川	*kawa/gawa river*
湖	*mizūmi/ko lake*
城	*shiro/jō castle*
海	*umi/kai sea*
山	*yama/san mountain*

***Midori-no-madoguchi** are located at Shinkansen stations to sell/reserve train tickets for Shinkansen and all other types of trains; **kippu-uriba** are located at non-Shinkansen stations and they do not sell/reserve train tickets for Shinkansen.

Most of the words listed above usually follow personal pronouns. For example, 富士山 **Fuji-san,** *Mt. Fuji,* 武田神社 **Takeda-jinja,** *Takeda shrine,* 姫路城 **Himeji-jō,** *Himeji Castle,* 隅田川 **Sumida-gawa,** *Sumida river,* 淀屋橋 **Yodoya-bashi,** *Yodoya bridge,* and so on. The characters 橋, 川, 湖, 城, 海 and 山, pronounced as **hashi, kawa, mizūmi, shiro, umi** and **yama** independently, are pronounced as **bashi, gawa, ko, jō, kai** and **san** when they follow personal pronouns most of the time.

You will also notice the following characters specifying locations in detail:

前 *mae front*	横 *yoko side*	上 **ue** *above*	下 **shita** *below*

For example, 東京駅前 **Tōkyō eki mae,** *Tokyo Station front,* 東京病院横 **Tōkyō byōin yoko,** *Tokyo Hospital side,* and so on. You may note that although **Tōkyō no eki no mae** is the expression you learned in lesson 6, **no** is usually dropped when reference is made to public transportation.

26.1. Imagine yourself at a train station. From the options given below, choose the signs you must follow to get to the following places:

1. You want to buy a train ticket. __________

2. You want to go to a washroom. __________

3. You want to take a bus. __________

4. You want to take a taxi. __________

5. You want to check your luggage. __________

6. You want to make a phone call. __________

7. You want to reserve a seat on a Shinkansen. __________

8. You want to get on the Shinkansen. __________

a. ↑ お手洗　　　　c. 新幹線のりば →　　　　e. 荷物一時預り所 →　　　　g. ← バス

b. ← タクシー　　　d. きっぷうりば →　　　　f. ← みどりの窓口　　　　h. ↑ 電話

26.2. Imagine yourself on a bus. Which sign do you look for on the bus display if you want to get off at the following locations?

1. The front of Tokyo train station __________

2. Osaka castle __________

3. The front of a hospital   _____________

4. Tokyo University   _____________

5. Tokyo Zoo   _____________

6. The front of a post office   _____________

7. Bank of Osaka   _____________

8. Bank of America   _____________

a. アメリカ銀行   c. 東京駅前   e. 東京大学   g. 郵便局前

b. 大阪城   d. 東京動物園   f. 大阪銀行   h. 病院前

Walking the Streets

Having rested well and congratulated yourself on getting to your sleeping quarters on the previous night, you are now more confident of yourself: you are ready to go out and test your skill in Japanese characters. As you walk the streets, you will notice many signs, for example:

駐車場	*chūshajō*	parking
出口	*deguchi*	exit
入口	*iriguchi*	entrance
危険	*kiken*	danger
禁煙	*kin-en*	no smoking
工事中	*kōjichū*	under construction (walk carefully)
横断禁止	*ōdan kinshi*	do not cross the street
消火器	*shōkaki*	fire hydrant
立入禁止	*tachiiri kinshi*	no admittance
止まれ	*tomare*	stop

A fire hydrant.

Instructions for garbage collection.

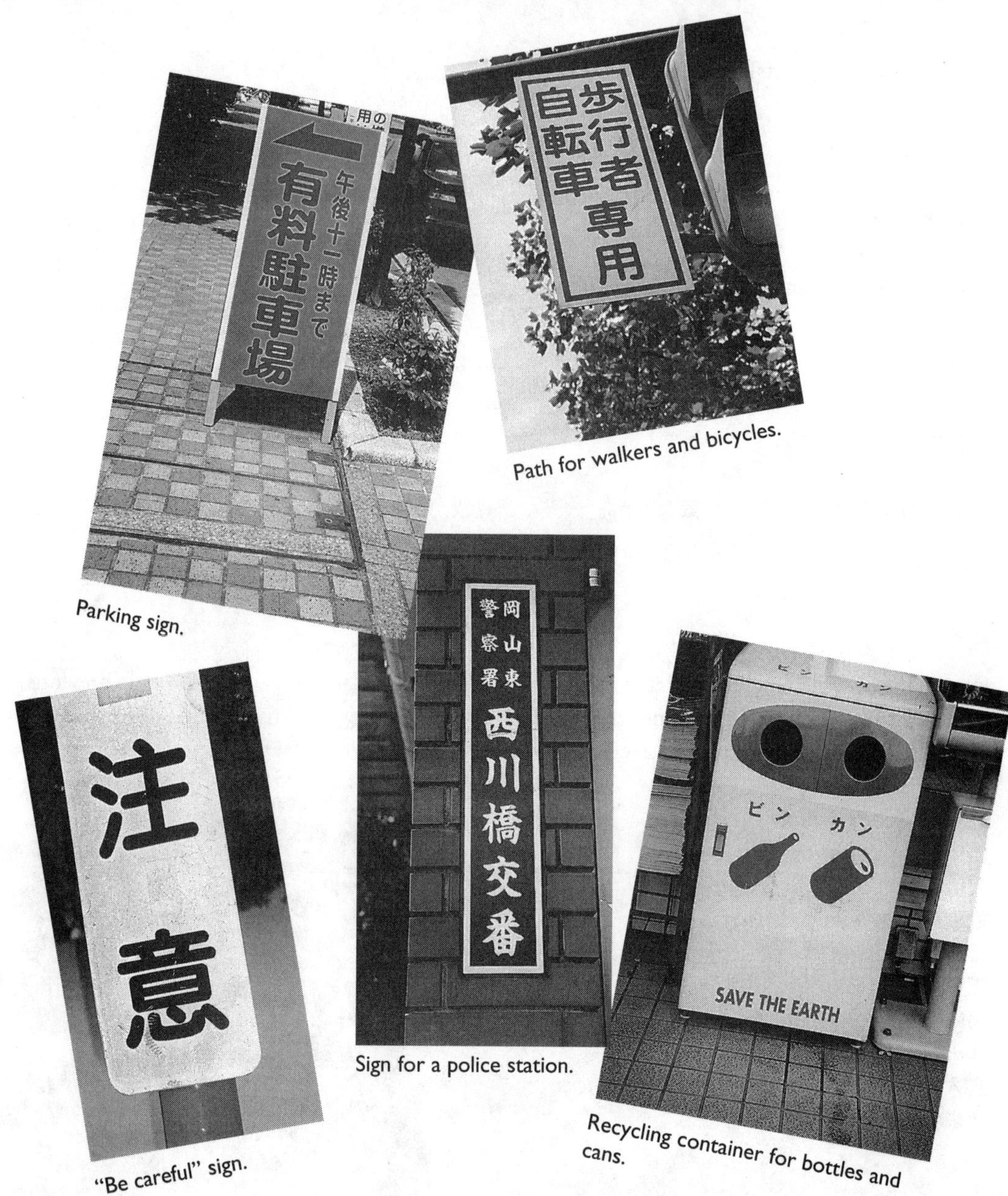

Parking sign.

Path for walkers and bicycles.

"Be careful" sign.

Sign for a police station.

Recycling container for bottles and cans.

Food Is Everywhere!

As you walk the streets, you cannot avoid noticing many show windows of restaurants with color-ful displays of food. No matter how you try to resist them, they keep on coming at you. Finally, you cannot resist the temptation any longer: whether you are hungry or not, you want to go into a restaurant and taste some of the alluring food. The eating and drinking establishments have the following signs to tell you whether they are open or closed.

営業中	*eigyōchū open*
準備中	*junbichū getting ready to open* (it may also indicate "closed for the day" as well, which is of course very annoying)

I can see you standing in front of a restaurant display, trying to decide what to have. The following list shows some Japanese dishes you are likely to see at restaurants. You have already learned what they are in lesson 3.

どんぶり／丼	*donburi/don*
ハンバーガー	*hanbāgā*
ジュース	*jūsu*
カレーライス	*karēraisu*
コーヒー	*kōhī*
おこのみ焼	*okonomiyaki*
パン	*pan*
ラーメン	*rāmen*
サンドイッチ	*sandoicchi*
サラダ	*sarada*
そば	*soba*
すき焼き	*sukiyaki*
寿司	*sushi*
ステーキ	*sutēki*
天ぷら	*tenpura*
トンカツ	*tonkatsu*
うどん	*udon*
焼そば	*yakisoba*
焼鳥	*yakitori*

Eigyōchū: "open."

Getting ready: meaning it is "closed."

Well, you have decided what you are going to eat, but you may be wondering how much it costs. Although prices in train stations, supermarkets, department stores, etc. are listed horizontally in Arabic numerals, many restaurants, especially the traditional ones, list prices vertically in kanji. So, let's go through some numbers in kanji.

〇	*zero*	0							
一	*ichi*	1	六	*roku*	6	百	*hyaku*	100	
二	*ni*	2	七	*nana/shichi*	7	千	*sen*	1,000	
三	*san*	3	八	*hachi*	8	萬	*man*	10,000	
四	*yon/shi*	4	九	*kyū/ku*	9				
五	*go*	5	十	*jū*	10	円	*en*	*yen*	

The typical listings for 200 yen are as follows.

二 百 円	二 〇 〇 円	２０ ０ 円

Having satisfied your appetite, you can now walk the streets more leisurely. The food displays won't distract you as much any more, and you will see many other shops for the first time. You can guess what they sell by looking through the show windows most of the time, but here is a short list of some of the shops you may see.

デパート	*depāto* department store
花屋	*hana-ya* flower shop
本屋	*hon-ya* bookstore
ケーキ屋	*kēki-ya* cake shop
肉屋	*niku-ya* butcher
お菓子屋	*(o)kashi-ya* confectionery shop
おもちゃ屋	*omocha-ya* toy shop
パン屋	*pan-ya* bread shop
魚屋	*sakana-ya* fish shop
スーパーマーケット	*sūpāmāketto* supermarket

Front of an ATM.

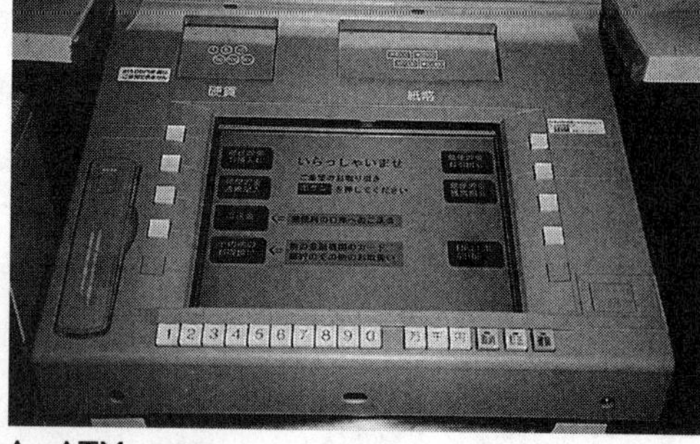

An ATM screen.

ATM Machines

Sooner or later, you may want to use an ATM machine to withdraw money. Operating an ATM machine in Japan is much the same as in the West. Although ATM machines have different configurations from bank to bank, they all have the same slots available. They are:

通帳入口	*tsūchō-ireguchi* entrance for a pass book
カード入口	*kādo-ireguchi* entrance for a card
紙幣出入口	*shihei-dashiireguchi* entrance and exit for paper money

The options available on an ATM screen are:

引き出し	*hikidashi* withdrawal
入金／預金	*nyūkin/yokin* payment/deposit
記帳	*kichō* entry in a bank book
残高照会	*zandaka-shōkai* checking the balance
確認	*kakunin* confirmation
訂正	*teisei* correction

You push a button for withdrawal or deposit or entry in your book. Then you insert either your card or pass book, and you punch in your PIN. Then you punch in the amount you want to de-

          Lesson 26: Pictures Tell It All!

posit or withdraw. Then you press **kakunin** if the screen shows you the correct amount, or press **teisei** to make a correction. Then you take money from, or put money in, the cash dispenser (**shihei-dashiireguchi**). The automated machine then (hopefully) dispenses a transaction statement.

Post Offices

Well, you have by now managed to survive in Japan fairly well: you can do almost anything necessary. Naturally, you want to broadcast your adequacy in the strange country to your friends at home, and you have written many post cards. All you need is to get some stamps in order to mail those cards. You already know that Japanese post offices have banking services such as saving accounts, money transfers, etc., insurance services such as life insurance, automobile insurance, etc., as well as the usual postal services. You must go to the window marked はがき・切手 for stamps, post cards, aerogrammes and the usual postal services. Just in case you cannot find はがき・切手 to buy stamps, or you want to use banking services, the following table lists some of the Japanese characters that you are likely to see at post offices.

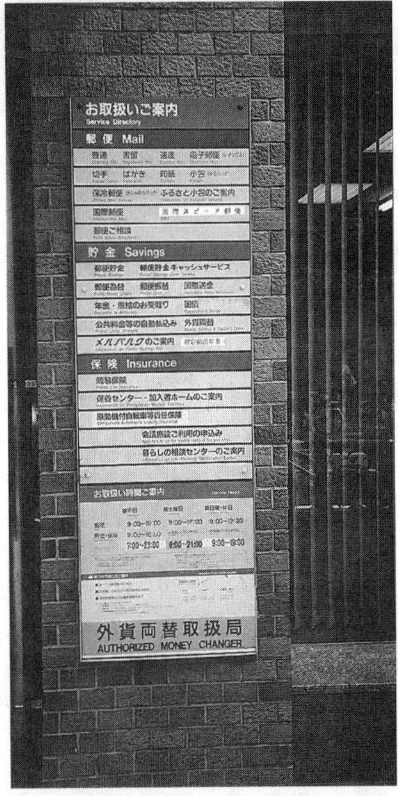

A sign outside a big post office, listing all the services.

郵便	*yūbin* mail		年金	*nenkin* old age pension
小包	*kozutsumi* parcels		恩給	*onkyū* pension from civil service
切手	*kitte* stamps		貯金	*chokin* savings
はがき	*hagaki* post cards		為替	*kawase* money order
印紙	*inshi* revenue stamps*		振替	*furikae* money transfer

Now, you want to mail those post cards to home. City mailboxes usually have two letter drops, one for letters and post cards, and another for special mail such as express, international, large and electronic mail (meaning telegrams). Instructions are written below each letter drop, and you must place your mail accordingly. The instructions you will see are essentially as follows.

てがみ	*tegami* letters
はがき	*hagaki* post cards
速達	*sokutatsu* express
国際	*kokusai* international (mail)
大型郵便	*ōgata-yūbin* large mail
電子郵便	*denshi-yūbin* electronic mail

*When you apply for a multiple entry visa to Japan while you are in Japan (you usually get a single entry visa when you apply for a visa from the U.S.), for example, you are required to pay a fee. On your application form, you put **inshi,** a revenue stamp, for the fee. **Inshi** is a very plain uninteresting looking stamp, which you buy at another section of the visa office. It indicates that you have paid the required fee.

26.3. Imagine yourself in a traditional Japanese restaurant. The menu is written in Japanese, vertically. Write down how much these items are in English.

1. tempura __________________

2. sukiyaki __________________

3. sushi __________________

4. udon __________________

5. yakitori __________________

五.	四.	三.	二.	一.
焼鳥	寿司	天ぷら	すき焼き	うどん
二千二百五十円	二千二百円	九百円	千三百円	七百五十円

In contemporary Chinese, each Chinese character (a kanji character in Japanese) has only one pronunciation.

   Lesson 26: Pictures Tell It All!

Appendix
English Grammar—A Summary

Since we discuss grammar throughout this book, let me refresh your memory of some English grammar points which are relevant. Some basic differences between the Japanese and English languages will be mentioned also.

Sentences

A sentence is made from a combination of words that make sense. There are four types of sentences:

1. I eat an apple.	(This sentence is a statement.)
2. Do you eat an apple?	(This sentence is a question.)
3. (You) eat the apple!	(This sentence is a command.)
4. What a delicious apple I ate!	(This sentence is an exclamation.)

Each sentence contains two parts: a subject and a predicate. The subject names the person(s), or thing(s), the sentence is speaking about. The predicate says something about the subject. Hence the subjects and the predicates for the four sentences above are as follows.

SUBJECT	PREDICATE
1. I	eat an apple
2. you	do eat an apple
3. (you)	eat the apple
4. I	ate what a delicious apple

Sentences 2 and 4 must be rearranged a bit in order to see which parts are subjects and which are predicates.

Japanese sentences are written either horizontally or vertically with no spaces between words. In this book, to make learning easier, I write horizontally with spaces between words just as in English. Although Japanese sentences have no capital letters, question marks or exclamation marks, I use capital letters. Japanese sentences have periods and commas just as in English.

Words

A word may belong to one of the eight groups: articles, nouns, verbs, pronouns, adjectives, adverbs, conjunctions and prepositions. Let us consider the following paragraph and sort the words into these groups.

The sky was blue. Tom and Betty ate very delicious apples. Then they went to school by bus.

Articles

There are two types of articles in English: definite and indefinite. The definite article is *the* and the indefinite articles are *a* and *an*. There are no articles in Japanese.

Nouns

Nouns are names of people, places, things and ideas. In the paragraph above, *sky, Tom, Betty, apples, school* and *bus* are nouns. Japanese nouns are very different from English nouns.

Japanese nouns have no special forms to show whether they are singular or plural (both *an apple* and *apples* have the same form in Japanese). Neither do they have definite *(the)* or indefinite *(a, an)* articles.

Hence **ringo** means *an apple, apples, some apples, the apple,* or *the apples*. Which translation to choose may usually be decided from the context without ambiguity.

Verbs

Verbs indicate what action or condition or relationship is going on. The verbs which indicate action are called *verbs of doing*, and verbs which indicate condition or relationship are called *verbs of being*. The verbs of being have basically the same meaning as the verb *to be* and they may also be called link-verbs. In the paragraph above, *ate* and *went* are verbs of doing and *was* is a verb of being.

There are two types of verbs of doing: transitive and intransitive. A *transitive verb* takes a direct object. A *direct object* is the person, thing, or matter to which the verb directs its action. For the sentence "Tom and Betty ate delicious apples," *ate* is a transitive verb and *delicious apples*, which is what Tom and Betty *ate*, is the direct object. An *intransitive verb* does not take a direct object. For example, *went* of "then they went to school by bus" is an intransitive verb of doing since *went* does not have a direct object. Intransitive verbs of doing make complete sense without direct objects. Some verbs of doing may be both transitive and intransitive. For example, *ate* of "I *ate* an apple" is a transitive verb while *ate* of "I *ate* in the garden" is an intransitive verb.

The verbs of being are all intransitive verbs because they do not have direct objects. Unlike intransitive verbs of doing, which make complete sense with subjects and verbs alone, intransitive verbs of being, such as *was* of "the sky was blue," need to be followed by a completing word, *blue*, called the *complement*, to complete the sense.

Verbs are said to have three persons. First person is the person/persons speaking of himself/herself or themselves (*I, we*), second person is the person/persons being spoken to (*you*) and third person is the person/persons or thing/things spoken of (*he, she, it, they*). In English, the number

 Appendix: English Grammar—A Summary

(singular or plural) and person (first, second or third) of the subject must agree with the number and person of the verb. For example, the subject *I* (first person singular) must have the verb *am*, while the subject *he* (third person singular) must have the verb *is*.

Pronouns

Pronouns are used instead of nouns to refer to people, places, things or ideas without naming them. In the example paragraph above, *they,* used instead of *Tom and Betty,* is a pronoun. There are several kind of pronouns and the ones you will be seeing in this book are:

1. Personal pronouns: e.g., *I, me, my, we, ours, they, them, theirs*

2. Demonstrative pronouns: e.g., *this, that, those, these*

3. Interrogative (question) pronouns: e.g., *who, whom, what, which*

Adjectives

Adjectives describe nouns by adding size, color, number and other qualities to them. In the paragraph above, *blue* and *delicious* are adjectives since *blue* describes the noun *sky* and *delicious* describes the noun *apples*. Adjectives may be used in two positions in sentences. They may precede nouns they describe ("*delicious* apple" for the example paragraph above) or they may follow the verb of being (link-verb) to complete predicates (as is the case of "sky was *blue*" in the above paragraph).

Adverbs

Adverbs describe verbs, adjectives and adverbs. In the paragraph above, *very* is an adverb describing the adjective *delicious*. Japanese adverbs precede verbs, adjectives and adverbs they describe.

Conjunctions

Conjunctions join words and sentences. In the paragraph above, *and* and *then* are conjunctions.

Prepositions

Prepositions are words placed in front of nouns or pronouns to express ideas such as place, time, manner, purpose and cause. In the paragraph above, *by* is a preposition since "*by* bus" describes the manner of going. Japanese prepositions are not placed before nouns and pronouns as in English, but are placed after them.

Glossary

abunai dangerous

achira that (indicates a person "away from the speaker and the listener")

agemasu give (to somebody)

ahiru duck

aidea idea

aimasu meet

aisatsu greeting

aisukurīmu ice cream

akachan baby

akai red

aki autumn

amai sweet (taste)

amari (not) very (with negative adjectives and adverbs describing negative verbs); (not) a lot, (not) much (with negative verbs)

ame candy

ame rain

Amerika America

Amerika-jin American person

amimono knitting

anata you

ano that (over there)

aoi blue

apāto apartment

araimasu wash

are that (indicates a thing/person "away from the speaker and the listener")

Arigatō Thank you

arimasu to-be-located/to-exist (used to indicate a position/location of a non-living subject)

arukimasu walk

asa morning

asa-gohan breakfast

asatte the day after tomorrow

ashi leg

ashita tomorrow

asobimasu play, amuse, enjoy

asoko that (place over there) (indicates "the place away from both the speaker and the listener")

atama head

atatakai warm

ato (time) after

atsui hot (of touch)

atsui hot (temperature)

atsui thick (of flat things)

atsumemasu collect

baka na foolish, stupid

-ban is put after a number to tell the order. For example, *ichi-ban* means *number one*; *ni-ban* means *number two*; etc.

ban evening

banana banana

ban-gohan dinner

banira vanilla

basu bus

bāsudē birthday

basu-sutoppu bus stop

benkyō study

benri na convenient

bentō meal in a box

bideo video

boku I, me (for boys)

bōshi hat

budō grape

burausu blouse

burūsu blues

buta pig

buta-niku pork

byōin hospital

cha Japanese green tea

chairoi brown

-chan is added after the names of small children and especially after the names of girls; e.g., *Amy-chan*, Amy.

chawan bowl (rice)

chekkuauto check out

chiisai small, little, quiet (sound, voice)

chikaku nearby

chiri geography

chizu map

chokorēto chocolate

chūgakkō secondary school

Chūgoku China

daidokoro kitchen

daigaku university, college

dai-kirai na very dislikable

daikon large white radish

dai-suki na very likable

dakara so, therefore

dakkusufundo dachshund

dame na not good

dare who

dare mo (not) anyone

dareka somebody

de in/with/by

deito date

dekimasu be made, be produced, be possible

demasu go out

densha electric train

depāto department store

desu is, am, are

Dewa mata See you

Dizunī Disney

-do degree

dō how, in what way

Dō itashimashite You are welcome

Dō shimashita ka What's wrong/ happened/the matter (with you)?

Dō shimasu ka What will you do (about it)?

dōbutsu animal

dōbutsuen zoo

Doitsu Germany

Doitsu-go German language

Doitsu-jin German person

doko where, which place

doko mo (not) anywhere

dokoka somewhere

Dōmo arigatō gozaimasu is a very polite phrase meaning *Thank you very much.*

donburi bowl of cooked rice with toppings of meat, fish, eggs and vegetables

dono which

dono "noun" *ka* some "noun"

dono "noun" *mo* (not) any "noun"

dore which one

dore mo (not) any of them

doreka something

doresu dress

dōro road, way, highway

do-yōbi Saturday

Dōzo Please

Dōzo yoroshiku Pleased to meet you (in introductions)

Dōzo yoroshiku Please do as I requested (after asking for a favor)

Dōzo yoroshiku ___ *ni Dōzo yoroshiku* Please give my regards to ___

e picture, painting

e is used as *to* in the sense of motion toward a "place."

eiga movie

Eigo English language

eki (railway) station

-en is put after a number to tell the amount of money, and is translated as _yen.

enpitsu pencil

erabimasu choose

fuben na inconvenient

fuku cloth

funabin surface mail

fune ship, boat

Furansu France

Furansu-go French language

Furansu-jin French person

furimasu fall (rain, snow)

furo bath

furoba bathroom

futoi thick (of cylindrical things), *fat*

futsuka 2nd

fuyu winter

gaijin foreigner

gaikoku abroad

gakkō school

gakusei student (of a school)

-gatsu is put after a number to tell the month.

-gawa -side

Genki desu ka How are you?

genki na healthy, hearty

getsu-yōbi Monday

ginkō bank

-go is added to the name of a country for its language (just as *-jin* is added for its people), e.g., *Furansu-go, French language.* There are exceptions to the rule such as *Eigo, English.*

go 5

Gochisōsama Thank you for the delicious food (after eating)

go-fun 5 minutes

go-gatsu May

gogo P.M.

gohan meal, boiled rice

go-ji 5 o'clock

go-kai fifth floor

gōkei total

Gomennasai Sorry

Gōruden-uīku Golden-Week

goshujin somebody else's husband

gozen A.M.

gyū-niku beef

hachi 8

hachi-fun 8 minutes

hachi-gatsu August

hachi-ji 8 o'clock

hai yes

Hai genki desu I am fine

Hai okagesamade I am fine, thank you

hairimasu come in, enter, join, get in

ha-isha dentist

hajimarimasu begin

Hajimemashite How do you do?

hajimemasu begin (something)

hajimete for the first time

hakarimasu measure, weigh

hakimasu put on (footwear, trousers)

hakusai Chinese cabbage

han half past (hour)

hana flower

hana nose

hanashi talk, conversation

hanashimasu speak

hana-ya flower shop

hanbāgā hamburger

handobaggu handbag

hansamu na handsome

hantai opposite

hap-pun 8 minutes

hare fine weather

haru spring

hashi chopsticks

hatarakimasu work

hatsuka 20th

hayai quick, rapid, early

hayaku quickly, rapidly, early

hebi snake

hen na strange, suspicious

heta na bad (at a particular skill such as a sport, a language, etc.)

heya room

hi day

hidari left

-hiki is put after a number to count animals such as dogs, tigers, rabbits, fishes and insects.

hikōjō airport

hikōki airplane

hikui low, short (height)

hima free, time to spare

Hinamatsuri The Festival of Dolls

hiroi spacious

hiru afternoon

hiru-gohan lunch

hito person

hō direction

hokenshō health insurance card

hōkō direction

hōku fork

hon book

hone bone

hon-ya bookstore

hoshii desirous

hosoi thin (of cylindrical things)

hoteru hotel

hyaku 100

hyaku-man 1,000,000

ichi 1

ichi-ban most, best, number one

ichi-gatsu January

ichigo strawberry

ichi-ji 1 o'clock

ie house, home

Igirisu Britain

Igirisu-jin British person

ii good

iie no

Iie kekkō desu No, thank you (rejecting with gratitude)

ike pond

ikimasu go

ik-kai first floor

ikura how much

ima at this moment

ima family room

imasu to-be-located/to-exist (indicates a position/location of a living subject)

imōto younger sister

inu dog

ippai full, plenty, one cupful, one drink (alcoholic)

ip-pun 1 minute

Irasshaimase Hello and welcome! Come in!

iro color

isha physician, medical doctor

isogashii busy

isu chair

Itadakimasu Thank you for the gift (when receiving it), Thank you for the food (before eating)

itai painful

Itaria Italy

Itaria-go Italian language

itsu when

itsu mo (not) anytime

itsuka 5th

itsuka someday

jagaimo potato

jazu jazz

jidō-kippu-uriba automatic ticket dispensing area

jidōsha automobile

jikan (spare) time

jikanhyō timetable

-jin is added to the name of a country to stand for its person/people.

jinja shrine

jitensha bicycle

jōzu na good (at a particular skill such as a sport, a language, etc.)

jū 10

jūdō judo

jū-gatsu October

jūgo-nichi 15th

jugyō lecture

jūhachi-nichi 18th

jūichi-gatsu November

jūichi-ji 11 o'clock

jūichi-nichi 11th

jū-ji 10 o'clock

juku cram school

jūku-nichi 19th

jū-man 100,000

jūni-gatsu December

jūni-ji 12 o'clock

jūni-nichi 12th

jup-pun 10 minutes

jūroku-nichi 16th

jūsan-nichi 13th

jūshichi-nichi 17th

jūsu juice

jūyokka 14th

ka or, ?

kaban briefcase

kaburimasu put on (hat)

kaeri return

kaerimasu return

kaeshimasu return (things borrowed)

kagaku science

kagi key

kaigi meeting

kaimasu buy

kaimono shopping

kaisha company

kaishain white-collar worker

kakimasu write, draw

kami hair

Kanada Canada

Kanada-jin Canadian person

kanai my wife

kane money

kangofu nurse

kao face

kara from

karada body

karai hot (spicy)

karate karate

karēraisu Indian curry

karimasu borrow

karui light (weight)

kasa umbrella

kashimasu lend

kata shoulder

kawa river

kawaii cute

ka-yōbi Tuesday

kayui itchy

kaze a cold

kazoku family

kēki cake

kēki-ya cake shop

kekkon marriage

kesa this morning

keshō make-up

kibun feeling

kiiroi yellow

kikimasu listen to, hear, ask for

kikoemasu be heard

kimarimasu be decided

kimasu come

kimasu put on (dress)

kimono kimono

kinō yesterday

kin-yōbi Friday

kirai na detestable, dislikeable

kirei na beautiful, clean

kirin giraffe

kisha train

kissaten coffee shop

kitanai dirty

kitte stamp

kōcha Indian tea

kochira this (indicates a person "near the speaker")

kodomo child

Kodomo no hi Children's Day

koe voice, cry

kōen park

kōgyō-daigaku technical college

kōhī coffee

kōjō factory

koko this (place) (indicates "the place near the speaker")

kōkō high school

kokonoka 9th

kōkūbin air mail

kokugo the national language

kon- this (-getsu, -shū)

konban this evening

Konbanwa Good evening

kon-getsu this month

Konnichiwa Good afternoon, Good day

kono this

kon-shū this week

koppu cup

kore this (indicates a thing/person "near the speaker")

Kore wa dō desu ka How about this? How do you like this?

korekara from now on

kōsaten intersection

koshō pepper

koto thing (abstract)

kōto coat

kotoshi this year

kowai frightful, frightening

kowaremasu break

kowashimasu break (something)

ku 9

kuchi mouth

kudamono fruit

kudamono-ya fruit shop

ku-gatsu September

ku-ji 9 o'clock

kuma bear

kumo cloud

kumori cloudy weather

-kun is added after the names of boys; e.g., Bob-kun, Bob.

kuni country

kurashikku myūjikku classical music

kurasu (lecture) class

kuremasu give (to me)

Kurisumasu Christmas

kuroi black

kuruma car

kurushii hard (full of suffering)

kusuri medicine

kutsu shoe
kutsushita sock, stocking
kyō today
kyonen last year
kyū 9
kyū-fun 9 minutes
kyūri cucumber
machi town
machimasu wait for
mada yet (used with negative verbs)
made until, till
made is used as *to* in the sense of *until*.
mae before/to (hour/minutes)
mae front part, position in front
mae (time) before
magarimasu turn
-mai is put after a number to count thin flat objects such as stamps, papers, tickets, plates, blankets, etc.
mai- every (-asa, -ban, -nen, -nichi, -shū)
mai-asa every morning
mai-ban every evening
mai-nen every year
mai-nichi every day
mai-shū every week
māmā so and so
man 10,000
manekimasu invite
manga comics, cartoon
manshon high-grade apartment
massugu straight through
mata again
matawa or
mazui unsavory taste
me eye
megane eyeglasses
mezurashii unusual, rare
michi road, path, way
midori-no-madoguchi Shinkansen train reservation office
miemasu be visible
migi right
mijikai short (length)
mikan tangerine
mikisā blender
mikka 3rd
mimai a visit (to inquire about the health)

mimasu see, watch
mimi ear
minikui ugly
minna everyone
miokurimasu see (a person) off
miruku milk
mise shop
misemasu show
mizu water
mizūmi lake
mo also/too
mō already
moku-yōbi Thursday
momo peach
mono thing (article)
Moshi-moshi Hello! (used only and usually on the telephone)
motto more
mottomo most, best
muika 6th
mukashi long time ago
muzukashii difficult
nagai long
naifu knife
naka middle, inside
nakimasu cry
nakushimasu lose
namae name
nan what
nana 7
nana-fun 7 minutes
nan-fun how many minutes?
nan-gatsu what month?
nani what
nani mo (not) anything
nanika something
nan-ji what time?, what hour?
nan-nen what year?
nan-nichi what day of the month?
nanoka 7th
nan-yōbi what day of the week?
naraimasu learn
narimasu become
nashi pear
natsu summer
naze why
ne isn't it?, don't you?, etc.

negai appeal, wish

neko cat

nemasu sleep

-nen is put after a number to tell the year.

netsu body temperature, fever

nezumi mouse, rat

ni 2

ni at/in/on

ni is used as *to* in the sense of motion towards an "event" and direction of attention or interest.

-nichi is put after some numbers to tell the day of the month.

nichi-yōbi Sunday

ni-fun 2 minutes

nigai bitter (taste)

ni-gatsu February

Nihon Japan

Nihon-go Japanese language

Nihon-jin Japanese person

niji rainbow

ni-ji 2 o'clock

nijūgo-nichi 25th

nijūhachi-nichi 28th

nijūichi-nichi 21st

nijūku-nichi 29th

nijūni-nichi 22nd

nijūroku-nichi 26th

nijūsan-nichi 23rd

nijūshichi-nichi 27th

nijūyokka 24th

niku meat

niku-ya butcher's shop

-nin is put after a number to count people.

ninjin carrot

Nippon Japan

niwa garden

nomimasu drink

nomimasu take (medicine)

nomimono drink

norimasu ride (on)

nōto notebook

nyūin admission into a hospital

nyūin shimasu be admitted into a hospital

obasan aunt

obāsan grandmother

Ohayōgozaimasu Good morning

oishii delicious, tasty

ojisan uncle

ojīsan grandfather

Okaerinasai Welcome back

okāsan mother

okashi confectionery, sweets, candy

okashi-ya confectionery shop

ōkii big

ōkii loud (sound, voice)

ōkiku big

okimasu wake up

okonomiyaki meat and vegetable pancake

okuremasu be late

okurimasu send

okusan somebody else's wife

Ōmisoka New Year's Eve

omocha-ya toy shop

omoi heavy

omoshiroi interesting, amusing

omoshiroku interestingly

onaka stomach, abdomen, belly

onēsan older (elder) sister

ongaku music

onīsan older (elder) brother

orenji orange

orimasu break (bone, stick)

orimasu get off

osoi late, slow

osoku late

otearai washroom (polite)

ōtobai motorcycle

otona adult

otōsan father

otōto younger brother

ototoi the day before yesterday

Oyasuminasai Good night

oyogimasu swim

ōzei many people

painappuru pineapple

pan bread

pan-ya bread shop

Pari Paris

pātī party

pen pen

pittari na perfectly fit

poppu songu popular song

purattohōmu platform
purezento present
pūru pool
rai- next (*-getsu, -nen, -shū*)
rai-getsu next month
rainen next year
rainen next year
raion lion
rai-shū next week
rajio radio
rāmen ramen (noodles in a hot soup with some garnishing)
ranchi lunch
reizōko refrigerator
rekishi history
resutoran restaurant
rikō na clever
ringo apple
rippa na splendid
risu squirrel
roku 6
roku-fun 6 minutes
roku-gatsu June
roku-ji 6 o'clock
romanchikku na romantic
Rondon London
rop-pun 6 minutes
ryokan Japanese inn
ryokō travel
ryōri cooking
ryūkōka popular song
sabishii lonely
saifu wallet, purse
sakana fish
sakana-ya fish shop
sakaya liquor store
sake Japanese rice wine
sakki a little while ago
sakuranbo cherry
samui cold (temperature)
-san is added after names; it is comparable to *Mr., Mrs., Miss* or *Ms.*; e.g., **Kelly-san,** Mr./Mrs./Miss/Ms. Kelly, **Betty-san,** Betty.
san 3
sandoicchi sandwich

san-gatsu March
sangurasu sunglasses
san-ji 3 o'clock
sanjūichi-nichi 31st
sanjū-nichi 30th
san-pun 3 minutes
sansū arithmetic
sara plate
sarada salad
saru monkey
satō sugar
Sayōnara Good-bye
se height, stature
seito student (in general)
semai limited (space)
-sen line __
sen- last (*-getsu, -shū*)
sen 1,000
sen (train) line
sen-getsu last month
senpūki electric fan
-sensei is added after the names of teachers (of any kind) and medical doctors.
sensei teacher
sen-shū last week
sentaku laundry
sētā sweater
shi 4
shichi 7
shichi-gatsu July
shichi-ji 7 o'clock
shi-gatsu April
shigoto work
shimasu do
shinbun newspaper
shingō traffic light
shinimasu die
shinsetsu na kind
shio salt
shio-karai salty
shiroi white
shita lower part, space under (something)
shiteiseki reserved seats
shizuka na quiet, peaceful
shōgakkō primary school
Shōgatsu New Year's Day

shōyu soy sauce

shujin my husband

shukudai homework

shumi hobby

shuto capitals

sō so, in that way

soba buckwheat noodle: eaten either with a cold dipping sauce or in a hot broth

sochira that (indicates a person "near the listener")

sōji cleaning

soko that (place) (indicates "the place near the listener")

sono that

sora sky

sore that (indicates a thing/person "near the listener")

sorekara after that, and then

soto outside

sūgaku mathematics

sugi after/past (hour/minutes)

sugu immediately

suiei swimming

suika watermelon

sui-yōbi Wednesday

sukāto skirt

sukī ski, skiing

suki na likable

sukimasu be empty, not to be crowded

sukiyaki meat and vegetables cooked in sweetened soy sauce

sukoshi a little

sukūtā scooter

Sumimasen Excuse me, Pardon me

sumimasu live at, take up residence at __

sumō sumo wrestling

sūpāmāketto supermarket

supōtsu sport

supūn spoon

sushi raw fish placed on top of vinegared rice balls; fish, vegetables and cooked eggs mixed in, or rolled with, vinegared rice

sutēki steak

suteki na lovely

sutereo stereo

sūtsu suit

suzushii cool (temperature)

tabemasu eat

tabemono food

-tachi is added to make a person into a plural form; e.g., **watashi-tachi**, we.

Tadaima I am back (now)

taihen very (with adjectives and adverbs); a lot, much (with verbs)

taiin discharge from a hospital

taiin shimasu be discharged from a hospital

taionkei clinical thermometer

taisetsu na precious

taisō gymnastics

takai expensive

takai high, tall

takaku expensively, highly

takusan much, many, a lot, plenty

takushī taxi

tamago egg

tamanegi round onion

Tanabata The Festival of Stars

tanoshii enjoyable

tanoshiku enjoyably

tanuki badger

tatemono building

te hand

tēburu table

tegami letter

-ten mark

ten mark, score

tenisu tennis

tenki weather

tenpura tempura (pieces of food coated with thin batter and then deep fried)

tera temple

terebi television

tesuto test

tetsudai help

-tō is put after a number to count animals such as whales, cows and horses.

to and

to together, along with

toire washroom

tōka 10th

tokei watch

tokemasu melt

toki time, moment

tokidoki sometimes

tokkyū super express

tokoro place

Tōkyō Tokyo

tomarimasu stay (overnight)

tomarimasu stop

tomato tomato

tomemasu stop (vehicles)

tomemasu stop (something)

tomodachi friend

tonari next door, position next to

tonkatsu pork cutlet

tora tiger

torakku truck

tori bird

torimasu score

torimasu take

tori-niku chicken meat

tōsutā toaster

totemo very (with adjectives and adverbs);
   a lot, much (with verbs)

tsuitachi 1st

tsukaremasu be tired

tsukiatari T-junction

tsukimasu arrive

tsukimasu be accompanied, be included

tsukue desk

tsukurimasu make

tsumaranai boring

tsumetai cold (of touch)

tsuri change

uchi house, home

ude arm

udon thick noodle in hot soup, garnished
   with meat and vegetables

ue upper part, space over (something)

uētā waiter

uētoresu waitress

ugokashimasu move (something)

ugokimasu move

uma horse

umaremasu to be born

umi sea

undō-gutsu sport shoes

unten driving

urimasu sell

urusai noisy

usagi rabbit

ushi cow

ushiro back part, position behind

usui thin (of flat things)

uta song

-wa is put after a number to count
   animals such as rabbits, and birds
   such as ducks and chickens.

wain wine

wakarimasu to be understandable

wanpīsu one-piece dress

warui bad

Washinton Washington

wasuremasu forget

watashi I, me (except boys)

-ya -shop

yagate soon, presently, before long

yakisoba fried noodles with meat and
   vegetables (Chinese chow mein)

yakitori small chicken pieces skewered and
   barbequed with sauce

yakusoku promise

yakyū baseball

yama mountain

yamemasu resign from, cease, stop

yamimasu stop (rain, snow)

yaoya vegetable shop

yasai vegetables

yasashii easy

yasashii gentle

yasui cheap

yasuku cheaply

yasumi holiday

yasumimasu be absent from, rest from, take
   time off from

yo !

-yōbi denotes the day of the week.

yōchien kindergarten

yoi good

yo-ji 4 o'clock

yōka 8th

yokka 4th

yoko side part, position beside

yoku well, thoroughly, fully, frequently,
   often, a lot

yomimasu read

yon 4

yon-fun *4 minutes*
yori *(more) than* __
yoru *night*
yubi *finger*
yūbinkyoku *post office*
yuki *snow*
yukkuri *slowly*
yūmei na *famous*

yūsuhosuteru *youth hostel*
zasshi *magazine*
zenbu *all, everything, completely*
zenzen *not at all, entirely* (used with negative verbs)
zero *0*
zō *elephant*
zubon *trousers*

Kazuko Imaeda has taught Japanese to people of all ages and walks of life for more than 10 years. Her language learning adventure started when she moved to Ireland from Japan at the age of 13, and learned to express herself in English by starting with a minimum amount of vocabulary and sentence structures. Now, she uses the same approach to teach Japanese to non-native speakers. With a B.A. in Mathematical Sciences from Trinity College in Dublin, Ireland and a M.Math degree in Applied Mathematics from the University of Waterloo, Canada, Imaeda has applied her mathematical mindset to creating this effective, logic-based system for learning Japanese. Imaeda also holds an M.A. degree from Trinity College. She currently splits her time between Waterloo, Canada and Southern California.